Living Life Fully's

Motivational Classics, vol. 1

Including:

Acres of Diamonds by Russell H. Conwell

"Self-Reliance" by Ralph Waldo Emerson

The Wayfarer on the Open Road by Ralph Waldo Trine

The Heart of the New Thought by Ella Wheeler Wilcox

"On the Duty of Civil Disobedience" by Henry David Thoreau

As a Man Thinketh by James Allen

Character: The Grandest Thing in the World by Orison Swett Marden

Plus assorted poems from Wordsworth, Browning, Longfellow, Frost, and Dickinson!

Tom Walsh, editor

Published by Living Life Fully Publications
United States of America
http://www.livinglifefully.com

Motivational Classics

Copyright © 2007 Living Life Fully Publications

ISBN: 978-0-6151-5447-3

All rights reserved. All material in this book is in the public domain; the only material copyrighted are all references to Living Life Fully and the structure, outline, and editing of the works, as well as the particular presentation of the collected materials.

Printed in the United States of America.

Living Life Fully Publications is a trademark of livinglifefully.com.

Table of Contents

Acres of Diamonds	5
"Self-Reliance"	36
The Wayfarer on the Open Road	56
The Heart of the New Thought	88
"On the Duty of Civil Disobedience"	123
As a Man Thinketh	145
Character	164

Poems

The Road Not Taken	Robert Frost	34
A Psalm of Life	Longfellow	54
I Wandered Lonely...	Wordsworth	86
My Heart Leaps up...	Wordsworth	86
Ode: Intimations...	Wordsworth	139
Out in the Fields with God	Browning	162
If I Can Stop One Heart...	Dickinson	162

A Very Short Introduction

Most people don't realize that there's nothing new under the sun (as a Spanish refrain reminds us). Most of what we see that's "new" is in the packaging only—the thoughts and ideas have been around as long as people have. The Law of Attraction isn't new, for example—it's been talked about for as long as people have been around. "The Secret" isn't a secret at all—many people have been teaching and living these principles for many years.

    In this book I hope to present you with valuable material that will get you to think about your own life and the way that you live it, the way that you see it, the way that you *feel* it. I hope that you can find something in here that will help you to thrive in life, creating for yourself a life of abundance. All of the works are in the public domain, which means they've been around for a very, very long time. Millions of people have found them to be extremely valuable, and that's not likely to change—these works all have certain enduring qualities that make them almost timeless.

    You'll find no biographical information here—that information is readily available online and elsewhere. Besides, the men and women who wrote these words aren't the focus here—the focus is on the ideas that they present, the thoughts that they tried so hard to teach us. Let us focus on the message—that which can truly help us—and not be distracted by the peripheral information.

    Please, enter the book with an open mind and an open heart, and learn from people who cared enough to share their insights with us. May your life be one of plenty, and may you have plenty of love to share with all whom you meet on your journey!

tom walsh
livinglifefully.com

Acres of Diamonds

Russell H. Conwell

ACRES OF DIAMONDS

Friends.—This lecture has been delivered under these circumstances: I visit a town or city, and try to arrive there early enough to see the postmaster, the barber, the keeper of the hotel, the principal of the schools, and the ministers of some of the churches, and then go into some of the factories and stores, and talk with the people, and get into sympathy with the local conditions of that town or city and see what has been their history, what opportunities they had, and what they had failed to do—and every town fails to do something--and then go to the lecture and talk to those people about the subjects which applied to their locality. "Acres of Diamonds"—the idea—has continuously been precisely the same. The idea is that in this country of ours every man has the opportunity to make more of himself than he does in his own environment, with his own skill, with his own energy, and with his own friends.

                              RUSSELL H. CONWELL

ACRES OF DIAMONDS

This is the most recent and complete form of the lecture. It happened to be delivered in Philadelphia, Dr. Conwell's home city. When he says "right here in Philadelphia," he means the home city, town, or village of every reader of this book, just as he would use the name of it if delivering the lecture there, instead of doing it through the pages which follow.

WHEN going down the Tigris and Euphrates rivers many years ago with a party of English travelers I found myself under the direction of an old Arab guide whom we hired up at Baghdad, and I have often thought how that guide resembled our barbers in certain mental characteristics. He thought that it was not only his duty to guide us down those rivers, and do what he was paid for doing, but also to entertain us with stories curious and weird, ancient and modern, strange and familiar. Many of them I have forgotten, and I am glad I have, but there is one I shall never forget.
    The old guide was leading my camel by its halter along the banks of those ancient rivers, and he told me story after story until I grew weary of his story-telling and ceased to listen. I have never been irritated with that guide when he lost his temper as I ceased listening. But I remember that he took off his Turkish cap and swung it in a circle to get my attention. I could see it through the corner of my eye, but I determined not to look straight at him for fear he would tell another story. But although I am not a woman, I did finally look, and as soon as I did he went right into another story.
    Said he, "I will tell you a story now which I reserve for my particular friends." When he emphasized the words "particular friends," I listened, and I have ever been glad I did. I really feel devoutly thankful, that there are 1,674 young men who have been carried through college by this lecture who are also glad that I did listen. The old guide told me that there once lived not far from the River Indus an ancient Persian by the name of Ali Hafed. He said that Ali Hafed owned a very large farm, that he had orchards, grain-fields, and gardens; that he had money at interest, and was a wealthy and contented man. He was contented because he was wealthy, and wealthy because he was contented. One day there visited that old Persian farmer one of these ancient Buddhist priests, one of the wise men of the East. He sat down by the fire and told the old farmer how this world of ours was made. He said that this world was once a mere bank of fog, and that the Almighty thrust His finger into this bank of fog, and began slowly to move His finger around, increasing the speed until at last He whirled this bank of fog into a solid ball of fire. Then it went rolling through the universe, burning its way through other banks of fog, and condensed the moisture without, until it fell in floods of rain upon its hot surface, and cooled the outward crust. Then the internal

fires bursting outward through the crust threw up the mountains and hills, the valleys, the plains and prairies of this wonderful world of ours. If this internal molten mass came bursting out and cooled very quickly it became granite; less quickly copper, less quickly silver, less quickly gold, and, after gold, diamonds were made.

Said the old priest, "A diamond is a congealed drop of sunlight." Now that is literally scientifically true, that a diamond is an actual deposit of carbon from the sun. The old priest told Ali Hafed that if he had one diamond the size of his thumb he could purchase the county, and if he had a mine of diamonds he could place his children upon thrones through the influence of their great wealth.

Ali Hafed heard all about diamonds, how much they were worth, and went to his bed that night a poor man. He had not lost anything, but he was poor because he was discontented, and discontented because he feared he was poor. He said, "I want a mine of diamonds," and he lay awake all night.

Early in the morning he sought out the priest. I know by experience that a priest is very cross when awakened early in the morning, and when he shook that old priest out of his dreams, Ali Hafed said to him: "Will you tell me where I can find diamonds?"

"Diamonds! What do you want with diamonds?"

"Why, I wish to be immensely rich."

"Well, then, go along and find them. That is all you have to do; go and find them, and then you have them."

"But I don't know where to go."

"Well, if you will find a river that runs through white sands, between high mountains, in those white sands you will always find diamonds."

"I don't believe there is any such river."

"Oh yes, there are plenty of them. All you have to do is to go and find them, and then you have them."

Said Ali Hafed, "I will go."

So he sold his farm, collected his money, left his family in charge of a neighbor, and away he went in search of diamonds. He began his search, very properly to my mind, at the Mountains of the Moon. Afterward he came around into Palestine, then wandered on into Europe, and at last when his money was all spent and he was in rags, wretchedness, and poverty, he stood on the shore of that bay at Barcelona, in Spain, when a great tidal wave came rolling in between the pillars of Hercules, and the poor, afflicted, suffering, dying man could not resist the awful temptation to cast himself into that incoming tide, and he sank beneath its foaming crest, never to rise in this life again.

When that old guide had told me that awfully sad story he stopped the camel I was riding on and went back to fix the baggage that was coming off another camel, and I had an opportunity to muse over his story while he was gone. I remember saying to myself, "Why did he reserve that story for his 'particular friends'?" There seemed to be no beginning, no middle, no end, nothing to it. That was the first story I had ever heard told in my life, and would be the first one I ever read, in which the hero was killed in the first chapter. I had but one chapter of that story, and the hero was dead.

When the guide came back and took up the halter of my camel, he went right ahead with the story, into the second chapter, just as though there had been no break. The man who purchased Ali Hafed's farm one day led his camel into the garden to drink, and as that camel put its nose into the shallow water of that garden brook, Ali Hafed's successor noticed a curious flash of light from the white sands of the stream. He pulled out a black stone having an eye of light reflecting all the hues of the rainbow. He took the pebble into the house and put it on the mantel which covers the central fires, and forgot all about it.

A few days later this same old priest came in to visit Ali Hafed's successor, and the moment he opened that drawing-room door he saw that flash of light on the mantel, and he rushed up to it, and shouted: "Here is a diamond! Has Ali Hafed returned?"

"Oh no, Ali Hafed has not returned, and that is not a diamond. That is nothing but a stone we found right out here in our own garden."

"But," said the priest, "I tell you I know a diamond when I see it. I know positively that is a diamond."

Then together they rushed out into that old garden and stirred up the white sands with their fingers, and lo! there came up other more beautiful and valuable gems than the first.

"Thus," said the guide to me, and, friends, it is historically true, "was discovered the diamond-mine of Golconda, the most magnificent diamond-mine in all the history of mankind, excelling the Kimberly itself. The Kohinoor, and the Orloff of the crown jewels of England and Russia, the largest on earth, came from that mine.

When that old Arab guide told me the second chapter of his story, he then took off his Turkish cap and swung it around in the air again to get my attention to the moral. Those Arab guides have morals to their stories, although they are not always moral. As he swung his hat, he said to me, "Had Ali Hafed remained at home and dug in his own cellar, or underneath his own wheat-fields, or in his own garden, instead of wretchedness, starvation, and death by suicide in a strange land, he would have had 'acres of diamonds.' For every acre of that old farm, yes, every shovelful, afterward revealed gems which since have decorated the crowns of monarchs."

When he had added the moral to his story I saw why he reserved it for his "particular friends." But I did not tell him I could see it. It was that mean old Arab's way of going around a thing like a lawyer, to say indirectly what he did not dare say directly, that "in his private opinion there was a certain young man then traveling down the Tigris River that might better be at home in America. I did not tell him I could see that, but I told him his story reminded me of one, and I told it to him quick, and I think I will tell it to you.

I told him of a man out in California in 1847 who owned a ranch. He heard they had discovered gold in southern California, and so with a passion for gold he sold his ranch to Colonel Sutter, and away he went, never to come back. Colonel Sutter put a mill upon a stream that ran through that ranch, and one day his little girl brought some wet sand from the raceway into their home and sifted it through her fingers before the fire, and in that falling sand a visitor saw the first shining scales of real gold that were ever discovered in California. The man who had owned that ranch wanted gold, and he could have secured it for the mere taking. Indeed, thirty-eight millions of dollars has been taken out of a very few acres since then. About eight years ago I delivered this lecture in a city that stands on that farm, and they told me that a one-third owner for years and years had been getting one hundred and twenty dollars in gold every fifteen minutes, sleeping or waking, without taxation. You and I would enjoy an income like that-- if we didn't have to pay an income tax.

But a better illustration really than that occurred here in our own Pennsylvania. If there is anything I enjoy above another on the platform, it is to get one of these German audiences in Pennsylvania before me, and fire that at them, and I enjoy it to-night. There was a man living in Pennsylvania, not unlike some Pennsylvanians you have seen, who owned a farm, and he did with that farm just what I should do with a farm if I owned one in Pennsylvania--he sold it. But before he sold it he decided to secure employment collecting coal-oil for his cousin, who was in the business in Canada, where they first discovered oil on this continent. They dipped it from the running streams at that early time. So this Pennsylvania farmer wrote to his cousin asking for employment. You see, friends, this farmer was not altogether a foolish man. No, he was not. He did not leave his farm until he had something else to do.

"Of all the simpletons the stars shine on I don't know of a worse one than the man who leaves one job before he has gotten another."

That has especial reference to my profession, and has no reference whatever to a man seeking a divorce. When he wrote to his cousin for employment, his cousin replied, "I cannot engage you because you know nothing about the oil business."

Well, then the old farmer said, "I will know," and with most commendable zeal (characteristic of the students of Temple University) he set himself at the study of the whole subject. He began away back at the second day of God's creation when this world was covered thick and deep with that rich vegetation which since has turned to the primitive beds of coal. He studied the subject until he found that the drainings really of those rich beds of coal furnished the coal-oil that was worth pumping, and then he found how it came up with the living springs. He studied until he knew what it looked like, smelled like, tasted like, and how to refine it. Now said he in his letter to his cousin, "I understand the oil business."

His cousin answered, "All right, come on."

So he sold his farm, according to the county record, for $833 (even money, "no cents"). He had scarcely gone from that place before the man who purchased the spot went out to arrange for the watering of the cattle. He found the previous owner had gone out years before and put a plank across the brook back of the barn, edgewise into the surface of the water just a few inches. The purpose of that plank at that sharp angle across the brook was to throw over to the other bank a dreadful-looking scum through which the cattle would not put their noses. But with that plank there to throw it all over to one side, the cattle would drink below, and thus that man who had gone to Canada had been himself damming back for twenty-three years a flood of coal-oil which the state geologists of Pennsylvania declared to us ten years later was even then worth a hundred millions of dollars to our state, and four years ago our geologist declared the discovery to be worth to our state a thousand millions of dollars. The man who owned that territory on which the city of Titusville now stands, and those Pleasantville valleys, had studied the subject from the second day of God's creation clear down to the present time. He studied it until he knew all about it, and yet he is said to have sold the whole of it for $833, and again I say, "no sense."

But I need another illustration. I found it in Massachusetts, and I am sorry I did because that is the state I came from. This young man in Massachusetts furnishes just another phase of my thought. He went to Yale College and studied mines and mining, and became such an adept as a mining engineer that he was employed by the authorities of the university to train students who were behind their classes. During his senior year he earned $15 a week for doing that work. When he graduated they raised his pay from $15 to $45 a week, and offered him a professorship, and as soon as they did he went right home to his mother.

If they had raised that boy's pay from $15 to $15.60 he would have stayed and been proud of the place, but when they put it up to $45 at one leap, he said, "Mother, I won't work for $45 a week. The idea of a man with a brain like mine working for $45 a week! Let's go out in California and stake out gold-mines and silver-mines, and be immensely rich."

Said his mother, "Now, Charlie, it is just as well to be happy as it is to be rich."

"Yes," said Charlie, "but it is just as well to be rich and happy, too." And they were both right about it. As he was an only son and she a widow, of course he had his way. They always do.

They sold out in Massachusetts, and instead of going to California they went to Wisconsin, where he went into the employ of the Superior Copper Mining Company at $15 a week again, but with the proviso in his contract that he should have an interest in any mines he should discover for the company. I don't believe he ever discovered a mine, and if I am looking in the face of any stockholder of that copper company you wish he had discovered something or other. I have friends who are not here because they could not afford a ticket, who did have stock in that company at the time this young man was employed there. This young man went out there, and I have not heard a word from him. I don't know what became of him, and I don't know whether he found any mines or not, but I don't believe he ever did.

But I do know the other end of the line. He had scarcely gotten out of the old homestead before the succeeding owner went out to dig potatoes. The potatoes were already growing in the ground when he bought the farm, and as the old farmer was bringing in a basket of potatoes it hugged very tight between the ends of the stone fence. You know in Massachusetts our farms are nearly all stone wall. There you are obliged to be very economical of front gateways in order to have some place to put the stone. When that basket hugged so tight he set it down on the ground, and then dragged on one side, and pulled on the other side, and as he was dragging that basket through this farmer noticed in the upper and outer corner of that stone wall, right next the gate, a block of native silver eight inches square. That professor of mines, mining, and mineralogy who knew so much about the subject that he would not work for $45 a week, when he sold that homestead in Massachusetts sat right on that silver to make the bargain. He was born on that homestead, was brought up there, and had gone back and forth rubbing the stone with his sleeve until it reflected his countenance, and seemed to say, "Here is a hundred thousand dollars right down here just for the taking." But he would not take it. It was in a home in Newburyport, Massachusetts, and there was no silver there, all away off--well, I don't know where, and he did not, but somewhere else, and he was a professor of mineralogy.

My friends, that mistake is very universally made, and why should we even smile at him. I often wonder what has become of him. I do not know at all, but I will tell you what I "guess" as a Yankee. I guess that he sits out there by his fireside to-night with his friends gathered around him, and he is saying to them something like this: "Do you know that man Conwell who lives in Philadelphia?"

"Oh yes, I have heard of him."

"Do you know that man Jones that lives in Philadelphia?"

"Yes, I have heard of him, too."

Then he begins to laugh, and shakes his sides and says to his friends, "Well, they have done just the same thing I did, precisely"-- and that spoils the whole joke, for you and I have done the same thing he did, and while we sit here and laugh at him he has a better right to sit out there and laugh at us. I know I have made the same mistakes, but, of course, that does not make any difference, because we don't expect the same man to preach and practice, too.

As I come here to-night and look around this audience I am seeing again what through these fifty years I have continually seen-men that are making precisely that same mistake. I often wish I could see the younger people, and would that the Academy had been filled to-night with our high-school scholars and our grammar-school scholars, that I could have them to talk to. While I would have preferred such an audience as that, because they are most susceptible, as they have not grown up into their prejudices as we have, they have not gotten into any custom that they cannot break, they have not met with any failures as we have; and while I could perhaps do such an audience as that more good than I can do grown-up people, yet I will do the best I can with the material I have. I say to you that you have "acres of diamonds" in Philadelphia right where you now live.

"Oh," but you will say, "you cannot know much about your city if you think there are any 'acres of diamonds' here."

I was greatly interested in that account in the newspaper of the young man who found that diamond in North Carolina. It was one of the purest diamonds that has ever been discovered, and it has several predecessors near the same locality. I went to a distinguished professor in mineralogy and asked him where he thought those diamonds came from. The professor secured the map of the geologic formations of our continent, and traced it. He said it went either through the underlying carboniferous strata adapted for such production, westward through Ohio and the Mississippi, or in more probability came eastward through Virginia and up the shore of the Atlantic Ocean. It is a fact that the diamonds were there, for they have been discovered and sold; and that they were carried down there during the drift period, from some northern locality. Now who can say but some person going down with his drill in Philadelphia will find some trace of a diamond-mine yet down here? Oh, friends! you cannot say that you are not over one of the greatest diamond-mines in the world, for such a diamond as that only comes from the most profitable mines that are found on earth.

But it serves simply to illustrate my thought, which I emphasize by saying if you do not have the actual diamond-mines literally you have all that they would be good for to you. Because now that the Queen of England has given the greatest compliment ever conferred upon American woman for her attire because she did not appear with any jewels at all at the late reception in England, it has almost done away with the use of diamonds anyhow. All you would care for would be the few you would wear if you wish to be modest, and the rest you would sell for money.

Now then, I say again that the opportunity to get rich, to attain unto great wealth, is here in Philadelphia now, within the reach of almost every man and woman who hears me speak tonight, and I mean just what I say. I have not come to this platform even under these circumstances to recite something to you. I have come to tell you what in God's sight I believe to be the truth, and if the years of life have been of any value to me in the attainment of common sense, I know I am right; that the men and women sitting here, who found it difficult perhaps to buy a ticket to this lecture or gathering to-night, have within their reach "acres of diamonds," opportunities to get largely wealthy. There never was a place on earth more adapted than the city of Philadelphia today, and never in the history of the world did a poor man without capital have such an opportunity to get rich quickly and honestly as he has now in our city. I say it is the truth, and I want you to accept it as such; for if you think I have come to simply recite something, then I would better not be here. I have no time to waste in any such talk, but to say the things I believe, and unless some of you get richer for what I am saying to-night my time is wasted.

I say that you ought to get rich, and it is your duty to get rich. How many of my pious brethren say to me, "Do you, a Christian minister, spend your time going up and down the country advising young people to get rich, to get money?"

"Yes, of course I do."

They say, "Isn't that awful! Why don't you preach the gospel instead of preaching about man's making money?"

"Because to make money honestly is to preach the gospel." That is the reason. The men who get rich may be the most honest men you find in the community.

"Oh," but says some young man here tonight, "I have been told all my life that if a person has money he is very dishonest and dishonorable and mean and contemptible."

"My friend, that is the reason why you have none, because you have that idea of people. The foundation of your faith is altogether false. Let me say here clearly, and say it briefly, though subject to discussion which I have not time for here, ninety-eight out of one hundred of the rich men of America are honest. That is why they are rich. That is why they are trusted with money. That is why they carry on great enterprises and find plenty of people to work with them. It is because they are honest men.

Says another young man, "I hear sometimes of men that get millions of dollars dishonestly."

Yes, of course you do, and so do I. But they are so rare a thing in fact that the newspapers talk about them all the time as a matter of news until you get the idea that all the other rich men got rich dishonestly.

My friend, you take and drive me--if you furnish the auto--out into the suburbs of Philadelphia, and introduce me to the people who own their homes around this great city, those beautiful homes with gardens and flowers, those magnificent homes so lovely in their art, and I will introduce you to the very best people in character as well as in enterprise in our city, and you know I will. A man is not really a true man until he owns his own home, and they that own their homes are made more honorable and honest and pure, and true and economical and careful, by owning the home.

For a man to have money, even in large sums, is not an inconsistent thing. We preach against covetousness, and you know we do, in the pulpit, and oftentimes preach against it so long and use the terms about "filthy lucre" so extremely that Christians get the idea that when we stand in the pulpit we believe it is wicked for any man to have money--until the collection-basket goes around, and then we almost swear at the people because they don't give more money. Oh, the inconsistency of such doctrines as that!

Money is power, and you ought to be reasonably ambitious to have it. You ought because you can do more good with it than you could without it. Money printed your Bible, money builds your churches, money sends your missionaries, and money pays your preachers, and you would not have many of them, either, if you did not pay them. I am always willing that my church should raise my salary, because the church that pays the largest salary always raises it the easiest. You never knew an exception to it in your life. The man who gets the largest salary can do the most good with the power that is furnished to him. Of course he can if his spirit be right to use it for what it is given to him.

I say, then, you ought to have money. If you can honestly attain unto riches in Philadelphia, it is your Christian and godly duty to do so. It is an awful mistake of these pious people to think you must be awfully poor in order to be pious.

Some men say, "Don't you sympathize with the poor people?" Of course I do, or else I would not have been lecturing these years. I won't give in but what I sympathize with the poor, but the number of poor who are to be sympathized with is very small. To sympathize with a man whom God has punished for his sins, thus to help him when God would still continue a just punishment, is to do wrong, no doubt about it, and we do that more than we help those who are deserving. While we should sympathize with God's poor--that is, those who cannot help themselves--let us remember there is not a poor person in the United States who was not made poor by his own shortcomings, or by the shortcomings of someone else. It is all wrong to be poor, anyhow. Let us give in to that argument and pass that to one side.

A gentleman gets up back there, and says, "Don't you think there are some things in this world that are better than money?" Of course I do, but I am talking about money now. Of course there are some things higher than money. Oh yes, I know by the grave that has left me standing alone that there are some things in this world that are higher and sweeter and purer than money. Well do I know there are some things higher and grander than gold. Love is the grandest thing on God's earth, but fortunate the lover who has plenty of money. Money is power, money is force, money will do good as well as harm. In the hands of good men and women it could accomplish, and it has accomplished, good.

I hate to leave that behind me. I heard a man get up in a prayer-meeting in our city and thank the Lord he was "one of God's poor." Well, I wonder what his wife thinks about that? She earns all the money that comes into that house, and he smokes a part of that on the veranda. I don't want to see any more of the Lord's poor of that kind, and I don't believe the Lord does. And yet there are some people who think in order to be pious you must be awfully poor and awfully dirty.

That does not follow at all. While we sympathize with the poor, let us not teach a doctrine like that.

Yet the age is prejudiced against advising a Christian man (or, as a Jew would say, a godly man) from attaining unto wealth. The prejudice is so universal and the years are far enough back, I think, for me to safely mention that years ago up at Temple University there was a young man in our theological school who thought he was the only pious student in that department. He came into my office one evening and sat down by my desk, and said to me: "Mr. President, I think it is my duty sir, to come in and labor with you."

"What has happened now?"

Said he, "I heard you say at the Academy, at the Peirce School commencement, that you thought it was an honorable ambition for a young man to desire to have wealth, and that you thought it made him temperate, made him anxious to have a good name, and made him industrious. You spoke about man's ambition to have money helping to make him a good man. Sir, I have come to tell you the Holy Bible says that 'money is the root of all evil.'"

I told him I had never seen it in the Bible, and advised him to go out into the chapel and get the Bible, and show me the place. So out he went for the Bible, and soon he stalked into my office with the Bible open, with all the bigoted pride of the narrow sectarian, or of one who founds his Christianity on some misinterpretation of Scripture. He flung the Bible down on my desk, and
fairly squealed into my ear: "There it is, Mr. President; you can read it for yourself."

I said to him: "Well, young man, you will learn when you get a little older that you cannot trust another denomination to read the Bible for you. You belong to another denomination. You are taught in the theological school, however, that emphasis is exegesis. Now, will you take that Bible and read it yourself, and give the proper emphasis to it?"

He took the Bible, and proudly read, "'The love of money is the root of all evil.'"

Then he had it right, and when one does quote aright from that same old Book he quotes the absolute truth. I have lived through fifty years of the mightiest battle that old Book has ever fought, and I have lived to see its banners flying free; for never in the history of this world did the great minds of earth so universally agree that the Bible is true-- all true--as they do at this very hour.

So I say that when he quoted right, of course he quoted the absolute truth. "The love of money is the root of all evil." He who tries to attain unto it too quickly, or dishonestly, will fall into many snares, no doubt about that. The love of money. What is that? It is making an idol of money, and idolatry pure and simple everywhere is condemned by the Holy Scriptures and by man's common sense. The man that worships the dollar instead of thinking of the purposes for which it ought to be used, the man who idolizes simply money, the miser that hordes his money in the cellar, or hides it in his stocking, or refuses to invest it where it will do the world good, that man who hugs the dollar until the eagle squeals has in him the root of all evil.

I think I will leave that behind me now and answer the question of nearly all of you who are asking, "Is there opportunity to get rich in Philadelphia?" Well, now, how simple a thing it is to see where it is, and the instant you see where it is it is yours. Some old gentleman gets up back there and says, "Mr. Conwell, have you lived in Philadelphia for thirty-one years and don't know that the time has gone by when you can make anything in this city?"

"No, I don't think it is."

"Yes, it is; I have tried it."

"What business are you in?"

"I kept a store here for twenty years, and never made over a thousand dollars in the whole twenty years."

"Well, then, you can measure the good you have been to this city by what this city has paid you, because a man can judge very well what he is worth by what he receives; that is, in what he is to the world at this time. If you have not made over a thousand dollars in twenty years in Philadelphia, it would have been better for Philadelphia if they had kicked you out of the city nineteen years and nine months ago. A man has no right to keep a store in Philadelphia twenty years and not make at least five hundred thousand dollars even though it be a corner grocery up-town."

You say, "You cannot make five thousand dollars in a store now." Oh, my friends, if you will
just take only four blocks around you, and find out what the people want and what you ought to supply and set them down with your pencil and figure up the profits you would make if you did supply them, you would very soon see it. There is wealth right within the sound of your voice.

Some one says: "You don't know anything about business. A preacher never knows a thing about business." Well, then, I will have to prove that I am an expert. I don't like to do this, but I have to do it because my testimony will not be taken if I am not an expert. My father kept a country store, and if there is any place under the stars where a man gets all sorts of experience in every kind of mercantile transactions, it is in the country store. I am not proud of my experience, but sometimes when my father was away he would leave me in charge of the store, though fortunately for him that was not very often. But this did occur many times, friends: A man would come in the store, and say to me, "Do you keep jack knives?"

"No, we don't keep jack-knives," and I went off whistling a tune. What did I care about that man, anyhow? Then another farmer would come in and say, "Do you keep jack knives?"

"No, we don't keep jack-knives." Then I went away and whistled another tune.

Then a third man came right in the same door and said, "Do you keep jack-knives?"

"No. Why is every one around here asking for jack-knives? Do you suppose we are keeping this store to supply the whole neighborhood with jack-knives?" Do you carry on your store like that in Philadelphia? The difficulty was I had not then learned that the foundation of godliness and the foundation principle of success in business are both the same precisely. The man who says, "I cannot carry my religion into business" advertises himself either as being an imbecile in business, or on the road to bankruptcy, or a thief, one of the three, sure. He will fail within a very few years. He certainly will if he doesn't carry his religion into business. If I had been carrying on my father's store on a Christian plan, godly plan, I would have had a jack-knife for the third man when he called for it. Then I would have actually done him a kindness, and I would have received a reward myself, which it would have been my duty to take.

There are some over-pious Christian people who think if you take any profit on anything you sell that you are an unrighteous man. On the contrary, you would be a criminal to sell goods for less than they cost. You have no right to do that. You cannot trust a man with your money who cannot take care of his own. You cannot trust a man in your family that is not true to his own wife. You cannot trust a man in the world that does not begin with his own heart, his own character, and his own life. It would have been my duty to have furnished a jack-knife to the third man, or the second, and to have sold it to him and actually profited myself. I have no more right to sell goods without making a profit on them than I have to overcharge him dishonestly beyond what they are worth. But I should so sell each bill of goods that the person to whom I sell shall make as much as I make.

To live and let live is the principle of the gospel, and the principle of every-day common sense. Oh, young man, hear me; live as you go along. Do not wait until you have reached my years before you begin to enjoy anything of this life. If I had the millions back, or fifty cents of it, which I have tried to earn in these years, it would not do me anything like the good that it does me now in this almost sacred presence tonight. Oh, yes, I am paid over and over a hundredfold to-night for dividing as I have tried to do in some measure as I went along through the years. I ought not speak that way, it sounds egotistic, but I am old enough now to be excused for that. I should have helped my fellow-men, which I have tried to do, and every one should try to do, and get the happiness of it. The man who goes home with the sense that he has stolen a dollar that day, that he has robbed a man of what was his honest due, is not going to sweet rest. He arises tired in the morning, and goes with an unclean conscience to his work the next day. He is not a successful man at all, although he may have laid up millions. But the man who has gone through life dividing always with his fellow-men, making and demanding his own rights and his own profits, and giving to every other man his rights and profits, lives every day, and not only that, but it is the royal road to great wealth. The history of the thousands of millionaires shows that to be the case.

The man over there who said he could not make anything in a store in Philadelphia has been carrying on his store on the wrong principle. Suppose I go into your store to-morrow morning and ask, "Do you know neighbor A, who lives one square away, at house No. 1240?"

"Oh yes, I have met him. He deals here at the corner store."

"Where did he come from?"

"I don't know."

"How many does he have in his family?"

"I don't know."

"What ticket does he vote?"

"I don't know."

"What church does he go to?"

"I don't know, and don't care. What are you asking all these questions for?"

If you had a store in Philadelphia would you answer me like that? If so, then you are conducting your business just as I carried on my father's business in Worthington, Massachusetts. You don't know where your neighbor came from when he moved to Philadelphia, and you don't care. If you had cared you would be a rich man now. If you had cared enough about him to take an interest in his affairs, to find out what he needed, you would have been rich. But you go through the world saying, "No opportunity to get rich," and there is the fault right at your own door.

But another young man gets up over there and says, "I cannot take up the mercantile business." (While I am talking of trade it applies to every occupation.)

"Why can't you go into the mercantile business?"

"Because I haven't any capital." Oh, the weak and dudish creature that can't see over its collar! It makes a person weak to see these little dudes standing around the corners and saying, "Oh, if I had plenty of capital, how rich I would get."

"Young man, do you think you are going to get rich on capital?"

"Certainly."

Well, I say, "Certainly not." If your mother has plenty of money, and she will set you up in business, you will "set her up in business," supplying you with capital. The moment a young man or woman gets more money than he or she has grown to by practical experience, that moment he has gotten a curse. It is no help to a young man or woman to inherit money. It is no help to your children to leave them money, but if you leave them education, if you leave them Christian and noble character, if you leave them a wide circle of friends, if you leave them an honorable name, it is far better than that they should have money. It would be worse for them, worse for the nation, that they should have any money at all. Oh, young man, if you have inherited money, don't regard it as a help. It will curse you through your years, and deprive you of the very best things of human life. There is no class of people to be pitied so much as the inexperienced sons and daughters of the rich of our generation. I pity the rich man's son. He can never know the best things in life.

One of the best things in our life is when a young man has earned his own living, and when he becomes engaged to some lovely young woman, and makes up his mind to have a home of his own. Then with that same love comes also that divine inspiration toward better things, and he begins to save his money. He begins to leave off his bad habits and put money in the bank. When he has a few hundred dollars he goes out in the suburbs to look for a home. He goes to the savings-bank, perhaps, for half of the value, and then goes for his wife, and when he takes his bride over the threshold of that door for the first time he says in words of eloquence my voice can never touch: "I have earned this home myself. It is all mine, and I divide with thee." That is the grandest moment a human heart may ever know.

But a rich man's son can never know that. He takes his bride into a finer mansion, it may be, but he is obliged to go all the way through it and say to his wife, "My mother gave me that, my mother gave me that, and my mother gave me this," until his wife wishes she had married his mother. I pity the rich man's son.

The statistics of Massachusetts showed that not one rich man's son out of seventeen ever dies rich. I pity the rich man's sons unless they have the good sense of the elder Vanderbilt, which sometimes happens. He went to his father and said, "Did you earn all your money?"

"I did, my son. I began to work on a ferry-boat for twenty-five cents a day."

"Then," said his son, "I will have none of your money," and he, too, tried to get employment on a ferry-boat that Saturday night. He could not get one there, but he did get a place for three dollars a week. Of course, if a rich man's son will do that, he will get the discipline of a poor boy that is worth more than a university education to any man. He would then be able to take care of the millions of his father. But as a rule the rich men will not let their sons do the very thing that made them great. As a rule, the rich man will not allow his son to work--and his mother! Why, she would think it was a social disgrace if her poor, weak, little lily-fingered, sissy sort of a boy had to earn his living with honest toil. I have no pity for such rich men's sons.

I remember one at Niagara Falls. I think I remember one a great deal nearer. I think there are gentlemen present who were at a great banquet, and I beg pardon of his friends. At a banquet here in Philadelphia there sat beside me a kind-hearted young man, and he said, "Mr. Conwell, you have been sick for two or three years. When you go out, take my limousine, and it will take you up to your house on Broad Street."

I thanked him very much, and perhaps I ought not to mention the incident in this way, but I follow the facts. I got on to the seat with the driver of that limousine, outside, and when we were going up I asked the driver, "How much did this limousine cost?"

"Six thousand eight hundred, and he had to pay the duty on it."

"Well," I said, "does the owner of this machine ever drive it himself?" At that the chauffeur laughed so heartily that he lost control of his machine. He was so surprised at the question that he ran up on the sidewalk, and around a corner lamp-post out into the street again. And when he got out into the street he laughed till the whole machine trembled.

He said: "He drive this machine! Oh, he would be lucky if he knew enough to get out when we get there."

I must tell you about a rich man's son at Niagara Falls. I came in from the lecture to the hotel, and as I approached the desk of the clerk there stood a millionaire's son from New York. He was an indescribable specimen of anthropologic potency. He had a skull-cap on one side of his head, with a gold tassel in the top of it, and a gold-headed cane under his arm with more in it than in his head. It is a very difficult thing to describe that young man. He wore an eye-glass that he could not see through, patent-leather boots that he could not walk in, and pants that he could not sit down in--dressed like a grasshopper. This human cricket came up to the clerk's desk just as I entered, adjusted his unseeing eye-glass, and spake in this wise to the clerk. You see, he thought it was "Hinglish, you know," to lisp.

"Thir, will you have the kindness to supply me with thome papah and enwelophs!"

The hotel clerk measured that man quick, and he pulled the envelopes and paper out of a drawer, threw them across the counter toward the young man, and then turned away to his books. You should have seen that young man when those envelopes came across that counter. He swelled up like a gobbler turkey, adjusted his unseeing eye-glass, and yelled: "Come right back here. Now thir, will you order a thervant to take that papah and enwelophs to yondah dethk." Oh, the poor, miserable, contemptible American monkey! He could not carry paper and envelopes twenty feet. I suppose he could not get his arms down to do it. I have no pity for such travesties upon human nature. If you have not capital, young man, I am glad of it. What you need is common sense, not copper cents.

The best thing I can do is to illustrate by actual facts well-known to you all. A. T. Stewart, a poor boy in New York, had $1.50 to begin life on. He lost 87 1/2 cents of that on the very first venture. How fortunate that young man who loses the first time he gambles. That boy said, "I will never gamble again in business," and he never did.

How came he to lose 87 ½ cents? You probably all know the story how he lost it—because he bought some needles, threads, and buttons to sell which people did not want, and had them left on his hands, a dead loss. Said the boy, "I will not lose any more money in that way." Then he went around first to the doors and asked the people what they did want. Then when he had found out what they wanted he invested his 62 ½ cents to supply a known demand. Study it wherever you choose--in business, in your profession, in your housekeeping, whatever your life, that one thing is the secret of success. You must first know the demand. You must first know what people need, and then invest yourself where you are most needed. A. T. Stewart went on that principle until he was worth what amounted afterward to forty millions of dollars, owning the very store in which Mr. Wanamaker carries on his great work in New York. His fortune was made by his losing something, which taught him the great lesson that he must only invest himself or his money in something that people need. When will you salesmen learn it? When will you manufacturers learn that you must know the changing needs of humanity if you would succeed in life? Apply yourselves, all you Christian people, as manufacturers or merchants or workmen to supply that human need. It is a great principle as broad as humanity and as deep as the Scripture itself.

The best illustration I ever heard was of John Jacob Astor. You know that he made the money of the Astor family when he lived in New York. He came across the sea in debt for his fare. But that poor boy with nothing in his pocket made the fortune of the Astor family on one principle. Some young man here to-night will say, "Well they could make those fortunes over in New York but they could not do it in Philadelphia!" My friends, did you ever read that wonderful book of Riis (his memory is sweet to us because of his recent death), wherein is given his statistical account of the records taken in 1889 of 107 millionaires of New York. If you read the account you will see that out of the 107 millionaires only seven made their money in New York. Out of the 107 millionaires worth ten million dollars in real estate then, 67 of them made their money in towns of less than 3,500 inhabitants. The richest man in this country today, if you read the real-estate values, has never moved away from a town of 3,500 inhabitants. It makes not so much difference where you are as who you are. But if you cannot get rich in Philadelphia you certainly cannot do it in New York.

Now John Jacob Astor illustrated what can be done anywhere. He had a mortgage once on a millinery-store, and they could not sell bonnets enough to pay the interest on his money. So he foreclosed that mortgage, took possession of the store, and went into partnership with the very same people, in the same store, with the same capital. He did not give them a dollar of capital. They had to sell goods to get any money. Then he left them alone in the store just as they had been before, and he went out and sat down on a bench in the park in the shade. What was John Jacob Astor doing out there, and in partnership with people who had failed on his own hands? He had the most important and, to my mind, the most pleasant part of that partnership on his hands.

For as John Jacob Astor sat on that bench he was watching the ladies as they went by; and where is the man who would not get rich at that business? As he sat on the bench if a lady passed him with her shoulders back and head up, and looked straight to the front, as if she did not care if all the world did gaze on her, then he studied her bonnet, and by the time it was out of sight he knew the shape of the frame, the color of the trimmings, and the crinklings in the feather. I sometimes try to describe a bonnet, but not always. I would not try to describe a modern bonnet. Where is the man that could describe one? This aggregation of all sorts of driftwood stuck on the back of the head, or the side of the neck, like a rooster with only one tail feather left.

But in John Jacob Astor's day there was some art about the millinery business, and he went to the millinery-store and said to them: "Now put into the show-window just such a bonnet as I describe to you, because I have already seen a lady who likes such a bonnet. Don't make up any more until I come back." Then he went out and sat down again, and another lady passed him of a different form, of different complexion, with a different shape and color of bonnet.

"Now," said he, "put such a bonnet as that in the show window." He did not fill his show-window up town with a lot of hats and bonnets to drive people away, and then sit on the back stairs and bawl because people went to Wanamaker's to trade. He did not have a hat or a bonnet in that show-window but what some lady liked before it was made up. The tide of custom began immediately to turn in, and that has been the foundation of the greatest store in New York in that line, and still exists as one of three stores. Its fortune was made by John Jacob Astor after they had failed in business, not by giving them any more money, but by finding out what the ladies liked for bonnets before they wasted any material in making them up. I tell you if a man could foresee the millinery business he could foresee anything under heaven!

Suppose I were to go through this audience tonight and ask you in this great manufacturing city if there are not opportunities to get rich in manufacturing. "Oh yes," some young man says, "there are opportunities here still if you build with some trust and if you have two or three millions of dollars to begin with as capital." Young man, the history of the breaking up of the trusts by that attack upon "big business" is only illustrating what is now the opportunity of the smaller man. The time never came in the history of the world when you could get rich so quickly manufacturing without capital as you can now.

But you will say, "You cannot do anything of the kind. You cannot start without capital." Young man, let me illustrate for a moment. I must do it. It is my duty to every young man and woman, because we are all going into business very soon on the same plan. Young man, remember if you know what people need you have gotten more knowledge of a fortune than any amount of capital can give you.

There was a poor man out of work living in Hingham, Massachusetts. He lounged around the house until one day his wife told him to get out and work, and, as he lived in Massachusetts, he obeyed his wife. He went out and sat down on the shore of the bay, and whittled a soaked shingle into a wooden chain. His children that evening quarreled over it, and he whittled a second one to keep peace. While he was whittling the second one a neighbor came in and said: "Why don't you whittle toys and sell them? You could make money at that."

"Oh," he said, "I would not know what to make."

"Why don't you ask your own children right here in your own house what to make?"

"What is the use of trying that?" said the carpenter. "My children are different from other people's children." (I used to see people like that when I taught school.) But he acted upon the hint, and the next morning when Mary came down the stairway, he asked, "What do you want for a toy?"

She began to tell him she would like a doll's bed, a doll's washstand, a doll's carriage, a little doll's umbrella, and went on with a list of things that would take him a lifetime to supply. So, consulting his own children, in his own house, he took the firewood, for he had no money to buy lumber, and whittled those strong, unpainted Hingham toys that were for so many years known all over the world. That man began to make those toys for his own children, and then made copies and sold them through the boot-and-shoe store next door. He began to make a little money, and then a little more, and Mr. Lawson, in his "Frenzied Finance" says that man is the richest man in old Massachusetts, and I think it is the truth. And that man is worth a hundred millions of dollars to-day, and has been only thirty-four years making it on that one principle—that one must judge that what his own children like at home other people's children would like in their homes, too; to judge the human heart by oneself, by one's wife or by one's children. It is the royal road to success in manufacturing. "Oh," but you say, "didn't he have any capital?" Yes, a penknife, but I don't know that he had paid for that.

I spoke thus to an audience in New Britain, Connecticut, and a lady four seats back went home and tried to take off her collar, and the collar-button stuck in the buttonhole. She threw it
out and said, "I am going to get up something better than that to put on collars."

Her husband said: "After what Conwell said to-night, you see there is a need of an improved collar-fastener that is easier to handle. There is a human need; there is a great fortune. Now, then, get up a collar-button and get rich." He made fun of her, and consequently made fun of me, and that is one of the saddest things which comes over me like a deep cloud of midnight sometimes—although I have worked so hard for more than half a century, yet how little I have ever really done. Notwithstanding the greatness and the handsomeness of your compliment to-night, I do not believe there is one in ten of you that is going to make a million of dollars because you are here tonight; but it is not my fault, it is yours. I say that sincerely. What is the use of my talking if people never do what I advise them to do?

When her husband ridiculed her, she made up her mind she would make a better collar-button, and when a woman makes up her mind "she will," and does not say anything about it, she does it. It was that New England woman who invented the snap button which you can find anywhere now. It was first a collar-button with a spring cap attached to the outer side. Any of you who wear modern waterproofs know the button that simply pushes together, and when you unbutton it you simply pull it apart. That is the button to which I refer, and which she invented. She afterward invented several other buttons, and then invested in more, and then was taken into partnership with great factories. Now that woman goes over the sea every summer in her private steamship--yes, and takes her husband with her! If her husband were to die, she would have money enough left now to buy a foreign duke or count or some such title as that at the latest quotations.

Now what is my lesson in that incident? It is this: I told her then, though I did not know her, what I now say to you, "Your wealth is too near to you. You are looking right over it"; and she had to look over it because it was right under her chin.

I have read in the newspaper that a woman never invented anything. Well, that newspaper ought to begin again. Of course, I do not refer to gossip--I refer to machines--and if I did I might better include the men. That newspaper could never appear if women had not invented something. Friends, think. Ye women, think! You say you cannot make a fortune because you are in some laundry, or running a sewing-machine, it may be, or walking before some loom, and yet you can be a millionaire if you will but follow this almost infallible direction.

When you say a woman doesn't invent anything, I ask, Who invented the Jacquard loom that wove every stitch you wear? Mrs. Jacquard. The printer's roller, the printing-press, were invented by farmers' wives. Who invented the cotton-gin of the South that enriched our country so amazingly? Mrs. General Greene invented the cotton-gin and showed the idea to Mr. Whitney, and he, like a man, seized it. Who was it that invented the sewing-machine? If I would go to school tomorrow and ask your children they would say, "Elias Howe."

He was in the Civil War with me, and often in my tent, and I often heard him say that he worked fourteen years to get up that sewing-machine. But his wife made up her mind one day that they would starve to death if there wasn't something or other invented pretty soon, and so in two hours she invented the sewing-machine. Of course he took out the patent in his name. Men always do that. Who was it that invented the mower and the reaper? According to Mr. McCormick's confidential communication, so recently published, it was a West Virginia woman, who, after his father and he had failed altogether in making a reaper and gave it up, took a lot of shears and nailed them together on the edge of a board, with one shaft of each pair loose, and then wired them so that when she pulled the wire one way it closed them, and when she pulled the wire the other way it opened them, and there she had the principle of the mowing-machine. If you look at a mowing-machine, you will see it is nothing but a lot of shears. If a woman can invent a mowing-machine, if a woman can invent a Jacquard loom, if a woman can invent a cotton-gin, if a woman can invent a trolley switch--as she did and made the trolleys possible; if a woman can invent, as Mr. Carnegie said, the great iron squeezers that laid the foundation of all the steel millions of the United States, "we men" can invent anything under the stars! I say that for the encouragement of the men.

Who are the great inventors of the world? Again this lesson comes before us. The great inventor sits next to you, or you are the person yourself. "Oh," but you will say, "I have never invented anything in my life." Neither did the great inventors until they discovered one great secret. Do you think it is a man with a head like a bushel measure or a man like a stroke of lightning? It is neither. The really great man is a plain, straightforward, every-day, common-sense man. You would not dream that he was a great inventor if you did not see something he had actually done. His neighbors do not regard him so great. You never see anything great over your back fence. You say there is no greatness among your neighbors. It is all away off somewhere else. Their greatness is ever so simple, so plain, so earnest, so practical, that the neighbors and friends never recognize it.

True greatness is often unrecognized. That is sure. You do not know anything about the greatest men and women. I went out to write the life of General Garfield, and a neighbor, knowing I was in a hurry, and as there was a great crowd around the front door, took me around to General Garfield's back door and shouted, "Jim! Jim!" And very soon "Jim" came to the door and let me in, and I wrote the biography of one of the grandest men of the nation, and yet he was just the same old "Jim" to his neighbor. If you know a great man in Philadelphia and you should meet him to-morrow, you would say, "How are you, Sam?" or "Good morning, Jim." Of course you would. That is just what you would do.

One of my soldiers in the Civil War had been sentenced to death, and I went up to the White House in Washington--sent there for the first time in my life to see the President. I went into the waiting-room and sat down with a lot of others on the benches, and the secretary asked one after another to tell him what they wanted. After the secretary had been through the line, he went in, and then came back to the door and motioned for me. I went up to that anteroom, and the secretary said: "That is the President's door right over there. Just rap on it and go right in."

I never was so taken aback, friends, in all my life, never. The secretary himself made it worse for me, because he had told me how to go in and then went out another door to the left and shut that. There I was, in the hallway by myself before the President of the United States of America's door. I had been on fields of battle, where the shells did sometimes shriek and the bullets did sometimes hit me, but I always wanted to run. I have no sympathy with the old man who says, "I would just as soon march up to the cannon's mouth as eat my dinner." I have no faith in a man who doesn't know enough to be afraid when he is being shot at. I never was so afraid when the shells came around us at Antietam as I was when I went into that room that day; but I finally mustered the courage--I don't know how I ever did--and at arm's-length tapped on the door. The man inside did not help me at all, but yelled out, "Come in and sit down!"

    Well, I went in and sat down on the edge of a chair, and wished I were in Europe, and the man at the table did not look up. He was one of the world's greatest men, and was made great by one single rule. Oh, that all the young people of Philadelphia were before me now and I could say just this one thing, and that they would remember it. I would give a lifetime for the effect it would have on our city and on civilization. Abraham Lincoln's principle for greatness can be adopted by nearly all. This was his rule: Whatsoever he had to do at all, he put his whole mind into it and held it all there until that was all done. That makes men great almost anywhere. He stuck to those papers at that table and did not look up at me, and I sat there trembling. Finally, when he had put the string around his papers, he pushed them over to one side and looked over to me, and a smile came over his worn face. He said: "I am a very busy man and have only a few minutes to spare. Now tell me in the fewest words what it is you want." I began to tell him, and mentioned the case, and he said: "I have heard all about it and you do not need to say any more. Mr. Stanton was talking to me only a few days ago about that. You can go to the hotel and rest assured that the President never did sign an order to shoot a boy under twenty years of age, and never will. You can say that to his mother anyhow."

    Then he said to me, "How is it going in the field?"

    I said, "We sometimes get discouraged."

    And he said: "It is all right. We are going to win out now. We are getting very near the light. No man ought to wish to be President of the United States, and I will be glad when I get through; then Tad and I are going out to Springfield, Illinois. I have bought a farm out there and I don't care if I again earn only twenty-five cents a day. Tad has a mule team, and we are going to plant onions."

    Then he asked me, "Were you brought up on a farm?"

    I said, "Yes; in the Berkshire Hills of Massachusetts."

    He then threw his leg over the corner of the big chair and said, "I have heard many a time, ever since I was young, that up there in those hills you have to sharpen the noses
of the sheep in order to get down to the grass between the rocks." He was so familiar, so everyday, so farmer-like, that I felt right at home with him at once.

    He then took hold of another roll of paper, and looked up at me and said, "Good morning."

I took the hint then and got up and went out. After I had gotten out I could not realize I had seen the President of the United States at all. But a few days later, when still in the city, I saw the crowd pass through the East Room by the coffin of Abraham Lincoln, and when I looked at the upturned face of the murdered President I felt then that the man I had seen such a short time before, who, so simple a man, so plain a man, was one of the greatest men that God ever raised up to lead a nation on to ultimate liberty. Yet he was only "Old Abe" to his neighbors. When they had the second funeral, I was invited among others, and went out to see that same coffin put back in the tomb at Springfield. Around
the tomb stood Lincoln's old neighbors, to whom he was just "Old Abe." Of course that is all they would say.

Did you ever see a man who struts around altogether too large to notice an ordinary working mechanic? Do you think he is great? He is nothing but a puffed-up balloon, held down by his big feet. There is no greatness there.

Who are the great men and women? My attention was called the other day to the history of a very little thing that made the fortune of a very poor man. It was an awful thing, and yet because of that experience he--not a great inventor or genius--invented the pin that now is called the safety-pin, and out of that safety-pin made the fortune of one of the great aristocratic families of this nation.

A poor man in Massachusetts who had worked in the nail-works was injured at thirty-eight, and he could earn but little money. He was employed in the office to rub out the marks on the bills made by pencil memorandums, and he used a rubber until his hand grew tired. He then tied a piece of rubber on the end of a stick and worked it like a plane. His little girl came and said, "Why, you have a patent, haven't you?" The father said afterward, "My daughter told me when I took that stick and put the rubber on the end that there was a patent, and that was the first thought of that." He went to Boston and applied for his patent, and every one of you that has a rubber-tipped pencil in your pocket is now
paying tribute to the millionaire. No capital, not a penny did he invest in it. All was income, all the way up into the millions.

But let me hasten to one other greater thought. "Show me the great men and women who live in Philadelphia." A gentleman over there will get up and say: "We don't have any great men in Philadelphia. They don't live here. They live away off in Rome or St. Petersburg or London or Manayunk, or anywhere else but here in our town." I have come now to the apex of my thought. I have come now to the heart of the whole matter and to the center of my struggle: Why isn't Philadelphia a greater city in its greater wealth? Why does New York excel Philadelphia? People say, "Because of her harbor." Why do many other cities of the United States get ahead of Philadelphia now? There is only one answer, and that is because our own people talk down their own city. If there ever was a community

on earth that has to be forced ahead, it is the city of Philadelphia. If we are to have a boulevard, talk it down; if we are going to have better schools, talk them down; if you wish to have wise legislation, talk it down; talk all the proposed improvements down. That is the only great wrong that I can lay at the feet of the
magnificent Philadelphia that has been so universally kind to me. I say it is time we turn around in our city and begin to talk up the things that are in our city, and begin to set them before the world as the people of Chicago, New York, St. Louis, and San Francisco do. Oh, if we only could get that spirit out among our people, that we can do things in Philadelphia and do them well!

Arise, ye millions of Philadelphians, trust in God and man, and believe in the great opportunities that are right here not over in New York or Boston, but here--for business, for everything that is worth living for on earth. There was never an opportunity greater. Let us talk up our own city.

But there are two other young men here tonight, and that is all I will venture to say, because it is too late. One over there gets up and says, "There is going to be a great man in Philadelphia, but never was one."

"Oh, is that so? When are you going to be great?"

"When I am elected to some political office." Young man, won't you learn a lesson in the primer of politics that it is a *prima facie* evidence of littleness to hold office under our form of government? Great men get into office sometimes, but what this country needs
is men that will do what we tell them to do. This nation--where the people rule--is governed by the people, for the people, and so long as it is, then the office-holder is but the servant of the people, and the Bible says the servant cannot be greater than the master. The Bible says, "He that is sent cannot be greater than Him who sent Him." The people rule, or should rule, and if they do, we do not need the greater men in office. If the great men in America took our offices, we would change to an empire in the next ten years.

I know of a great many young women, now that woman's suffrage is coming, who say, "I am going to be President of the United States some day." I believe in woman's suffrage, and there is no doubt but what it is coming, and I am getting out of the way, anyhow. I may want an office by and by myself; but if the ambition for an office influences the women in their desire to vote, I want to say right here what I say to the
young men, that if you only get the privilege of casting one vote, you don't get anything that is worth while. Unless you can control more than one vote, you will be unknown, and your influence so dissipated as practically not to be felt. This country is not run by votes. Do you think it is? It is governed by influence. It is governed by the ambitions and the enterprises which control votes. The young woman that thinks she is going
to vote for the sake of holding an office is making an awful blunder.

That other young man gets up and says, "There are going to be great men in this country and in Philadelphia."

"Is that so? When?"

"When there comes a great war, when we get into difficulty through watchful waiting in Mexico; when we get into war with England over some frivolous deed, or with Japan or China or New Jersey or some distant country. Then I will march up to the cannon's mouth; I will sweep up among the glistening bayonets; I will leap into the arena and tear down the flag and bear it away in triumph. I will come home with stars on my shoulder, and hold every office in the gift of the nation, and I will be great." No, you won't. You think you are going to be made great by an office, but remember that if you are not great before you get the office, you won't be great when you secure it. It will only be a burlesque in that shape.

We had a Peace Jubilee here after the Spanish War. Out West they don't believe this, because they said, "Philadelphia would not have heard of any Spanish War until fifty years hence." Some of you saw the procession go up Broad Street. I was away, but the family wrote to me that the tally-ho coach with Lieutenant Hobson upon it stopped right at the front door and the people shouted, "Hurrah for Hobson!" and if I had been there I would have yelled too, because he deserves much more of his country than he has ever received. But suppose I go into school and say, "Who sunk the *Merrimac* at Santiago?"
and if the boys answer me, "Hobson," they will tell me seven-eighths of a lie. There were seven other heroes on that steamer, and they, by virtue of their position, were continually exposed to the Spanish fire, while Hobson, as an officer, might reasonably be behind the smokestack. You have gathered in this house your most intelligent people, and yet, perhaps, not one here can name the other seven men.

We ought not to so teach history. We ought to teach that, however humble a man's station may be, if he does his full duty in that place he is just as much entitled to the American people's honor as is the king upon his throne. But we do not so teach. We are now teaching everywhere that the generals do all the fighting.

I remember that, after the war, I went down to see General Robert E. Lee, that magnificent Christian gentleman of whom both North and South are now proud as one of our great Americans. The general told me about his servant, "Rastus," who was an enlisted colored soldier. He called him in one day to make fun of him, and said,
"Rastus, I hear that all the rest of your company are killed, and why are you not killed?" Rastus winked at him and said, " 'Cause when there is any fightin' goin' on I stay back with the generals."

I remember another illustration. I would leave it out but for the fact that when you go to the library to read this lecture, you will find this has been printed in it for twenty-five years. I shut my eyes--shut them close--and lo! I see the faces of my youth. Yes, they sometimes say to me, "Your hair is not white; you are working night and day without seeming ever to stop; you can't be old." But when I shut my eyes, like any other man of my years, oh, then come trooping back the faces of the loved and lost of long ago, and I know, whatever men may say, it is evening-time.

I shut my eyes now and look back to my native town in Massachusetts, and I see the cattle-show ground on the mountain-top; I can see the horse-sheds there. I can see the Congregational church; see the town hall and mountaineers' cottages; see a great assembly of people turning out, dressed resplendently, and I can see flags flying and handkerchiefs waving and hear bands playing. I can see that company of soldiers that had re-enlisted marching up on that cattle-show ground. I was but a boy, but I was captain of that company and puffed out with pride. A cambric needle would have burst me all to pieces. Then I thought it was the greatest event that ever came to man on earth. If you have ever thought you would like to be a king or queen, you go and be received by the mayor.

The bands played, and all the people turned out to receive us. I marched up that Common so proud at the head of my troops, and we turned down into the town hall. Then they seated my soldiers down the center aisle and I sat down on the front seat. A great assembly of people a hundred or two--came in to fill the town hall, so that they stood up all around. Then the town officers came in and formed a half-circle. The mayor of the town sat in the middle of the platform. He was a man who had never held office before; but he was a good man, and his friends have told me that I might use this without giving them offense. He was a good man, but he thought an office made a man great. He came up and took his seat, adjusted his powerful spectacles, and looked around, when he suddenly spied me sitting there on the front seat. He came right forward on the platform and invited me up to sit with the town officers. No town officer ever took any notice of me before I went to war, except to advise the teacher to thrash me, and now I was invited up on the stand with the town officers. Oh my! the town mayor was then the emperor, the king of our day and our time. As I came up on the platform they gave me a chair about this far, I would say, from the front.

When I had got seated, the chairman of the Selectmen arose and came forward to the table, and we all supposed he would introduce the Congregational minister, who was the only orator in town, and that he would give the oration to the returning soldiers. But, friends, you should have seen the surprise which ran over the audience when they discovered that the old fellow was going to deliver that speech himself. He had never made a speech in his life, but he fell into the same error that hundreds of other men have fallen into. It seems so strange that a man won't learn he must speak his piece as a boy if he intends to be an orator when he is grown, but he seems to think all he has to do is to hold an office to be a great orator.

So he came up to the front, and brought with him a speech which he had learned by heart walking up and down the pasture, where he had frightened the cattle. He brought the manuscript with him and spread it out on the table so as to be sure he might see it. He adjusted his spectacles and leaned over it for a moment and marched back on that platform, and then came forward like this--tramp, tramp, tramp. He must have studied the subject a great deal, when you come to think of it, because he assumed an "elocutionary" attitude. He rested heavily upon his left heel, threw back his shoulders, slightly advanced the right foot, opened the organs of speech, and advanced his right foot at an angle of forty-five. As he stood in that elocutionary attitude, friends, this is just the way that speech went. Some people say to me, "Don't you exaggerate?" That would be impossible. But I am here for the lesson and not for the story, and this is the way it went:

"Fellow-citizens--" As soon as he heard his voice his fingers began to go like that, his knees began to shake, and then he trembled all over. He choked and swallowed and came around to the table to look at the manuscript. Then he gathered himself up with clenched fists and came back: "Fellow-citizens, we are Fellow-citizens, we are—we are—we are—we are—we are—we are very happy—we are very happy—we are very happy. We are very happy to welcome back to their native town these soldiers who have fought and bled--and come back again to their native town. We are especially—we are especially—we are especially. We are especially pleased to see with us to-day this young hero" (that meant me)—"this young hero who in imagination" (friends, remember he said that; if he had not said "in imagination" I would not be egotistic enough to refer to it at all)—"this young hero who in imagination we have seen leading—we have seen leading—leading. We have seen leading his troops on to the deadly breach. We have seen his shining—we have seen his shining—his shining—his shining sword—flashing. Flashing in the sunlight, as he shouted to his troops, `Come on'!"

Oh dear, dear, dear! how little that good man knew about war. If he had known anything about war at all he ought to have known what any of my G.A.R. comrades here tonight will tell you is true, that it is next to a crime for an officer of infantry ever in time of danger to go ahead of his men. "I, with my shining sword flashing in the sunlight, shouting to my troops, `Come on'!" I never did it. Do you suppose I would get in front of my men to be shot in front by the enemy and in the back by my own men? That is no place for an officer. The place for the officer in actual battle is behind the line. How
often, as a staff officer, I rode down the line, when our men were suddenly called to the line of battle, and the Rebel yells were coming out of the woods, and shouted: "Officers to the rear! Officers to the rear!" Then every officer gets behind the line of private soldiers, and the higher the officer's rank the farther behind he goes. Not because

he is any the less brave, but because the laws of war require that. And yet he shouted, "I, with
my shining sword--" In that house there sat the company of my soldiers who had carried that boy across the Carolina rivers that he might not wet his feet. Some of them had gone far out to get a pig or a chicken. Some of them had gone to death under the shell-swept pines in the mountains of Tennessee, yet in the good man's speech they were scarcely known. He did refer to them, but only incidentally. The hero of the hour was this boy. Did the nation owe him anything? No, nothing then and nothing now. Why was he
the hero? Simply because that man fell into that same human error— that this boy was great because he was an officer and these were only private soldiers.

Oh, I learned the lesson then that I will never forget so long as the tongue of the bell of time continues to swing for me. Greatness consists not in the holding of some future office, but really consists in doing great deeds with little means and the accomplishment of vast purposes from the private ranks of life. To be great at all one must be great here, now, in Philadelphia. He who can give to this city better streets and better sidewalks, better schools and more colleges, more happiness and more civilization, more of God, he
will be great anywhere. Let every man or woman here, if you never hear me again, remember this, that if you wish to be great at all, you must begin where you are and what you are, in Philadelphia, now. He that can give to his city any blessing, he who can be a good citizen while he lives here, he that can make better homes, he that can be a blessing whether he works in the shop or sits behind the counter or keeps house, whatever be his
life, he who would be great anywhere must first be great in his own Philadelphia.

The Road Not Taken
Robert Frost

Two roads diverged in a yellow wood,
And sorry I could not travel both
And be one traveler, long I stood
And looked down one as far as I could
To where it bent in the undergrowth;

Then took the other, as just as fair,
And having perhaps the better claim,
Because it was grassy and wanted wear;
Though as for that the passing there
Had worn them really about the same,

And both that morning equally lay
In leaves no step had trodden black.
Oh, I kept the first for another day!
Yet knowing how way leads on to way,
I doubted if I should ever come back.

I shall be telling this with a sigh
Somewhere ages and ages hence:
Two roads diverged in a wood, and I--
I took the one less traveled by,
And that has made all the difference.

Self-Reliance

Ralph Waldo Emerson

SELF-RELIANCE
"Ne te quaesiveris extra."

"Man is his own star; and the soul that can
Render an honest and a perfect man,
Commands all light, all influence, all fate;
Nothing to him falls early or too late.
Our acts our angels are, or good or ill,
Our fatal shadows that walk by us still."

Epilogue to Beaumont and Fletcher's Honest Man's Fortune.

Cast the bantling on the rocks,
Suckle him with the she-wolf's teat,
Wintered with the hawk and fox.
Power and speed be hands and feet.

SELF-RELIANCE

I READ the other day some verses written by an eminent painter which were original and not conventional. The soul always hears an admonition in such lines, let the subject be what it may. The sentiment they instill is of more value than any thought they may contain. To believe your own thought, to believe that what is true for you in your private heart is true for all men,--that is genius. Speak your latent conviction, and it shall be the universal sense; for the inmost in due time becomes the outmost, and our first thought is rendered back to us by the trumpets of the Last Judgment. Familiar as the voice of the mind is to each, the highest merit we ascribe to Moses, Plato and Milton is that they set at naught books and traditions, and spoke not what men, but what they thought. A man should learn to detect and watch that gleam of light which flashes across his mind from within, more than the lustre of the firmament of bards and sages. Yet he dismisses without notice his thought, because it is his. In every work of genius we recognize our own rejected thoughts; they come back to us with a certain alienated majesty. Great works of art have no more affecting lesson for us than this. They teach us to abide by our spontaneous impression with good- humored inflexibility then most when the whole cry of voices is on the other side. Else to-morrow a stranger will say with masterly good sense precisely what we have thought and felt all the time, and we shall be forced to take with shame our own opinion from another.
    There is a time in every man's education when he arrives at the conviction that envy is ignorance; that imitation is suicide; that he must take himself for better for worse as his portion; that though the

wide universe is full of good, no kernel of nourishing corn can come to him but through his toil bestowed on that plot of ground which is given to him to till. The power which resides in him is new in nature, and none but he knows what that is which he can do, nor does he know until he has tried. Not for nothing one face, one character, one fact, makes much impression on him, and another none. This sculpture in the memory is not without pre-established harmony. The eye was placed where one ray should fall, that it might testify of that particular ray. We but half express ourselves, and are ashamed of that divine idea which each of us represents. It may be safely trusted as proportionate and of good issues, so it be faithfully imparted, but God will not have his work made manifest by cowards. A man is relieved and gay when he has put his heart into his work and done his best; but what he has said or done otherwise shall give him no peace. It is a deliverance which does not deliver. In the attempt his genius deserts him; no muse befriends; no invention, no hope.

Trust thyself: every heart vibrates to that iron string. Accept the place the divine providence has found for you, the society of your contemporaries, the connection of events. Great men have always done so, and confided themselves childlike to the genius of their age, betraying their perception that the absolutely trustworthy was seated at their heart, working through their hands, predominating in all their being. And we are now men, and must accept in the highest mind the same transcendent destiny; and not minors and invalids in a protected corner, not cowards fleeing before a revolution, but guides, redeemers and benefactors, obeying the Almighty effort and advancing on Chaos and the Dark.

What pretty oracles nature yields us on this text in the face and behavior of children, babes, and even brutes! That divided and rebel mind, that distrust of a sentiment because our arithmetic has computed the strength and means opposed to our purpose, these have not. Their mind being whole, their eye is as yet unconquered, and when we look in their faces we are disconcerted. Infancy conforms to nobody; all conform to it; so that one babe commonly makes four or five out of the adults who prattle and play to it. So God has armed youth and puberty and manhood no less with its own piquancy and charm, and made it enviable and gracious and its claims not to be put by, if it will stand by itself. Do not think the youth has no force, because he cannot speak to you and me. Hark! in the next room his voice is sufficiently clear and emphatic. It seems he knows how to speak to his contemporaries. Bashful or bold then, he will know how to make us seniors very unnecessary.

The nonchalance of boys who are sure of a dinner, and would disdain as much as a lord to do or say aught to conciliate one, is the healthy attitude of human nature. A boy is in the parlor what the pit is in the playhouse; independent, irresponsible, looking out from his corner on such people and facts as pass by, he tries and sentences them on their merits, in the swift, summary way of boys, as good, bad, interesting, silly, eloquent, troublesome. He cumbers himself never about consequences, about interests; he gives an independent, genuine verdict. You must court him; he does not court you. But the man is as it were clapped into jail by his consciousness. As soon as he has once acted or spoken with éclat he is a committed person, watched by the sympathy or the hatred of hundreds, whose affections must now enter into his account. There is no Lethe for this. Ah, that he could pass again into his neutrality! Who can thus avoid all pledges and, having observed, observe again from the same unaffected, unbiased, unbribable, unaffrighted innocence,-- must always be formidable. He would utter opinions on all passing affairs, which being seen to be not private but necessary, would sink like darts into the ear of men and put them in fear.

These are the voices which we hear in solitude, but they grow faint and inaudible as we enter into the world. Society everywhere is in conspiracy against the manhood of every one of its members. Society is a joint-stock company, in which the members agree, for the better securing of his bread to each shareholder, to surrender the liberty and culture of the eater. The virtue in most request is conformity. Self-reliance is its aversion. It loves not realities and creators, but names and customs.

Whoso would be a man, must be a nonconformist. He who would gather immortal palms must not be hindered by the name of goodness, but must explore if it be goodness. Nothing is at last sacred but the integrity of your own mind. Absolve you to yourself, and you shall have the suffrage of the world. I remember an answer which when quite young I was prompted to make to a valued adviser who was wont to importune me with the dear old doctrines of the church. On my saying, "What have I to do with the sacredness of traditions, if I live wholly from within?" my friend suggested,--"But these impulses may be from below, not from above." I replied, "They do not seem to me to be such; but if I am the Devil's child, I will live then from the Devil." No law can be sacred to me but that of my nature. Good and bad are but names very readily transferable to that or this; the only right is what is after my constitution; the only wrong what is against it. A man is to carry himself in the presence of all opposition as if every thing were titular and ephemeral but he.

I am ashamed to think how easily we capitulate to badges and names, to large societies and dead institutions. Every decent and well-spoken individual affects and sways me more than is right. I ought to go upright and vital, and speak the rude truth in all ways. If malice and vanity wear the coat of philanthropy, shall that pass? If an angry bigot assumes this bountiful cause of Abolition, and comes to me with his last news from Barbadoes, why should I not say to him, 'Go love thy infant; love thy wood-chopper; be good-natured and modest; have that grace; and never varnish your hard, uncharitable ambition with this incredible tenderness for black folk a thousand miles off. Thy love afar is spite at home.' Rough and graceless would be such greeting, but truth is handsomer than the affectation of love. Your goodness must have some edge to it,--else it is none. The doctrine of hatred must be preached, as the counteraction of the doctrine of love, when that pules and whines. I shun father and mother and wife and brother when my genius calls me. I would write on the lintels of the door-post, *Whim*. I hope it is somewhat better than whim at last, but we cannot spend the day in explanation.

Expect me not to show cause why I seek or why I exclude company. Then again, do not tell me, as a good man did to-day, of my obligation to put all poor men in good situations. Are they my poor? I tell thee thou foolish philanthropist that I grudge the dollar, the dime, the cent, I give to such men as do not belong to me and to whom I do not belong. There is a class of persons to whom by all spiritual affinity I am bought and sold; for them I will go to prison if need be; but your miscellaneous popular charities; the education at college of fools; the building of meeting-houses to the vain end to which many now stand; alms to sots, and the thousand-fold Relief Societies;--though I confess with shame I sometimes succumb and give the dollar, it is a wicked dollar which by and by I shall have the manhood to withhold.

Virtues are, in the popular estimate, rather the exception than the rule. There is the man and his virtues. Men do what is called a good action, as some piece of courage or charity, much as they would pay a fine in expiation of daily non-appearance on parade. Their works are done as an apology or extenuation of their living in the world,--as invalids and the insane pay a high board. Their virtues are penances. I do not wish to expiate, but to live. My life is for itself and not for a spectacle. I much prefer that it should be of a lower strain, so it be genuine and equal, than that it should be glittering and unsteady. I wish it to be sound and sweet, and not to need diet and bleeding. I ask primary evidence that you are a man, and refuse this appeal from the man to his actions. I know that for myself it makes no difference whether I do or forbear those actions which are reckoned excellent. I cannot consent to pay for a privilege where I have intrinsic right. Few and mean as my gifts may be, I actually am, and do not need for my own assurance or the assurance of my fellows any secondary testimony.

What I must do is all that concerns me, not what the people think. This rule, equally arduous in actual and in intellectual life, may serve for the whole distinction between greatness and meanness. It is the harder because you will always find those who think they know what is your duty better than you know it. It is easy in the world to live after the world's opinion; it is easy in solitude to live after our own; but the great man is he who in the midst of the crowd keeps with perfect sweetness the independence of solitude.

The objection to conforming to usages that have become dead to you is that it scatters your force. It loses your time and blurs the impression of your character. If you maintain a dead church, contribute to a dead Bible-society, vote with a great party either for the government or against it, spread your table like base housekeepers,--under all these screens I have difficulty to detect the precise man you are: and of course so much force is withdrawn from your proper life. But do your work, and I shall know you. Do your work, and you shall reinforce yourself. A man must consider what a blindman's-buff is this game of conformity. If I know your sect, I anticipate your argument.

I hear a preacher announce for his text and topic the expediency of one of the institutions of his church. Do I not know beforehand that not possibly can he say a new and spontaneous word? Do I not know that with all this ostentation of examining the grounds of the institution he will do no such thing? Do I not know that he is pledged to himself not to look but at one side, the permitted side, not as a man, but as a parish minister? He is a retained attorney, and these airs of the bench are the emptiest affectation. Well, most men have bound their eyes with one or another handkerchief, and attached themselves to some one of these communities of opinion. This conformity makes them not false in a few particulars, authors of a few lies, but false in all particulars. Their every truth is not quite true. Their two is not the real two, their four not the real four; so that every word they say chagrins us and we know not where to begin to set them right.

Meantime nature is not slow to equip us in the prison-uniform of the party to which we adhere. We come to wear one cut of face and figure, and acquire by degrees the gentlest asinine expression. There is a mortifying experience in particular, which does not fail to wreak itself also in the general history; I mean "the foolish face of praise," the forced smile which we put on in company where we do not feel at ease in answer to conversation which does not interest us. The muscles, not spontaneously moved but moved by a low usurping willfulness, grow tight about the outline of the face with the most disagreeable sensation.

For nonconformity the world whips you with its displeasure. And therefore a man must know how to estimate a sour face. The by-standers look askance on him in the public street or in the friend's parlor. If this aversion had its origin in contempt and resistance like his own he might well go home with a sad countenance; but the sour faces of the multitude, like their sweet faces, have no deep cause, but are put on and off as the wind blows and a newspaper directs. Yet is the discontent of the multitude more formidable than that of the senate and the college. It is easy enough for a firm man who knows the world to brook the rage of the cultivated classes. Their rage is decorous and prudent, for they are timid, as being very vulnerable themselves. But when to their feminine rage the indignation of the people is added, when the ignorant and the poor are aroused, when the unintelligent brute force that lies at the bottom of society is made to growl and mow, it needs the habit of magnanimity and religion to treat it godlike as a trifle of no concernment.

The other terror that scares us from self-trust is our consistency; a reverence for our past act or word because the eyes of others have no other data for computing our orbit than our past acts, and we are loath to disappoint them.

But why should you keep your head over your shoulder? Why drag about this corpse of your memory, lest you contradict somewhat you have stated in this or that public place? Suppose you should contradict yourself; what then? It seems to be a rule of wisdom never to rely on your memory alone, scarcely even in acts of pure memory, but to bring the past for judgment into the thousand-eyed present, and live ever in a new day. In your metaphysics you have denied personality to the Deity, yet when the devout motions of the soul come, yield to them heart and life, though they should clothe God with shape and color. Leave your theory, as Joseph his coat in the hand of the harlot, and flee.

A foolish consistency is the hobgoblin of little minds, adored by little statesmen and philosophers and divines. With consistency a great soul has simply nothing to do. He may as well concern himself with his shadow on the wall. Speak what you think now in hard words and to-morrow speak what to-morrow thinks in hard words again, though it contradict every thing you said to-day.--'Ah, so you shall be sure to be misunderstood.'--Is it so bad then to be misunderstood? Pythagoras was misunderstood, and Socrates, and Jesus, and Luther, and Copernicus, and Galileo, and Newton, and every pure and wise spirit that ever took flesh. To be great is to be misunderstood.

I suppose no man can violate his nature. All the sallies of his will are rounded in by the law of his being, as the inequalities of Andes and Himmaleh are insignificant in the curve of the sphere. Nor does it matter how you gauge and try him. A character is like an acrostic or Alexandrian stanza;--read it forward, backward, or across, it still spells the same thing. In this pleasing contrite wood-life which God allows me, let me record day by day my honest thought without prospect or retrospect, and, I cannot doubt, it will be found symmetrical, though I mean it not and see it not. My book should smell of pines and resound with the hum of insects. The swallow over my window should interweave that thread or straw he carries in his bill into my web also. We pass for what we are. Character teaches above our wills. Men imagine that they communicate their virtue or vice only by overt actions, and do not see that virtue or vice emit a breath every moment.

There will be an agreement in whatever variety of actions, so they be each honest and natural in their hour. For of one will, the actions will be harmonious, however unlike they seem. These varieties are lost sight of at a little distance, at a little height of thought. One tendency unites them all. The voyage of the best ship is a zigzag line of a hundred tacks. See the line from a sufficient distance, and it straightens itself to the average tendency. Your genuine action will explain itself and will explain your other genuine actions. Your conformity explains nothing. Act singly, and what you have already done singly will justify you now. Greatness appeals to the future. If I can be firm enough to-day to do right and scorn eyes, I must have done so much right before as to defend me now. Be it how it will, do right now. Always scorn appearances and you always may. The force of character is cumulative. All the foregone days of virtue work their health into this.

What makes the majesty of the heroes of the senate and the field, which so fills the imagination? The consciousness of a train of great days and victories behind. They shed an united light on the advancing actor. He is attended as by a visible escort of angels. That is it which throws thunder into Chatham's voice, and dignity into Washington's port, and America into Adams's eye. Honor is venerable to us because it is no ephemera. It is always ancient virtue. We worship it to-day because it is not of to-day. We love it and pay it homage because it is not a trap for our love and homage, but is self-dependent, self-derived, and therefore of an old immaculate pedigree, even if shown in a young person.

I hope in these days we have heard the last of conformity and consistency. Let the words be gazetted and ridiculous henceforward. Instead of the gong for dinner, let us hear a whistle from the Spartan fife. Let us never bow and apologize more. A great man is coming to eat at my house. I do not wish to please him; I wish that he should wish to please me. I will stand here for humanity, and though I would make it kind, I would make it true. Let us affront and reprimand the smooth mediocrity and squalid contentment of the times, and hurl in the face of custom and trade and office, the fact which is the upshot of all history, that there is a great responsible Thinker and Actor working wherever a man works; that a true man belongs to no other time or place, but is the centre of things. Where he is, there is nature. He measures you and all men and all events.

Ordinarily, every body in society reminds us of somewhat else, or of some other person. Character, reality, reminds you of nothing else; it takes place of the whole creation. The man must be so much that he must make all circumstances indifferent. Every true man is a cause, a country, and an age; requires infinite spaces and numbers and time fully to accomplish his design;--and posterity seem to follow his steps as a train of clients. A man Caesar is born, and for ages after we have a Roman Empire. Christ is born, and millions of minds so grow and cleave to his genius that he is confounded with virtue and the possible of man. An institution is the lengthened shadow of one man; as, Monachism, of the Hermit Antony; the Reformation, of Luther; Quakerism, of Fox; Methodism, of Wesley; Abolition, of Clarkson. Scipio, Milton called "the height of Rome"; and all history Resolves itself very easily into the biography of a few stout and earnest persons.

Let a man then know his worth, and keep things under his feet. Let him not peep or steal, or skulk up and down with the air of a charity-boy, a bastard, or an interloper in the world which exists for him. But the man in the street, finding no worth in himself which corresponds to the force which built a tower or sculptured a marble god, feels poor when he looks on these. To him a palace, a statue, or a costly book have an alien and forbidding air, much like a gay equipage, and seem to say like that, 'Who are you, Sir?' Yet they all are his, suitors for his notice, petitioners to his faculties that they will come out and take possession. The picture waits for my verdict; it is not to command me, but I am to settle its claims to praise. That popular fable of the sot who was picked up dead drunk in the street, carried to the duke's house, washed and dressed and laid in the duke's bed, and, on his waking, treated with all obsequious ceremony like the duke, and assured that he had been insane, owes its popularity to the fact that it symbolizes so well the state of man, who is in the world a sort of sot, but now and then wakes up, exercises his reason and finds himself a true prince.

Our reading is mendicant and sycophantic. In history our imagination plays us false. Kingdom and lordship, power and estate, are a gaudier vocabulary than private John and Edward in a small house and common day's work; but the things of life are the same to both; the sum total of both is the same. Why all this deference to Alfred and Scanderbeg and Gustavus? Suppose they were virtuous; did they wear out virtue? As great a stake depends on your private act to-day, as followed their public and renowned steps. When private men shall act with original views, the lustre will be transferred from the actions of kings to those of gentlemen.

The world has been instructed by its kings, who have so magnetized the eyes of nations. It has been taught by this colossal symbol the mutual reverence that is due from man to man. The joyful loyalty with which men have everywhere suffered the king, the noble, or the great proprietor to walk among them by a law of his own, make his own scale of men and things and reverse theirs, pay for benefits not with money but with honor, and represent the law in his person, was the hieroglyphic by which they obscurely signified their consciousness of their own right and comeliness, the right of every man.

The magnetism which all original action exerts is explained when we inquire the reason of self-trust. Who is the Trustee? What is the aboriginal Self, on which a universal reliance may be grounded? What is the nature and power of that science- baffling star, without parallax, without calculable elements, which shoots a ray of beauty even into trivial and impure actions, if the least mark of independence appear? The inquiry leads us to that source, at once the essence of genius, of virtue, and of life, which we call Spontaneity or Instinct. We denote this primary wisdom as Intuition, whilst all later teachings are tuitions. In that deep force, the last fact behind which analysis cannot go, all things find their common origin. For the sense of being which in calm hours rises, we know not how, in the soul, is not diverse from things, from space, from light, from time, from man, but one with them and proceeds obviously from the same source whence their life and being also proceed.

We first share the life by which things exist and afterwards see them as appearances in nature and forget that we have shared their cause. Here is the fountain of action and of thought. Here are the lungs of that inspiration which giveth man wisdom and which cannot be denied without impiety and atheism. We lie in the lap of immense intelligence, which makes us receivers of its truth and organs of its activity. When we discern justice, when we discern truth, we do nothing of ourselves, but allow a passage to its beams. If we ask whence this comes, if we seek to pry into the soul that causes, all philosophy is at fault. Its presence or its absence is all we can affirm.

Every man discriminates between the voluntary acts of his mind and his involuntary perceptions, and knows that to his involuntary perceptions a perfect faith is due. He may err in the expression of them, but he knows that these things are so, like day and night, not to be disputed. My wilful actions and acquisitions are but roving;--the idlest reverie, the faintest native emotion, command my curiosity and respect. Thoughtless people contradict as readily the statement of perceptions as of opinions, or rather much more readily; for they do not distinguish between perception and notion. They fancy that I choose to see this or that thing. But perception is not whimsical, but fatal. If I see a trait, my children will see it after me, and in course of time all mankind,-- although it may chance that no one has seen it before me. For my perception of it is as much a fact as the sun.

The relations of the soul to the divine spirit are so pure that it is profane to seek to interpose helps. It must be that when God speaketh he should communicate, not one thing, but all things; should fill the world with his voice; should scatter forth light, nature, time, souls, from the centre of the present thought; and new date and new create the whole. Whenever a mind is simple and receives a divine wisdom, old things pass away,--means, teachers, texts, temples fall; it lives now, and absorbs past and future into the present hour. All things are made sacred by relation to it,--one as much as another. All things are dissolved to their centre by their cause, and in the universal miracle petty and particular miracles disappear. If therefore a man claims to know and speak of God and carries you backward to the phraseology of some old mouldered nation in another country, in another world, believe him not. Is the acorn better than the oak which is its fullness and completion? Is the parent better than the child into whom he has cast his ripened being? Whence then this worship of the past? The centuries are conspirators against the sanity and authority of the soul. Time and space are but physiological colors which the eye makes, but the soul is light: where it is, is day; where it was, is night; and history is an impertinence and an injury if it be any thing more than a cheerful apologue or parable of my being and becoming.

Man is timid and apologetic; he is no longer upright; he dares not say 'I think,' 'I am,' but quotes some saint or sage. He is ashamed before the blade of grass or the blowing rose. These roses under my window make no reference to former roses or to better ones; they are for what they are; they exist with God to-day. There is no time to them. There is simply the rose; it is perfect in every moment of its existence. Before a leaf-bud has burst, its whole life acts; in the full-blown flower there is no more; in the leafless root there is no less. Its nature is satisfied and it satisfies nature in all moments alike. But man postpones or remembers; he does not live in the present, but with reverted eye laments the past, or, heedless of the riches that surround him, stands on tiptoe to foresee the future. He cannot be happy and strong until he too lives with nature in the present, above time.

This should be plain enough. Yet see what strong intellects dare not yet hear God himself unless he speak the phraseology of I know not what David, or Jeremiah, or Paul. We shall not always set so great a price on a few texts, on a few lives. We are like children who repeat by rote the sentences of grandames and tutors, and, as they grow older, of the men of talents and character they chance to see,--painfully recollecting the exact words they spoke; afterwards, when they come into the point of view which those had who uttered these sayings, they understand them and are willing to let the words go; for at any time they can use words as good when occasion comes. If we live truly, we shall see truly. It is as easy for the strong man to be strong, as it is for the weak to be weak. When we have new perception, we shall gladly disburden the memory of its hoarded treasures as old rubbish. When a man lives with God, his voice shall be as sweet as the murmur of the brook and the rustle of the corn.

And now at last the highest truth on this subject remains unsaid; probably cannot be said; for all that we say is the far-off remembering of the intuition. That thought by what I can now nearest approach to say it, is this. When good is near you, when you have life in yourself, it is not by any known or accustomed way; you shall not discern the footprints of any other; you shall not see the face of man; you shall not hear any name;--the way, the thought, the good shall be wholly strange and new. It shall exclude example and experience. You take the way from man, not to man. All persons that ever existed are its forgotten ministers. Fear and hope are alike beneath it. There is somewhat low even in hope. In the hour of vision there is nothing that can be called gratitude, nor properly joy. The soul raised over passion beholds identity and eternal causation, perceives the self-existence of Truth and Right, and calms itself with knowing that all things go well. Vast spaces of nature, the Atlantic Ocean, the South Sea; long intervals of time, years, centuries, are of no account. This which I think and feel underlay every former state of life and circumstances, as it does underlie my present, and what is called life, and what is called death.

Life only avails, not the having lived. Power ceases in the instant of repose; it resides in the moment of transition from a past to a new state, in the shooting of the gulf, in the darting to an aim. This one fact the world hates; that the soul becomes; for that for ever degrades the past, turns all riches to poverty, all reputation to a shame, confounds the saint with the rogue, shoves Jesus and Judas equally aside. Why then do we prate of self-reliance? Inasmuch as the soul is present there will be power not confident but agent. To talk of reliance is a poor external way of speaking. Speak rather of that which relies because it works and is. Who has more obedience than I masters me, though he should not raise his finger. Round him I must revolve by the gravitation of spirits. We fancy it rhetoric when we speak of eminent virtue. We do not yet see that virtue is Height, and that a man or a company of men, plastic and permeable to principles, by the law of nature must overpower and ride all cities, nations, kings, rich men, poets, who are not.

This is the ultimate fact which we so quickly reach on this, as on every topic, the resolution of all into the ever-blessed ONE. Self-existence is the attribute of the Supreme Cause, and it constitutes the measure of good by the degree in which it enters into all lower forms. All things real are so by so much virtue as they contain. Commerce, husbandry, hunting, whaling, war, eloquence, personal weight, are somewhat, and engage my respect as examples of its presence and impure action. I see the same law working in nature for conservation and growth. Power is, in nature, the essential measure of right. Nature suffers nothing to remain in her kingdoms which cannot help itself. The genesis and maturation of a planet, its poise and orbit, the bended tree recovering itself from the strong wind, the vital resources of every animal and vegetable, are demonstrations of the self-sufficing and therefore self-relying soul.

Thus all concentrates: let us not rove; let us sit at home with the cause. Let us stun and astonish the intruding rabble of men and books and institutions, by a simple declaration of the divine fact. Bid the invaders take the shoes from off their feet, for God is here within. Let our simplicity judge them, and our docility to our own law demonstrate the poverty of nature and fortune beside our native riches.

But now we are a mob. Man does not stand in awe of man, nor is his genius admonished to stay at home, to put itself in communication with the internal ocean, but it goes abroad to beg a cup of water of the urns of other men. We must go alone. I like the silent church before the service begins, better than any preaching. How far off, how cool, how chaste the persons look, begirt each one with a precinct or sanctuary! So let us always sit. Why should we assume the faults of our friend, or wife, or father, or child, because they sit around our hearth, or are said to have the same blood? All men have my blood and I have all men's. Not for that will I adopt their petulance or folly, even to the extent of being ashamed of it. But your isolation must not be mechanical, but spiritual, that is, must be elevation. At times the whole world seems to be in conspiracy to importune you with emphatic trifles. Friend, client, child, sickness, fear, want, charity, all knock at once at thy closet door and say,--'Come out unto us.' But keep thy state; come not into their confusion. The power men possess to annoy me I give them by a weak curiosity. No man can come near me but through my act. "What we love that we have, but by desire we bereave ourselves of the love."

If we cannot at once rise to the sanctities of obedience and faith, let us at least resist our temptations; let us enter into the state of war and wake Thor and Woden, courage and constancy, in our Saxon breasts. This is to be done in our smooth times by speaking the truth. Check this lying hospitality and lying affection. Live no longer to the expectation of these deceived and deceiving people with whom we converse. Say to them, 'O father, O mother, O wife, O brother, O friend, I have lived with you after appearances hitherto. Henceforward I am the truth's. Be it known unto you that henceforward I obey no law less than the eternal law. I will have no covenants but proximities. I shall endeavour to nourish my parents, to support my family, to be the chaste husband of one wife,--but these relations I must fill after a new and unprecedented way. I appeal from your customs. I must be myself. I cannot break myself any longer for you, or you. If you can love me for what I am, we shall be the happier. If you cannot, I will still seek to deserve that you should. I will not hide my tastes or aversions. I will so trust that what is deep is holy, that I will do strongly before the sun and moon whatever inly rejoices me and the heart appoints. If you are noble, I will love you: if you are not, I will not hurt you and myself by hypocritical attentions. If you are true, but not in the same truth with me, cleave to your companions; I will seek my own. I do this not selfishly but humbly and truly.

It is alike your interest, and mine, and all men's, however long we have dwelt in lies, to live in truth. Does this sound harsh to-day? You will soon love what is dictated by your nature as well as mine, and if we follow the truth it will bring us out safe at last.'--But so may you give these friends pain. Yes, but I cannot sell my liberty and my power, to save their sensibility. Besides, all persons have their moments of reason, when they look out into the region of absolute truth; then will they justify me and do the same thing.

The populace think that your rejection of popular standards is a rejection of all standard, and mere antinomianism; and the bold sensualist will use the name of philosophy to gild his crimes. But the law of consciousness abides. There are two confessionals, in one or the other of which we must be shriven. You may fulfil your round of duties by clearing yourself in the direct, or in the reflex way. Consider whether you have satisfied your relations to father, mother, cousin, neighbor, town, cat, and dog; whether any of these can upbraid you. But I may also neglect this reflex standard and absolve me to myself. I have my own stern claims and perfect circle. It denies the name of duty to many offices that are called duties. But if I can discharge its debts it enables me to dispense with the popular code. If any one imagines that this law is lax, let him keep its commandment one day.

And truly it demands something godlike in him who has cast off the common motives of humanity and has ventured to trust himself for a taskmaster. High be his heart, faithful his will, clear his sight, that he may in good earnest be doctrine, society, law, to himself, that a simple purpose may be to him as strong as iron necessity is to others!

If any man consider the present aspects of what is called by distinction society, he will see the need of these ethics. The sinew and heart of man seem to be drawn out, and we are become timorous, desponding whimperers. We are afraid of truth, afraid of fortune, afraid of death and afraid of each other. Our age yields no great and perfect persons. We want men and women who shall renovate life and our social state, but we see that most natures are insolvent, cannot satisfy their own wants, have an ambition out of all proportion to their practical force and do lean and beg day and night continually. Our housekeeping is mendicant, our arts, our occupations, our marriages, our religion we have not chosen, but society has chosen for us. We are parlor soldiers. We shun the rugged battle of fate, where strength is born.

If our young men miscarry in their first enterprises they lose all heart. If the young merchant fails, men say he is ruined. If the finest genius studies at one of our colleges and is not installed in an office within one year afterwards in the cities or suburbs of Boston or New York, it seems to his friends and to himself that he is right in being disheartened and in complaining the rest of his life. A sturdy lad from New Hampshire or Vermont, who in turn tries all the professions, who teams it, farms it, peddles, keeps a school, preaches, edits a newspaper, goes to Congress, buys a township, and so forth, in successive years, and always like a cat falls on his feet, is worth a hundred of these city dolls. He walks abreast with his days and feels no shame in not 'studying a profession,' for he does not postpone his life, but lives already. He has not one chance, but a hundred chances. Let a Stoic open the resources of man and tell men they are not leaning willows, but can and must detach themselves; that with the exercise of self-trust, new powers shall appear; that a man is the word made flesh, born to shed healing to the nations; that he should be ashamed of our compassion, and that the moment he acts from himself, tossing the laws, the books, idolatries and customs out of the window, we pity him no more but thank and revere him;--and that teacher shall restore the life of man to splendor and make his name dear to all history.

It is easy to see that a greater self-reliance must work a revolution in all the offices and relations of men; in their religion; in their education; in their pursuits; their modes of living; their association; in their property; in their speculative views.

1. In what prayers do men allow themselves! That which they call a holy office is not so much as brave and manly. Prayer looks abroad and asks for some foreign addition to come through some foreign virtue, and loses itself in endless mazes of natural and supernatural, and mediatorial and miraculous. Prayer that craves a particular commodity, any thing less than all good, is vicious. Prayer is the contemplation of the facts of life from the highest point of view. It is the soliloquy of a beholding and jubilant soul. It is the spirit of God pronouncing his works good. But prayer as a means to effect a private end is meanness and theft. It supposes dualism and not unity in nature and consciousness. As soon as the man is at one with God, he will not beg. He will then see prayer in all action. The prayer of the farmer kneeling

in his field to weed it, the prayer of the rower kneeling with the stroke of his oar, are true prayers heard throughout nature, though for cheap ends. Caratach, in Fletcher's Bonduca, when admonished to inquire the mind of the god Audate, replies,--

"His hidden meaning lies in our endeavors;
Our valors are our best gods."

Another sort of false prayers are our regrets. Discontent is the want of self-reliance: it is infirmity of will. Regret calamities if you can thereby help the sufferer; if not, attend your own work and already the evil begins to be repaired. Our sympathy is just as base. We come to them who weep foolishly and sit down and cry for company, instead of imparting to them truth and health in rough electric shocks, putting them once more in communication with their own reason. The secret of fortune is joy in our hands. Welcome evermore to gods and men is the self-helping man. For him all doors are flung wide; him all tongues greet, all honors crown, all eyes follow with desire. Our love goes out to him and embraces him because he did not need it. We solicitously and apologetically caress and celebrate him because he held on his way and scorned our disapprobation. The gods love him because men hated him. "To the persevering mortal," said Zoroaster, "the blessed Immortals are swift."

As men's prayers are a disease of the will, so are their creeds a disease of the intellect. They say with those foolish Israelites, 'Let not God speak to us, lest we die. Speak thou, speak any man with us, and we will obey.' Everywhere I am hindered of meeting God in my brother, because he has shut his own temple doors and recites fables merely of his brother's, or his brother's brother's God. Every new mind is a new classification. If it prove a mind of uncommon activity and power, a Locke, a Lavoisier, a Hutton, a Bentham, a Fourier, it imposes its classification on other men, and lo! a new system. In proportion to the depth of the thought, and so to the number of the objects it touches and brings within reach of the pupil, is his complacency. But chiefly is this apparent in creeds and churches, which are also classifications of some powerful mind acting on the elemental thought of duty, and man's relation to the Highest. Such is Calvinism, Quakerism, Swedenborgism.

The pupil takes the same delight in subordinating every thing to the new terminology as a girl who has just learned botany in seeing a new earth and new seasons thereby. It will happen for a time that the pupil will find his intellectual power has grown by the study of his master's mind. But in all unbalanced minds the classification is idolized, passes for the end and not for a speedily exhaustible means, so that the walls of the system blend to their eye in the remote horizon with the walls of the universe; the luminaries of heaven seem to them hung on the arch their master built. They cannot imagine how you aliens have any right to see,--how you can see; 'It must be somehow that you stole the light from us.' They do not yet perceive that light, unsystematic, indomitable, will break into any cabin, even into theirs. Let them chirp awhile and call it their own. If they are honest and do well, presently their neat new pinfold will be too strait and low, will crack, will lean, will rot and vanish, and the immortal light, all young and joyful, million-orbed, million- colored, will beam over the universe as on the first morning.

2. It is for want of self-culture that the superstition of Travelling, whose idols are Italy, England, Egypt, retains its fascination for all educated Americans. They who made England, Italy, or Greece venerable in the imagination did so by sticking fast where they were, like an axis of the earth. In manly hours we feel that duty is our place. The soul is no traveller; the wise man stays at home, and when his necessities, his duties, on any occasion call him from his house, or into foreign lands, he is at home still and shall make men sensible by the expression of his countenance that he goes, the missionary of wisdom and virtue, and visits cities and men like a sovereign and not like an interloper or a valet.

I have no churlish objection to the circumnavigation of the globe for the purposes of art, of study, and benevolence, so that the man is first domesticated, or does not go abroad with the hope of finding somewhat greater than he knows. He who travels to be amused, or to get somewhat which he does not carry, travels away from himself, and grows old even in youth among old things. In Thebes, in Palmyra, his will and mind have become old and dilapidated as they. He carries ruins to ruins.

Travelling is a fool's paradise. Our first journeys discover to us the indifference of places. At home I dream that at Naples, at Rome, I can be intoxicated with beauty and lose my sadness. I pack my trunk, embrace my friends, embark on the sea and at last wake up in Naples, and there beside me is the stern fact, the sad self, unrelenting, identical, that I fled from. I seek the Vatican and the palaces. I affect to be intoxicated with sights and suggestions, but I am not intoxicated. My giant goes with me wherever I go.

3. But the rage of travelling is a symptom of a deeper unsoundness affecting the whole intellectual action. The intellect is vagabond, and our system of education fosters restlessness. Our minds travel when our bodies are forced to stay at home. We imitate; and what is imitation but the travelling of the mind? Our houses are built with foreign taste; our shelves are garnished with foreign ornaments; our opinions, our tastes, our faculties, lean, and follow the Past and the Distant. The soul created the arts wherever they have flourished. It was in his own mind that the artist sought his model. It was an application of his own thought to the thing to be done and the conditions to be observed. And why need we copy the Doric or the Gothic model? Beauty, convenience, grandeur of thought and quaint expression are as near to us as to any, and if the American artist will study with hope and love the precise thing to be done by him, considering the climate, the soil, the length of the day, the wants of the people, the habit and form of the government, he will create a house in

which all these will find themselves fitted, and taste and sentiment will be satisfied also.

Insist on yourself; never imitate. Your own gift you can present every moment with the cumulative force of a whole life's cultivation; but of the adopted talent of another you have only an extemporaneous half possession. That which each can do best, none but his Maker can teach him. No man yet knows what it is, nor can, till that person has exhibited it. Where is the master who could have taught Shakspeare? Where is the master who could have instructed Franklin, or Washington, or Bacon, or Newton? Every great man is a unique. The Scipionism of Scipio is precisely that part he could not borrow. Shakspeare will never be made by the study of Shakspeare. Do that which is assigned you, and you cannot hope too much or dare too much. There is at this moment for you an utterance brave and grand as that of the colossal chisel of Phidias, or trowel of the Egyptians, or the pen of Moses or Dante, but different from all these. Not possibly will the soul, all rich, all eloquent, with thousand-cloven tongue, deign to repeat itself; but if you can hear what these patriarchs say, surely you can reply to them in the same pitch of voice; for the ear and the tongue are two organs of one nature. Abide in the simple and noble regions of thy life, obey thy heart and thou shalt reproduce the Foreworld again.

4. As our Religion, our Education, our Art look abroad, so does our spirit of society. All men plume themselves on the improvement of society, and no man improves.

Society never advances. It recedes as fast on one side as it gains on the other. It undergoes continual changes; it is barbarous, it is civilized, it is christianized, it is rich, it is scientific; but this change is not amelioration. For every thing that is given something is taken. Society acquires new arts and loses old instincts. What a contrast between the well-clad, reading, writing, thinking American, with a watch, a pencil and a bill of exchange in his pocket, and the naked New Zealander, whose property is a club, a spear, a mat and an undivided twentieth of a shed to sleep under! But compare the health of the two men and you shall see that the white man has lost his aboriginal strength. If the traveller tell us truly, strike the savage with a broad axe and in a day or two the flesh shall unite and heal as if you struck the blow into soft pitch, and the same blow shall send the white to his grave.

The civilized man has built a coach, but has lost the use of his feet. He is supported on crutches, but lacks so much support of muscle. He has a fine Geneva watch, but he fails of the skill to tell the hour by the sun. A Greenwich nautical almanac he has, and so being sure of the information when he wants it, the man in the street does not know a star in the sky.

The solstice he does not observe; the equinox he knows as little; and the whole bright calendar of the year is without a dial in his mind. His note-books impair his memory; his libraries overload his wit; the insurance-office increases the number of accidents; and it may be a question whether machinery does not encumber; whether we have not lost by refinement some energy, by a Christianity entrenched in establishments and forms some vigor of wild virtue. For every Stoic was a Stoic; but in Christendom where is the Christian?

There is no more deviation in the moral standard than in the standard of height or bulk. No greater men are now than ever were. A singular equality may be observed between the great men of the first and of the last ages; nor can all the science, art, religion, and philosophy of the nineteenth century avail to educate greater men than Plutarch's heroes, three or four and twenty centuries ago. Not in time is the race progressive. Phocion, Socrates, Anaxagoras, Diogenes, are great men, but they leave no class. He who is really of their class will not be called by their name, but will be his own man, and in his turn the founder of a sect. The arts and inventions of each period are only its costume and do not invigorate men. The harm of the improved machinery may compensate its good. Hudson and Behring accomplished so much in their fishing-boats as to astonish Parry and Franklin, whose equipment exhausted the resources of science and art. Galileo, with an opera-glass, discovered a more splendid series of celestial phenomena than any one since. Columbus found the New World in an undecked boat. It is curious to see the periodical disuse and perishing of means and machinery which were introduced with loud laudation a few years or centuries before. The great genius returns to essential man. We reckoned the improvements of the art of war among the triumphs of science, and yet Napoleon conquered Europe by the bivouac, which consisted of falling back on naked valor and disencumbering it of all aids. The Emperor held it impossible to make a perfect army, says Las Cases, "without abolishing our arms, magazines, commissaries and carriages, until, in imitation of the Roman custom, the soldier should receive his supply of corn, grind it in his hand-mill, and bake his bread himself."

Society is a wave. The wave moves onward, but the water of which it is composed does not. The same particle does not rise from the valley to the ridge. Its unity is only phenomenal. The persons who make up a nation to-day, next year die, and their experience with them.

And so the reliance on Property, including the reliance on governments which protect it, is the want of self-reliance. Men have looked away from themselves and at things so long that they have come to esteem the religious, learned and civil institutions as guards of property, and they deprecate assaults on these, because they feel them to be assaults on property. They measure their esteem of each other by what each has, and not by what each is. But a cultivated man becomes ashamed of his property, out of new respect for his nature. Especially he hates what he has if he see that it is accidental,--came to him by inheritance, or gift, or crime; then he feels that it is not having; it does not belong to him, has no root in him and merely lies there because no revolution or no robber takes it away. But that which a man is, does always by necessity acquire, and what the man acquires is living property, which does not wait the beck of rulers, or mobs, or revolutions, or fire, or storm, or bankruptcies, but perpetually renews itself wherever the man breathes.

"Thy lot or portion of life," said the Caliph Ali, "is seeking after thee; therefore be at rest from seeking after it." Our dependence on these foreign goods leads us to our slavish respect for numbers. The political parties meet in numerous conventions; the greater the concourse and with each new uproar of announcement, The delegation from Essex! The Democrats from New Hampshire! The Whigs of Maine! the young patriot feels himself stronger than before by a new thousand of eyes and arms. In like manner the reformers summon conventions and vote and resolve in multitude. Not so, O friends! will the God deign to enter and inhabit you, but by a method precisely the reverse. It is only as a man puts off all foreign support and stands alone that I see him to be strong and to prevail. He is weaker by every recruit to his banner. Is not a man better than a town? Ask nothing of men, and, in the endless mutation, thou only firm column must presently appear the upholder of all that surrounds thee. He who knows that power is inborn, that he is weak because he has looked for good out of him and elsewhere, and so perceiving, throws himself unhesitatingly on his thought, instantly rights himself, stands in the erect position, commands his limbs, works miracles; just as a man who stands on his feet is stronger than a man who stands on his head.

So use all that is called Fortune. Most men gamble with her, and gain all, and lose all, as her wheel rolls. But do thou leave as unlawful these winnings, and deal with Cause and Effect, the chancellors of God. In the Will work and acquire, and thou hast chained the wheel of Chance, and shalt sit hereafter out of fear from her rotations. A political victory, a rise of rents, the recovery of your sick or the return of your absent friend, or some other favorable event raises your spirits, and you think good days are preparing for you. Do not believe it. Nothing can bring you peace but yourself. Nothing can bring you peace but the triumph of principles.

A Psalm of Life
Henry Wadsworth Longfellow

Tell me not, in mournful numbers,
Life is but an empty dream!
For the soul is dead that slumbers,
And things are not what they seem.

Life is real! Life is earnest!
And the grave is not its goal;
Dust thou art, to dust returnest,
Was not spoken of the soul.

Not enjoyment, and not sorrow,
Is our destined end or way;
But to act, that each to-morrow
Find us farther than to-day.

Art is long, and Time is fleeting,
And our hearts, though stout and brave,
Still, like muffled drums, are beating
Funeral marches to the grave.

In the world's broad field of battle,
In the bivouac of Life,
Be not like dumb, driven cattle!
Be a hero in the strife!

Trust no Future, howe'er pleasant!
Let the dead Past bury its dead!
Act,--act in the living Present!
Heart within, and God o'erhead!

Lives of great men all remind us
We can make our lives sublime,
And, departing, leave behind us
Footprints on the sands of time;--

Footprints, that perhaps another,
Sailing o'er life's solemn main,
A forlorn and shipwrecked brother,
Seeing, shall take heart again.

Let us, then, be up and doing,
With a heart for any fate;
Still achieving, still pursuing,
Learn to labor and to wait.

The Wayfarer on the Open Road

Ralph Waldo Trine

A CREED OF THE OPEN ROAD

To be observed today, to be changed tomorrow, or abandoned, according to tomorrow's light.

To live to our highest in all things that pertain to us, and to lend a hand as best we can to all others for this same end.

To aid in righting the wrongs that cross our path by pointing the wrong-doer to a better way, and thus aid him in becoming a power for good.

To turn toward and to keep our faces always to the light, knowing that we are then always safe, and that we shall travel with joy the open road.

To love the fields and the wild flowers, the stars, the far-open sea, the soft, warm earth, and to live much with them alone; but to love struggling and weary men and women and every pulsing, living creature better.

To do our own thinking, listening quietly to the opinions of others, but to be sufficiently men and women to act always upon our own convictions. To do our duty as we see it, regardless of the opinions of others, seeming gain or loss, temporary blame or praise.

To remain in nature always sweet and simple and humble and therefore strong.
To play the part of neither fool nor knave by attempting to judge another, but to give that same time to living more worthily ourselves.

To get up immediately when we stumble, face again to the light, and travel on without wasting even a moment in regret.

To love and to hold due reverence for all people and all things, but to stand in awe or fear of nothing save our own wrong doing.

To recognize the good lying at the heart of all people, of all things, waiting for expression all in its own good way and time.

To know that it is the middle ground that brings pleasure and satisfaction, and that excesses have to be paid for always with heavy and sometimes with frightful costs. To know that work, occupation, something definite and useful to do, is one of the established conditions of happiness in life.

To realize always clearly that thoughts are forces, that like creates like and like attracts like, and that to determine one's thinking therefore is to determine his life.

To take and to live always in the attitude of mind that compels gladness, looking for and thus drawing to us continually the best in all people and all things, being thereby the creators of our own good fortunes.

To know that the ever-conscious realization of the essential oneness of each life with the Divine Life is the Greatest of all knowledge, and that to open ourselves as opportune channels for the Divine Power to work in and through us is the open door to the highest attainment, and to the best there is in life.

In brief—to be honest, to be fearless, to be just, joyous, kind. This will make our part in life's great and as yet not fully understood play one of greatest glory, and we need then stand in fear of nothing—life nor death; for death is life. Or rather, it is the quick transition to life in another form; the putting off of the old coat and the putting on of the new; a passing not from light to darkness, but from light to light according as we have lived here; a taking up of life in another form where we leave it off here; a part in life not to be shunned or dreaded or feared, but to be welcomed with a glad and ready smile when it comes in its own good way and time.

1. To live to our highest in all things that pertain to us, and to lend a hand as best we can to all others for this same end.

DOES it pay? Are there any real, substantial reasons that we live to our highest?

The fact that we have ideals and aspirations, and that we always feel better the more fully we follow them, indicates that it pays. That we are conscious that something is not right, and that we suffer when we do violence to that which we know or which we feel to be the better thing, indicates that there is a law written in the universe through the inexorable operation of which we are pushed onward and upward, unless we are wise enough to go of our own accord.

As excessive eating or drinking, as excesses of every nature bring with them something that convinces an ordinarily bright mind that they don't pay, is an indication that there is a law of moderation, the observance of which brings good, the violation of which brings its opposite, pain and loss; as to live in discord with, in hatred or envy or jealousy of one's fellows brings its own peculiar destructive results, indicating that there is a law of love, of kindness, of mutuality, that will admit of no violation without striking home its punishments and inflicting its losses, so the lack of self-respect, the sense of loss, the general feeling that we have missed the higher and the satisfying in pursuing or being contented with the lower and the transient, indicates that the higher, the better, really pays, and that to follow it is a manifestation of simply good everyday common sense.

We shall come to our own sometime, and our own is the highest and best that we know; we shall come by being led in that we voluntarily follow our highest ideals and aspirations, our dreams, if you please, or we shall come by being pushed through suffering and loss and even anguish of soul, until we find all too concretely that the better pays, and more, that it will have obedience.

The thing that pays, and that makes for a well-balanced, useful, and happy life, is not necessarily and is not generally a somber, pious morality, or any standard of life that keeps us from a free, happy, spontaneous use and enjoyment of all normal and healthy faculties, functions, and powers, the enjoyment of all innocent pleasures—use, but not abuse, enjoyment, but enjoyment through self-mastery and not through license or perverted use, for it can never come that way. Of great suggestive value to us all should be this thought of Thoreau: "Do not be too moral. You may cheat yourself out of much life so. Aim above morality. Be not simply good; be good for something."

As there is, moreover, the great law of love, of service, of mutuality, written at the very core of human life, then in the degree that we are wise we will lend the hand whenever and wherever we can to all others in their strivings for the same life that we find is the better part, and as the influence, the help of example, is greater always than the kind intentions of precept, every strong though struggling life becomes the greatest possible help to every other.

2. To aid in righting the wrongs that cross our path by pointing the wrong-doer to a better way, and thus aid him in becoming a power for good.

WRONGS and injustices of one type or another come to our notice almost daily. They seem worthy of condemnation, many times of punishment. Wise however is he who is able to differentiate between the perpetrator of the wrong and the wrong that is done.

Only he who is perfect himself is in a consistent position even to judge another, to say nothing of condemning. The truly wise therefore will be slow to judge, and he will refuse to condemn. This must ever be so until he who would judge be perfect himself. We are all in the process of attaining—none have yet arrived.

The one whose zeal for justice is so keen can, moreover, rest at least in part peace when he is able once for all to realize that every wrong-doing carries with it its own punishment, that such is a fundamental law, and that by virtue of it the perpetrator of a wrong or an injustice suffers many times more than the one against whom it is directed.

All sin and error, all wrong and injustice, with its attendant suffering and loss, is the result of selfishness. Selfishness is always the result of ignorance—a mind undeveloped or developed only in spots. Therefore to aid in bringing one to a realization of his higher and better self and the laws that operate there, that lie may act and live continually from that center, is after all the effective and the fundamentally common-sense way of aiding in righting the wrongs that help in warping, in crippling, the happiness and the sweetness that belong inherently to every life.

Now and then there is one so steeped in selfishness, so ignorant therefore of the prevailing laws of life, that it is necessary to take the power of oppression or injustice out of his hands, at least for the time being; but the springs of tenderness, of compassion, of love for the right, though sometimes deeply covered or apparently non-existent, can be made in time to burst forth and to overflow by the truly wise, so that even such may in time, as has so often and so abundantly been the case, become one of the noblest, one of the most valuable, of earth's sons or daughters.

When the highest speaks to the highest in another, sooner or later the response is sure. In this way birth is given to ever-widening circles of influence that make for the good, the honest, the righteous, therefore the happy, in this at times hard and complex, but on the whole, good old world of ours.

3. To turn toward and to keep our faces always to the light, knowing that we are then always safe, and that we shall travel with joy the open road.

A KNOWLEDGE of the fact that we grow into the likeness of those things we contemplate, of those things that we live mostly with in our mental world, is one of the greatest assets of human life. Thought is at the bottom of all progress or retrogression, of all that is desirable or undesirable in life. We have it entirely in our own hands to determine what type of thought we entertain and habitually live with; thereby it is that we are the makers of our own good or ill fortunes.

A knowledge also of the fact that it is not what we actually accomplish at any particular time or times, but what we earnestly endeavor to accomplish, makes the road easier and should make all effort even a joy. It is the law of the reflex nerve system that whenever one does or endeavors to do any given thing in a certain way, a modicum of power is added whereby it is a trifle easier at the next effort, an added trifle at the next and the next, until that which is difficult and is done only with great effort in the beginning becomes easy of accomplishment—that which we do haltingly and stumblingly at first, bye and bye, so to speak, does itself, and with scarcely or even without any conscious effort on our part. This is the law; it is the secret of habit forming, character building, of all attainment.

The first thing then is the earnest desire, which, in other words, is the turning of the face to the light, then the mere traveling on day by day, calmly resting in the assurance that all is well with us now and that this course diligently and calmly pursued will lead us eventually to the sunlit hills and up to and into the very Gates of Paradise.

He who has the quest of the good in his heart has merely to travel on a step at a time, knowing that the second will be made clear when the first is taken. Patience and steadfastness and withal happiness and much laughter, mingled with whatever tears there may be along the way, will make even the most humble life the highest that can be lived. Such a life can end only in triumph; nay, it is a triumph during its progress, and even its failures are parts of its triumph.

4. To love the fields and the wild flowers, the stars, the far-open sea, the soft, warm earth, and to live much with them alone; but to love struggling and weary men and women and every pulsing, living creature better.

OUR complex modern life, especially in our larger centers, gets us running so many times into grooves that we are prone to miss, and sometimes for long periods, the all-round, completer life. We are led at times almost to forget that the stars come nightly to the sky, or even that there is a sky; that there are hedgerows and groves where the birds are always singing and where we can lie on our backs and watch the treetops swaying above us and the clouds floating by an hour or hours at a time; where one can live with his soul or, as Whitman has put it, where one can loaf and invite his soul.

We need changes from the duties and the cares of our accustomed everyday life. They are necessary for healthy, normal living. We need occasionally to be away from our friends, our relatives, from the members of our immediate households. Such changes are good for us; they are good for them. We appreciate them better, they us, when we are away from them for a period, or they from us.

We need these changes occasionally in order to find new relations—this in a twofold sense. By such changes there come to our minds more clearly the better qualities of those with whom we are in constant association; we lose sight of the little frictions and irritations that arise; we see how we can be more considerate, appreciative, kind.

In one of those valuable essays of Prentice Mulford entitled "Who Are Our Relations?" he points us to the fact, and with so much insight and common sense, that our relations are not always or necessarily those related to us by blood ties, those of our immediate households, but those most nearly allied to us in mind and in spirit, many times those we have never seen, but that we shall sometime, somewhere be drawn to through the ceaselessly working Law of Attraction, whose basis is that like attracts like. And so in staying too closely with the accustomed relations we may miss the knowledge and the companionship of those equally or even more closely related.

We need these changes to get the kinks out of our minds, our nerves, our muscles—the cobwebs off our faces. We need them to whet again the edge of appetite. We need them to invite the mind and the soul to new possibilities and powers. We need them in order to come back with new implements, or with implements redressed, sharpened, for the daily duties. It is like the chopper working too long with axe unground. There comes the time when an hour at the stone will give it such persuasive power that he can chop and cord in the day what he otherwise would in two or more, and with far greater ease and satisfaction.

We need periods of being by ourselves—alone. Sometimes a fortnight or even a week will do wonders for one, unless he or she has drawn too heavily upon the account. The simple custom, moreover, of taking an hour, or even a half hour, alone in the quiet, in the midst of the daily routine of life, would be the source of inestimable gain for countless numbers.

If such changes can be in closer contact with the fields and with the flowers that are in them, the stars and the sea that lies open beneath them, the woods and the wild things that are of them, one cannot help but find himself growing in love for and an ever fuller appreciation of these, and being at the same time so remade and unfolded that his love, his care, and his consideration for all mankind and for every living creature, will be the greater.

5. To do our own thinking, listening quietly to the opinions of others, but to be sufficiently men and women to act always upon our own convictions.

SINCERITY and honesty in thought is a characteristic essential to a commanding, to say nothing of a self-respecting, manhood or womanhood. It distinguishes always the man and the woman of influence.

Essentially true are the words of Robert Louis Stevenson: "If you teach a man to keep his eyes upon what others think of him, unthinkingly to lead the life and hold the principles of the majority of his contemporaries, you must discredit in his eyes the authoritative voice of his own soul. He may be a docile citizen; he will never be a man. It is ours, on the other hand, to disregard this babble and chattering of other men better and worse than we are, and to walk straight before us by what light we have. They may be right; but so, before heaven, are we. They may know; but we know also, and by that knowledge we must stand or fall. There is such a thing as loyalty to a man's own better self; and from those who have not that, God help me, how am I to look for loyalty to others?" To live not as slaves to, nor as unthinking or blind followers of the thought of others, under the mental domination of no man or woman or organization, in family life, in religious life, in community life, on the one hand, and to be not bigoted nor to pose as eccentric in thought and consequent act on the other, to yield and to use good sense in yielding quickly and quietly in non-essentials where peace and harmony will be preserved and where injury will be done no one thereby, is the part of the wise.

True and abundantly suggestive is the thought of Edward Carpenter:

"Him who is not detained by mortal adhesions, who walks in the world, yet not of it—Taking part in everything with equal mind, with free limbs and senses unentangled—Giving all, accepting all, using all, enjoying all, asking nothing, shocked at nothing—Him all creatures worship—all men and women bless."

Equally true on the other hand are the words of Joubert: "Those who never retract their opinions love themselves more than they love truth."

Any organization, religious or whatever its nature, that seeks to take from its followers or keep its adherents from perfect freedom and independence—in other words, common honesty—in thought and life does them untold injury, as well as sows thereby the seeds of its own destruction and disintegration. If old and decrepit, fast losing ground and making frantic efforts to hold its adherents, it indicates that the law is finally at work compelling restitution of that which it has filched, the disintegration of that which was untruthfully and unholily built.

If young and even though still apparently growing and rapidly increasing, it is merely a matter of time when violated law will strike its account and its at-one-time most enthusiastic followers will say, "Away with it all! Its falsity and its injury outweighs its good; that which robs me of my man-hood henceforth is not for me!"

Far better to build more truthfully even though it means a little more slowly—it pays in the end. Only those things that are essentially true at their foundations are the permanent.

6. To do our duty as we see it, regardless of the opinion of others—seeming gain or loss, temporary blame or praise.

INDEPENDENCE in the performance of one's duty as he sees it, in living his life as it comes to him to live it, is the natural concomitant of sincerity and independence in thought. To live one's life as it comes to him, to live it in essentials, considerate always of the feelings, the beliefs, the customs, the welfare of others in non-essentials, brings a completeness and a balance to life that makes for contentment as well as for growth and continual attainment.

Handing one's individuality over to the beliefs of the whims or the customs of others is productive of good to no one. Kingly and never too oft-repeated are the words of intrepid Walt Whitman: "From this hour I ordain myself loos'd of limits and imaginary lines, Going where I list, my own master total and absolute, Listening to others, considering well what they say, Pausing, searching, receiving, contemplating, Gently, but with undeniable will divesting Myself of the holds that would hold me."

Essentially the same truth had Channing in mind when he said: "In proportion as a man suppresses his conviction to save his orthodoxy from suspicion, or distorts language from its common use that he may stand well with his party, in that proportion he clouds and degrades his intellect, as well as undermines the integrity of his character." The blind following of party simply because one chances to belong to a particular party, and many times because his father or uncle—in some tomorrow his mother or his aunt—belonged to it, has been one of the chief causes of the most notorious political corruption and debauchery. It is due to this fact more than to anything else that bosses and machines have been able to get and to retain the hold they have gotten, and in the name of party fealty have been able to thieve the rights and the natural possessions of the people for their own aggrandizement and enrichment. It is only when you and I and all average men fully comprehend the moral obligation that is contained in the phrase, "Independence in party action," that we will see the power of corruption that they now hold slipping from their hands. It is when we not only make it known by quick and decisive action that we will support our own party when its platform is essentially the best and when it is constructed for the purpose of being fulfilled and not for the pure purpose of deception, in whole or in part, and again when its candidates are the best men that can be named; but that we will as quickly support the opposing party when platform and candidates in it are the better, that we will give birth to a revolution of tremendous import in our political and social traditions and life.

Then when we are able to get away from the idea that government is something separate and apart from us, but that in a very fundamental sense we are government so to speak, and when we set about doing for ourselves that which we now hand over to others to be done for us, and many times fully and treacherously done, we will have political institutions of which we and all men will be justly and unreservedly proud.

7. To remain in nature always sweet and simple and humble, and therefore strong.

SWEETNESS Of nature, simplicity in manners and conduct, humility without self-abasement, give the truly kingly quality to men, the queenly to women, the winning to children, whatever the rank or the station may be. The life dominated by this characteristic, or rather these closely allied characteristics, is a natural wellspring of joy to itself and sheds a continual benediction upon all who come within the scope of its influence. It makes for a life of great beauty in itself, and it imparts courage and hope and buoyancy to all others.

If the life find its lot in the more common, the more lowly walks, then for one to go about the daily work and duties doing all things well and with cheerful mind and heart, happy in the present and with full faith as to the working out of all things well and as is for the greatest good in the future, such a life is one of most royal success.

And oh the vast numbers of such kingly and queenly lives in our so-called common walks—men and women doing their daily work, rearing their children, meeting their problems, even their losses or apparent losses, with smiles on their lips and faith and therefore courage in their hearts, turning what would otherwise be drudgery and heartless and unremitting toil into triumphant living. It is this great army that constitutes the very backbone of our nation—of any nation. The very contemplation of this multitude is in itself an inspiration; and it recalls us to a renewed and more steadfast faith in our common human nature.

On the other hand there is no quality that constitutes a more accurate earmark of real greatness and nobility of character in the case of the prosperous and successful, the better known, than the preservation of due humility and simplicity; the life of every man truly great is permeated always with these qualities. An undue sense of one's importance or of one's achievements or possessions, or an undue propensity for show or desire for recognition, indicates always a weak mental strain that may make an otherwise successful and honorable life a failure.

And why should there be anything but simplicity on the part of even the greatest? There will be due humility in it bye and bye; everything here will come to naught; and after its separation from the body the life will pass on into the next state, taking with it only, by way of desirable possessions, all attainment made through the unfoldment of its higher self, all that it has gained by way of self-mastery and nobility of character—and of these attributes none are more enduring, as well as more to be desired, than kindness and humility.

Truly descriptive of the well-balanced man are these lines of Lowell: "The wisest man could ask no more of fate than to be simple, modest, manly, true, Safe from the many, honored by the few; Nothing to crave in Church or World or Stale, But inwardly in secret to be great."

The one who has true inward greatness thinks little of and cares less for what we term fame. For truly, "Fame means nothing to those who take an inward view of life, for they see that at best it is but the symbol of intrinsic worth."

8. To play the part of neither fool nor knave by attempting to judge another, but to give that same time to living more worthily ourselves.

HE WHO is perfect is in the position, were he so minded, of judging another. No man is perfect; no man therefore stands fully in such position.

The fool or the knave alone will do so. The fool because he hasn't sense sufficiently keen to grasp the inconsistency, the foolhardiness of one, imperfect himself, assuming to judge the life of another likewise imperfect. The knave because although keen enough to realize his own shortcomings, his own imperfect life, he voluntarily assumes the role of the hypocrite in passing judgment upon another.

Only the perfect and the all-wise is in the position to judge the innermost life—the springs of the outer life of his fellowmen. Such, however, would be most deliberate in his conclusions and most lenient in his judgments. Deliberate because of his knowledge of the warrings, the weaknesses, and the at times poor or one-sided equipment in the majority of lives which makes their efforts seem almost god-like, could we see all, even when for the time being the entire battle would seem lost. Deliberate, also, because of his refusal to pass judgment upon a life not yet complete. Lenient in his judgment because of the remembrance of his own weaknesses and struggles and failures—better known to himself than to any others—that he passed through in attaining his present perfect state.

It is so easy to see and to point to the fallings of another; it is so difficult to be in the position where there is absolute perfection in ourselves. It is so easy in conversation, idly, jokingly, or with little motives or malices that lie hidden at least in our own minds—and we are sufficiently ostrich-like many times to think in the minds of others—to dwell upon the peculiarities, the shortcomings of the one or ones under consideration. If with a sense always of one's own peculiarities and shortcomings, then it may be partly excusable or at least endurable, but without this it is a humorous manifestation of either ignorant or knavish conceit; and when it comes to the gossip he or she is generally a liar, consciously or unconsciously.

The grander natures and the more thoughtful are always looking for and in conversation dwelling on the better things in others. It is the rule with but few, if any exceptions, that the more noble and worthy and thoughtful the nature, the more it is continually looking for the best there is to be found in every life. Instead of judging or condemning, or acquiring the habit that eventually leads to this, it is looking more closely to and giving its time to living more worthily itself.

It is in this way continually unfolding and expanding in beauty and in power; it is finding an ever-increasing happiness by the admiration and the love that such a life is always, even though all unconsciously, calling to itself from all sources. It is the life that pays by many fold.

9. To get up immediately when we stumble, face again to the light, and travel on without wasting even a moment in regret.

WE are on the way from the imperfect to the perfect; someday, in this life or in some other, we shall reach our destiny. It is as much the part of folly to waste time and cripple our forces in vain, unproductive regrets in regard to the occurrences of the past as it is to cripple our forces through fears and forebodings for the future.

There is no experience in any life which if rightly regarded, rightly turned and thereby wisely used, cannot be made of value; many times things thus turned and used can be made sources of inestimable gain; ofttimes they become veritable blessings in disguise.

All have stumbled—all do stumble. All have fallen; every one of us has fallen flat, at some time, in one way or another, each along the lines of his own peculiar mental or physical makeup. Many a man, many a woman, has had a good round half dozen years or even more clipped from his or her life in moping, in vain and absolutely foolish regrets for this or that occurrence or series of occurrences in the past, thereby blocking initiative and neutralizing powers that rightly used would have led speedily to actualizing the attainment of the conditions desired.

Happy, happy and thrice blessed are we when we are wise enough to learn this quickly, and when we stumble, when we stumble and fall—yes flat—to give sufficient time in looking over the ground in quick attention to the object or the circumstances that caused it, and then with renewed effort getting ourselves together again and going straight on without losing another moment of time in vain, in costly get-nowhere regrets. We should be as lenient in judgment of ourselves as we are of others, remembering that all in all we are no better and no worse than the majority of men. We should give ourselves no mental and thereby physical handicaps that will hinder or possibly prevent us in attaining the best that the fullest life holds for us.

Of special value to the one prone to waste time and to turn much of life's joy into bitterness is the thought of Emerson: "Finish every day and be done with it. You have done what you could. Some blunders and absurdities no doubt crept in; forget them as soon as you can. Tomorrow is a new day; begin it well and serenely, and with too high a spirit to be cumbered with your old nonsense. Today is all that is good and fair. It is too dear with its hopes and invitations to waste a moment on the yesterdays."

And again: "Our strength grows out of our weakness. The indignation which arms itself with secret forces does not awaken until we are pricked and stung and sorely assailed. A great man is always willing to be little. Whilst he sits on the cushion of advantages he goes to sleep. When he is pushed, tormented, defeated, he has a chance to learn something; he has been put on his wits, on his manhood; he has gained facts, learns his ignorance, is cured of the insanity of conceit, has got moderation and real skill."

10. To love and to hold due reverence for all people and all things, but to stand in awe or fear of nothing save our own wrong-doing.

GOD never made any man or any institution a dispenser of truth or the custodian of the mental life of another. He instituted laws and forces whereby one man by ordering his life in accordance with the highest laws and forces of his being, living so to speak in the upper stories of his being, has become the revealer of truth and the exampler of truth to other men.

In the degree, however, that he has been worthy of receiving and successful in living, and thus in transmitting such revelations, in that degree has he kept his own personality in the background in order that the truth might be free from encumbrances now and from encrustations bye and bye. In other words, in the degree that he has loved truth more and self or self-aggrandizement less has he lost sight of himself in order that the truth might be unencumbered and freely and effectively delivered.

To hold undue reverence for or to stand in awe or fear of another is an exhibition, though perchance unconscious, of a lack of faith in or a degradation of our own native powers and forces, which if rightly unfolded and used might open to us revelations and lead us to heights even beyond those of the one we mentally crouch before.

There is probably no mental habit, native or acquired, that brings us so much that is undesirable in life as fear. It has been, it is today, the one great bugbear in almost countless lives, and until we redeem ourselves from this filcher of the best in life, we stand in fear at one time or another of almost everything. There is fear when happy that happiness will not remain; fear—when miserable that this condition will always remain; fear for our friends in that we shall lose them; fear of our enemies, if sufficiently unwise as to have them, in that they are continually at work in harm to us or to our reputations in the minds of others; fear of poverty in that what is ours today will not be ours tomorrow; fear of the elements; fear of sickness; fear of the transition we call death, either in our own case or in the case of those near to us. We fear that the bogy man, whatever his form and equipment and purpose, is continually on the wake for us. And so our conversation runs in terms of fear, and the prevailing mental attitude of fear has become the fixed habit of countless thousands.

It moreover stamps itself and registers its baneful influences in the very bodies of its victims. Fear retards and even paralyzes healthy action, the same as worry—closely allied to it—stagnates, corrodes, and pulls it down. When, moreover, we once understand the subtle power of thought—thought as a force—and its law in that like builds like and like attracts like, we can see how we endow the very things we fear with power to get their hold and work their ills upon us. Thus we create within us and we attract to us, many times all unconsciously, conditions the very opposite of those we would have in our lives.

Fear is, so to speak, the direct opposite of faith, and faith is perhaps the strongest and most effective mental-spiritual force that we can possess or grow. To take the positive, the cheerful attitude of mind, bidding good-bye to fear and setting about resolutely for the actualization of those conditions that are good and desirable, we thus set into operation silent but subtle and all-powerful forces that will work for us continual good. In this way fear will gradually lose its hold and we will find ourselves becoming masters instead of, as formerly, creatures of circumstance.

11. To recognize the good lying at the heart of all people, of all things, waiting for expression, all in its own good way and time.

WE are in a life of growth and unfoldment, in a world of change and incompleteness; each thing is good in its place, and each thing has its own particular and peculiar purpose. Each life is divine at its center and some time will show forth in the full beauty of holiness, which is wholeness or completeness—divine self-realization.

Aptness or tardiness in recognizing the source and also the laws of our being, combined with varied innate tendencies to start with or combined with the influences of varied environments, is ordinarily the reason why one life differs from another at any given period in its moral, ethical tone or fibre. Quickness also or tardiness in coming into a conscious living realization of the essential oneness of each life and all life with the divine, the source, the center, the substance of all life that there is manifested in existence, and the avenues of wisdom and of power that such realization opens, determines the relative condition of any life at any given time.

Sometimes, frequently, a year in the life thus awake to its real nature gives by way of insight, growth, unfoldment, therefore of peace, of happiness, of usefulness, more than a previous fifty years rolled together, and when it comes to a life that we are inclined to belittle, to judge harshly, to throw stones at, it behooves us to be guarded as the wise are guarded, for when the awakening and the consequent rapid march of such a soul begins it may quickly pass beyond those that we today deem much higher and much more important, beyond ourselves.

In a certain sense, in the broad sense, all is good. Yes, apparent misfortune and even what we ordinarily term evil, in that it is the good in the making. If we have faith, if we have patience and perseverance, there is no condition, no experience that rightly viewed and rightly turned and used will not bring us stores of good.

Everything that comes into each life has its place and its purpose, its part to play, and were it not necessary or were it not good in the long run that it come it would not come. If there is a divine order in the universe, if there is law—and in a sense there is absolutely nothing but law—it cannot be otherwise. A clear comprehension of this fact, or if this be impossible, a mere belief in it, is of tremendous value in helping us to meet understandingly and to work intelligently and bravely in the midst of adverse or undesirable conditions, that we may push on and through them to those that are more valuable and desirable. It is of value by way of enabling us to adjust ourselves in friendly relations with our environment or with existing conditions as long as it is well or possibly essential that we remain there, and to look for and to get the good that is unquestionably there for us.

By living thus in harmony, if not always in fullest sympathy with such conditions, we adopt the best possible method of getting from them the greatest good, and pushing on through them, not only with the least possible handicap, but with added wisdom and power. And possibly to some to whom the way may seem already long, this thought from Browning may be of value:

"The common problem, yours, mine, everyone's, is not to fancy what were fair in life provided it could be—but finding first what may be, then find how to make it fair up to our means: a very different thing."

12. To know that it is the middle ground that brings pleasure and satisfaction, and that excesses have to be paid for ofttimes with heavy and sometimes with frightful costs.

ALL things, good in themselves, are for use and enjoyment; but all things must be rightly used in order that there may be full and lasting enjoyment. A law written into the very fibre of human life, so to speak, is to the effect that excesses, the abuse of anything good in itself, will end disastrously, so that one's pleasures and enjoyments will have to be gathered up for repairs, or perchance his shattered mind or body also, and in case of the latter then the former will have to bide their time or wait indefinitely for their resumption.

Wise indeed is he who fully recognizes this law that never has and that never will allow itself to be violated or undone, but that will shatter, sometimes with telling and open blows, more often perhaps with blows subtle and guarded, but just as telling, the happiness or even the mind and the body of the one who would do violence to or who would fail to recognize its mandate—Moderation.

On the other hand, to see evil in things good in themselves is the perversion of another law that carries with it its own peculiar penalty. The one tends to make the prig, the self-righteous, out of a good, wholesome man or woman, the same as the other makes eventually the voluptuary. The one errs in the one direction the same as the other in another direction. Each pays the penalty for his folly, the one by cutting himself off from much innocent and valuable God intended enjoyment, at the same time casting a continual shadow over the lives of others; the other by way of settling heavy bills of costs for his excesses.

It should be then neither license nor perverted use on the one hand, nor asceticism or priggishness on the other—the full use of all normal and natural functions, faculties, and powers, innocent and good in themselves, that all may be brought to their fullest growth and development, but never excessive or perverted use.

The tendency of the great majority, especially in our present-day American life, is on the side of the too serious, the too busy, the too absorbing in the business, in the work. This induces all unconsciously, in time, a prevailing type of thought and mental activity that takes, so to speak, the buoyancy, the elasticity out of both mind and body, so that age and its accompanying features manifest, assert, and fix themselves in many, or to speak more truly, in the majority of cases, long before their time. By way of balance, by way of disarming these, we need more of the play element, more of the open air, the sunshine, the exercise element in our lives. It would save thousands from stiffening of joints and muscles, hardened arteries, dyspepsia, apoplexy, nerve exhaustion, melancholia, premature age, premature death.

"Happy recreation has a very subtle influence upon one's ability, which is emphasized and heightened and multiplied by it. How our courage is braced up, our determination, our ambition, our whole outlook on life changed by it! There seems to be a subtle fluid from humor and fun which penetrates the entire being, bathes all the mental faculties, and washes out the brain-ash and debris from exhausted cerebrum and muscles. . . . A joyful, happy, fun-loving environment develops powers, resources, and possibilities which would remain latent in a cold, dull, repressing atmosphere."

Look where we will, in or out and around us, we will find that it is the middle ground—neither poverty nor excessive riches, good wholesome use without license, a turning into the bye-ways along the main road where innocent and healthy God-sent and God-intended pleasures and enjoyments are to be found; but never getting far enough away to lose sight of the road itself. The middle ground it is that the wise man or woman plants foot upon.

13. To know that work, occupation, something definite and useful to do, is one of the established conditions of happiness in life.

IT is difficult to know, much more to tell, why there is such a law; but perchance it is that work, definite, useful activity, and along with it the satisfaction of accomplishment, is necessary to growth and development, and unquestionably growth, development, attainment is the purpose, the object of life. However this may be, we know one thing, that we always feel better when we can look back when night comes and feel that the day has been good in accomplishment, or at least in effort, and that it has not been allowed to pass without some good, some useful thing accomplished, to its credit.

Are we alone in the thought that work is one of the established conditions of successful and therefore healthy, happy living? Of its purpose, or rather its place, Hugh Black has given utterance to this thought: "One thing is certain, that, though work itself will not insure happiness, yet without it happiness is impossible. It is an essential condition of a contented life. This has been the experience of all, and there is no more useful lesson for youth to learn early."

It was Amiel who said: "It is work that gives flavor to life. Mere existence without object and without effort is a poor thing. Idleness leads to languor, and languor to disgust." Zola, putting it a little too strongly perhaps, showing nevertheless his thought regarding it, says: "Work! It is the sole law of the world "; and again: "Let each one accept his task, a task which should fill his life. It may be very humble; it will not be the less useful. Never mind what it is, so long as it exists and keeps you erect. When you have regulated it without excess—just the quantity you are able to accomplish each day—it will cause you to live in health and in joy."

Putting his general thought along the same line in more poetic form, Barry Cornwall wrote:
"There is not a creature from England's king
To the peasant that delves the soil,
That knows half the pleasures the seasons bring,
If he have not his share of toil."

A still more inclusive truth Bayard Taylor has put in the verse;
"Sloth is sin and toil is worship, and the soul demands an aim;
Who neglects the ordination, he shall not escape the blame."

But here again it is the middle ground—neither idleness nor excessive toil. Work, whatever its nature—so-called great or menial, cabinet minister or street cleaner, celebrated singer or homekeeper or shirt stitcher—work that is glorified and made a fair contributor to a genuinely religious life by the spirit we carry into it, by the way we do it. It is this and this alone that determines whether it is really great or menial—work, earnest and sincere, that is broken by periods of rest and leisure, so that the latter become replete with enjoyment and value. This combining of work with rest and play, of rest and play with work, gives zest and spirit to both and brings again in this phase of our being the balance to life.

God, however, deliver us from the too earnest people, those whose work is so important that they can never find place for the time off, whose earnestness leads to inflation, or to a stealing of responsibility for many important—or less important—things from God, who have no time for the appreciation or the development of a sense of humour and the occasional levity, who eliminate the innocent pleasures and leisures and joys that a good, sensible, well-rounded and withal useful life takes as its portion. By being too valuable to our fellowmen we may often become of but little value to them, and eventually to ourselves; here again, therefore, it is the middle ground.

The chief use, perhaps, of passing through the period of self-importance, of excessive earnestness, especially if it be in comparative youth, is that then we are through with it, we are able in reflection to get an occasional enjoyment by being able to see the humour of it all, and we are able also to appreciate it quickly and to see the humour of it in the occasional other one who is still in its throes.

For the all-round life there must be the balance also as to the kinds of work. The hand, manual, ground worker, to insure the most happy and satisfying life for himself, to say nothing of his greater value to his community, to the state, must turn periodically into the intellectual bye-ways, through investigation, study, reading, a greater intelligence of the best and latest developments and findings in his own work, as well as keeping in touch with general progress. This will determine whether he remain or become a mere machine or an intelligent, commanding worker, as also a valuable citizen.

The brain worker, the business man, and especially the one doing creative mental work, if he would know the all-round joy of living, must have that to turn to whereby his hands, his body, get their normal, healthy activity, and if it be useful, constructive work, or work in or of the soil, the greater the interest and value. This would save almost countless thousands of good men and good women that overwrought, nervous, brain- and nerve-fagged condition that renders full enjoyment of anything impossible, that causes a craving for and a turning to stimulants, excitement, extravagances that only increase their difficulties. It would save them to the simple, healthy, homely, and lasting joys that nature rewards never with satiety, but with good sleep, good appetite, good digestion, in brief, that greatest of all earthly blessings—good health.

14. To realize always clearly that thoughts are forces, that like creates like and like attracts like, and that to determine one's thinking, therefore, is to determine his life.

THAT we have within us the force or the power that makes us what we are, and that we have it in our own hands to determine how that force, that power, shall be used is a revelation, if not clearly realized before, of tremendous import to any life.
One of the most valuable, not discoveries, but rather rediscoveries, of the present decade, or still better, perhaps, clear formulations of a long-known truth, is the fact that thoughts are forces, that they have form and quality and substance and power, that they are the silent, unseen, but subtle agents at work that are daily and hourly producing and determining, and with almost absolute precision, the conditions in our lives. As is the inner, therefore, so always and necessarily is the outer. What one lives in his thought world is continually forming and thus determining his outer material world.

The clearly established law of thought as a force is that like creates like and like attracts like. The hopeful, cheerful, confident find themselves continually growing in faith, in confident, healthy optimism, in courage; they are also continually attracting and drawing to themselves, thus gaining as friends and helpers those of similar qualities and possessions, and they are likewise inspiring these qualities in others. Courage and faith beget energy and power; energy and power rightly directed bring success. Such, as a rule, are the successful people—successful simply by way of natural law.

The fearing, grumbling, worrying, vacillating do not succeed in anything and generally live by burdening, in some form or another, someone else. They stand in the way of, they prevent their own success; they fail in living even an ordinary healthy, normal life; they cast a blighting influence over and they act as a hindrance to all with whom they at any time come in contact. The pleasures we take captive in life, the growth and advancement we make, the pleasure and benefit our company or acquaintanceship brings to others, the very desirability of our companionship on the part of others—all depend upon the types of thought we entertain and live most habitually with.

Not only is there the direct connection—that of cause and effect— between the types of thought we most habitually entertain and the value and joy of living in our own lives, as well as the pleasure we give and the influence we exert upon others, but the intimate relations existing between certain mental states and the various bodily functions are beginning now to be so clearly understood and can be so easily traced and established, that no clear thinking, open mind can fail to recognize the great power constantly at work for disease or for health; and if certain given mental states or habits induce diseased conditions and structure, as they do, then certain other mental states, especially when consciously and definitely directed, can antidote and remove obstructions so that the operation of the life forces within can undo and cure the same.

There is a general order of thought that may be described as the normal, health bringing, pleasure bringing, the desirable, valuable. Of this order are faith, hope, love, magnanimity, charity, nobility of feeling and purpose, good temper, goodwill, clear, clean, hopeful, healthful thought. These are evidently the God-intended, for they are productive of wholesome activity, of health and strength and peace of mind, of soul, and of body.

There is a general order of thought that may be described as abnormal, perverted, and carrying with it a slow, corroding, poisoning effect upon or a quick death-sting for all that is good, healthy, and desirable in life. Of this order are fear, worry, anxiety, resentment, envy, jealousy, hatred, revenge, ill-temper, nagging, fault-finding, lust. The effect of this order of thought if lived in to any extent is that of a retarding, corroding, poisoning effect upon mind, soul, and through them the body—upon the latter not by way of fanciful influence, but by way of direct chemical corroding and poisoning, with its resultant effect upon tissues and structure. Thus one in time becomes the victim of the products, the children of his own brain—his thoughts.

Says one of our modern keen thinkers and forceful writers: "We are beginning to see that we can renew our bodies by renewing our thoughts; change our bodies by changing our thoughts; that by holding the thought of what we wish to become, we can become what we desire. Instead of being the victims of fate we can order our fate, we can largely determine what it shall be. Our destiny changes with our thought. We shall become what we wish to become when our habitual thought corresponds with the desire.... He is a fortunate man who early learns the secret of scientific brain-building, and who acquires the inestimable art of holding the right suggestion in his mind, so that he can triumph over the dominant note in his environment when it is unfriendly to his highest good. . . . The whole body is really a projected mind, objectified, made tangible. It is an outpicturing of the mind in material form. When we look at a person we actually see the mind, or what his thinking has made him. . . . The life follows the thought. There is no law clearer than that. There is no getting away from it." (*Dr. Orison Swett Marden in *Success Magazine*, August, 1908.)

After a certain age is reached in any life, the prevailing tone and condition of that life is the resultant of the mental habits of that life. If one has mental equipment sufficient to find and to make use of the Science of Thought in its application to scientific mind and body building, habit and character building, there is little by way of heredity, environment, attainment of which he or she will not be the master. One thing is very certain—the mental points of view, the mental tendencies and habits at twenty-eight and thirty eight will have externalized themselves and will have stamped the prevailing conditions of any life at forty-eight and fifty-eight and sixty-eight.

15. To take and to live always in the attitude of mind that compels gladness, looking for and thus drawing to us continually the best in all people and all things, being thereby the creators of our own good fortunes.

CHEERFULNESS, looking on the bright side of things, seeing the humorous side of situations when others see only the "too-bad," the "provoking," the "spasm," the "isn't-it-terrible," is a matter of habit quite as much as it is a matter of aptitude. If one lacks the habit he fails in one of the most important or even essential qualities of his life; so, on the other hand, to cultivate it to its highest is to become possessor of a quality in life most eagerly to be sought.

The optimistic, cheerful, hopeful habit of mind and thought is continually putting into and keeping in operation silent subtle forces that are continually changing from the unseen into the seen, from the ideal into the actual, and attracting to us, from without, conditions of a nature kindred to the type of thought force that we give birth to and set into operation. Ordinarily we find in people those qualities we are mostly looking for; if we show to them our best, their best will open and show itself to us.

There is no quality that exerts more good, is of greater service to all mankind during the course of the ordinary life, than the mind and the heart that goes out in an all embracing love for all, that is the generator and the circulator of a genuine, hearty, wholesome sympathy and courage and good cheer, that is not disturbed or upset by the passing occurrence little or great, but that is serene, tranquil, and conquering to the end, that is looking for the best, that is finding the best, and that is inspiring the best in all. There is, moreover, no quality that when genuine brings such rich returns to its possessor by virtue of the thoughts and the feelings that it inspires and calls forth from others and that come back laden with their peaceful, stimulating, healthful influences for him.

On the other hand, the peevish, gloomy, grumbling, paniky, critical—the small—cast a sort of deadening, unwholesome influence wherever they go. They get, however, what they give, for they inspire and call back to themselves thoughts and feelings of the kind they are sufficiently stupid to allow a dominating influence in their own lives. People ruled by the mood of gloom attract to themselves gloomy people and gloomy conditions, those that are of no help to them, but rather a hindrance.

The cheerful, confident, tranquil in all circumstances are continually growing in these same qualities, for the mind grows by and in the direction of that which it feeds upon. This process of mental chemistry is continually working in our lives, bringing us desirable or undesirable conditions according to our prevailing mental states.

The course of determining resolutely to expect only those things which we desire, or which will be ultimately for our larger good, of thinking health and strength rather than disease and weakness, an abundance for all our needs rather than poverty, success rather than failure, of looking for and calling from others the best there is in them, is one of the greatest aids also to bodily health and perfection. As a rule one seldom knows of those of this trend or determination of mind complaining of physical ailments, because they are generally free from the long list of ailments and disabilities that have their origin in perverted emotional and mental states, that by being regularly fed are allowed to externalize themselves and become settled conditions.

This attitude of mind is the one also that carries us through when the dark day comes and things look their worst. It enables us to take the long view, to throw the thought on beyond the present day, difficulty, or depression to the time when it will have worked itself out all well and good. Such times come to all. We must be brave and bravely take our share.

It is how we bear ourselves at such times that determines our real worth and use, whether we have stamina, backbone, courage—real character—and if at such times we can stand unfaltering, uncomplaining, desirous of neither sympathy nor pity, patient but resolute, and doing today what today reveals to be done and so ready for the morrow when it comes, there can be but one outcome. The Higher Powers of all the universe stand back of such a life, they uphold it, they sustain it, they stamp it with success, they crown it with adoration and with honour.

16. To know that the ever-conscious realization of the essential oneness of each life with the Divine Life is the highest of all knowledge, and that to open ourselves as opportune channels for the Divine Power to work in and through us is the open door to the highest attainment, and to the best there is in life.

FOR a life of the larger growth and attainment, for a life that finds itself ready for whatever the emergency that confronts it along the way, it is essential that it find a basis, or as has been aptly said, its center. It must be, moreover, a basis, a center that its own intelligence, its own thought can find and give acceptance to, not something imposed from without by some other mind, or body of men, or institution.

To me there is nothing more rational, more reasonable than to find one's start in being—that Spirit of Infinite Life and Power that is the intelligence, the unfolder, the creator if you please, of all there is in this universe of evident design of law and order. It is a universe where there is, in a sense, nothing but law, law constantly working through the agency of cause and effect, and in which for even the most ordinary intelligence to think that there is only, or that there is the slightest element of chance, is practically incomprehensible.

If all is in absolute accordance with law and plan and order, there is an intelligence, a power that is back of and that gives life and form and sustaining force to that law and order. To me this is being manifesting itself in existence, the Supreme Intelligence—God. The Creator manifesting itself—himself if you prefer—in creation, so that Creator and creation are one, in the sense that Creator is the life, the spirit of all there is in existence—in creation. There is the one life, this Spirit of Infinite Life and Power that is back of all, working in and through all, the Life of all. To speak therefore of our life as separate and apart from this Infinite Life, as separate from the life of God, is impossible. To speak of it as equal to the life of God is unreasonable. In nature, in essence, in quality it is essentially one and the same, therefore Divine in its origin, in its essence. In degree of manifestation and in power it is totally different, and here is the one essential feature of this all important fact in its bearing upon our lives. It is possible for us to remain closed to, in ignorance of, the source and nature of our real being, and to live without a conscious connection with this Source.

It is the mind that relates the soul of man, the real eternal self, with this Source. It is through the instrumentality of the mind that we are enabled to make this conscious connection. It is this that distinguishes us from the inanimate world; our minds, moreover, are given us for use.

It is possible for us through the channel of our minds so to relate ourselves to, and to grow ever more conscious of, the real identity of our lives with their Divine Source that we become receivers and liberators, so to speak, of the attributes of the Divine Life. Among the attributes of this Life are wisdom, power, love, harmony. In the degree that we make and keep this conscious connection we make ourselves natural channels for a continually greater degree of Divine Intelligence and Power to manifest in and through us.

It is in a way like the plant. When in its right relations with that to which it must rightly relate itself for unfoldment and growth—soil with sufficient moisture and sunlight—its life and growth go on naturally and unimpeded, and it finally reaches its destiny—fullness of unfoldment and growth, which means maturity. If but poorly related to or if separated from these, it struggles for a while and finally withers and dies.

Let us recur to the statement: In the degree that we make and keep this conscious connection with our Source do we make ourselves natural channels for a continually greater degree of Divine Intelligence and Power to manifest in and through us. And what, it is but right to ask, is the basis of such a statement outside of the statement itself? The fact that it is the uniform experience of all who become awake to this New Consciousness, as multitudes are becoming awake to it today. It has likewise been the experience of thousands in the world's history, both men and women, whose names and works are familiar to all, of the mystical, of the truly religious—not necessarily institutional and generally not—trend of mind and purpose of life. The religious mind and life, because the fundamental principle, in brief the essence of all real religion, whatever its form or time or name, is: The consciousness of God in the soul of man. It is the full realization, "In Him we live and move and have our being." It is the Christ state that Jesus realized and lived continually in because of the complete realization of the oneness of his life with the Father's life. "I and the Father are one." "The words that I speak unto you I speak not of myself, but the Father that dwelleth in me, He doeth the works"—and it is thus that he becomes the Saviour of other men, by virtue of pointing out to them this same way.

This brings also the child simplicity, for in ourselves we are nothing; we have every conceivable type of limitation. In the degree that the God life with its attendant wisdom and power dwells in us through our opening the way, in that degree do our latent possibilities change to actualized power. In other words, we determine our own limitations. In the degree that we come into the knowledge of our real selves our limitations rise and we come thereby into actual possession of our own.

And what, it is only right again to ask, has this to do with the healthy, bountiful, practical, everyday life that is the real thing before us? This consciousness of the God life in the soul, so that it becomes the constant guiding force in our lives, is nothing more nor less than the finding of the Kingdom. It is testing the reality of the injunction of Jesus, he who knew whereof he spoke when he said, "Seek ye first the Kingdom of God and His righteousness, and all these things shall be added unto you." It is the inclusive thing which brings all things of detail in its train.

It brings insight, intuition, wisdom, for it is the very source of wisdom. It brings power, for the secret of all power is the right co-ordination of the agents of expression with the power that works from within. It brings influence, for all men feel instinctively and are influenced, even unconsciously, by such a life.

It is productive of bodily health and vigour, for spirit, from its very nature, can admit of no disease or inharmony, and it externalizes, in the body of him who realizes himself a spiritual being, health and harmony. If inharmony and disease have gotten their hold before, they are quickly or more gradually eliminated according to the degree of this realization by the reversal of the process whereby they came. It brings power as an agent in healing the bodily ills of another because the mind spiritually alive is able more readily to reach and impress the subconscious mind of another, the agency through which all mental or spiritual healing in oneself or in another is accomplished. In the degree of the completeness of this realization is the element of time in such cases eliminated, as was so abundantly true in Jesus' case, whose (to us) wonderful works of healing were all in accordance with law—and this same law that we are considering.

It brings material things in full abundance, for wisdom offers the key and power unlocks the door; all material things are in the universe now waiting simply for the right combination, the right type of demand, to draw them to their rightful owners. It saves one, moreover, from the excessive accumulation of material things, for the life thus awake realizes that they are not and never, except to our detriment, can be made an end in themselves, but are simply a means to an end.

It eliminates fear, forebodings, worry, for these can have no existence in such a life. It gives a calmness, a poise, a serenity to life that proclaims the man or the woman master of the greatest of all arts—the Art of Living. Such a life has no fear and scarcely a thought of death, for it realizes that the only death to be feared, or that has in any sense a reality, is that feeling or that sense of separateness from the life of God. It has full consciousness of the fact that it is living the eternal life now, that it can never be in that life more in reality than now, and that in all eternity it can never be more conscious of God's presence than is in its power at this very moment. It acknowledges the reality of Jesus wonderful insight when he said: "Say not lo here nor lo there, know ye not that the Kingdom of Heaven is within you?" It is conscious of the fact that it is surrounded, guided, upheld by a force that is not to be explained, perhaps, as to the mode of its working. "No weapon that is formed against thee shall prosper." As real to it as the air it breathes is the ever-conscious fact, "Thou wilt keep him in perfect peace whose mind is stayed on Thee."

Ralph Waldo Trine 1866 - 1958

I Wandered Lonely as a Cloud
William Wordsworth

I wandered lonely as a cloud
That floats on high o'er vales and hills,
When all at once I saw a crowd,
A host, of golden daffodils,

Beside the lake, beneath the trees
Fluttering and dancing in the breeze.
Continuous as the stars that shine
And twinkle on the Milky Way,

They stretched in never-ending line
Along the margin of a bay:
Ten thousand saw I at a glance
Tossing their heads in sprightly dance.

The waves beside them danced, but they
Out-did the sparkling waves in glee: -
A poet could not but be gay
In such a jocund company:

I gazed -and gazed -but little thought
What wealth the show to me had brought.
For oft, when on my couch I lie
In vacant or in pensive mood,

They flash upon that inward eye
Which is the bliss of solitude;
And then my heart with pleasure fills
And dances with the daffodils.

My Heart Leaps up When I Behold
William Wordsworth

My heart leaps up when I behold
A rainbow in the sky:
So was it when my life began,
So is it now I am a man,
So be it when I shall grow old
Or let me die!
The Child is father of the Man:
And I could wish my days to be
Bound each to each by natural piety.

The Heart of the New Thought

Ella Wheeler Wilcox

1. Let the Past Go

Do not begin the new year by recounting to yourself or others all your losses and sorrows. Let the past go.

Should some good friend present you with material for a lovely garment, would you insult her by throwing it aside and describing the beautiful garments you had worn out in past times?

The new year has given you the fabric for fresh start in life; why dwell upon the events which have gone, the joys, blessings and advantages of the past!

Do not tell me it is too late to be successful or happy. Do not tell me you are sick or broken in spirit; the spirit cannot be sick or broken, because it is of God.

It is your mind which makes your body sick. Let the spirit assert itself and demand health and hope and happiness in this new year.

Forget the money you have lost, the mistakes you have made, the injuries you have received, the disappointments you have experienced.

Real sorrow, the sorrow which comes from the death of dear ones, or some great cross well borne, you need not forget. But think of these things as sent to enrich your nature, and to make you more human and sympathetic. You are missing them if you permit yourself instead to grow melancholy and irritable.

It is weak and unreasonable to imagine destiny has selected you for special suffering. Sorrow is no respecter of persons. Say to yourself with the beginning of this year that you are going to consider all your troubles as an education for your mind and soul; and that out of the experiences which you have passed through you are going to build a noble and splendid character, and a successful career.

Do not tell me you are too old. Age is all imagination. Ignore years and they will ignore you.

Eat moderately, and bathe freely in water as cold as nature's rainfall. Exercise thoroughly and regularly.

Be alive, from crown to toe. Breathe deeply, filling every cell of the lungs for at least five minutes, morning and night, and when you draw in long, full breaths, believe you are inhaling health, wisdom and success.

Anticipate good health. If it does not come at once, consider it a mere temporary delay, and continue to expect it.

Regard any physical ailment as a passing inconvenience, no more. Never for an instant believe you are permanently ill or disabled.

The young men of France are studying alchemy, hoping to learn the secret of the transmutation of gold. If you will study your own spirit and its limitless powers, you will gain a greater secret than any alchemist ever held; a secret which shall give you whatever you desire.

Think of your body as the silver jewel box, your mind as the silver lining, your spirit as the gem. Keep the box burnished and clear of dust, but remember always that the jewel within is the precious part of it.

Think of yourself as on the threshold of unparalleled success. A whole, clear, glorious year lies before you! In a year you can regain health, fortune, restfulness, happiness!

Push on! Achieve, achieve!

2. The Sowing of the Seed

When you start in the "New Thought" do not expect sudden illumination. Do not imagine that you are to become perfectly well, perfectly cheerful, successful, and a healer, in a few days.

Remember all growth is slow. Mushrooms spring up in a night, but oaks grow with deliberation and endure for centuries.

Mental and spiritual power must be gained by degrees.

It you attained maturity before you entered this field of "New Thought," it is folly to suppose a complete transformation of your whole being will take place in a week—a month—or a year. All you can reasonably look for is a gradual improvement, just as you might do if you were attempting to take up music or a science.

The New Thought is a science, the Science of Right Thinking. But the brain cells which have been shaped by the old thoughts of despondency and fear, cannot all at once be reformed. It will be a case of "Try, try again."

Make your daily assertions, "I am love, health, wisdom, cheerfulness, power for good, prosperity, success, usefulness, opulence." Never fail to assert these things at least twice a day; twenty times is better. But if you do not attain to all immediately, if your life does not at once exemplify your words, let it not discourage you.

The saying of the words is the watering of the seeds. After a time they will begin to sprout, after a longer time to cover the barren earth with grain, after a still longer time to yield a harvest.

If you have been accustomed to feeling prejudices and dislikes easily, you will not all at once find it easy to illustrate your assertion, "I am love." If you have indulged yourself in thoughts of disease, the old aches and pains will intrude even while you say "I am health!"

If you have groveled in fear and a belief that you were born to poverty and failure, courage and success and opulence will be of slow growth. Yet they will grow and materialize, as surely as you insist and persist. Declare they are yours, right in the face of the worst disasters. There is nothing that so confuses and frustrates misfortune as to stare it down with unflinching eyes.

If you waken some morning in the depths of despondency and gloom, do not say to yourself: "I may as well give up this effort to adopt the New Thought—I have made a failure of it evidently." Instead sit down quietly, and assert calmly that you are cheerfulness, hope, courage, faith and success.

Realize that your despondency is only temporary; an old habit, which is reasserting itself, but over which you will gradually gain the ascendancy. Then go forth into the world and busy yourself in some useful occupation, and before you know it is on the way, hope will creep into your heart, and the gray cloud will lift from your mind. Physical pains will loosen their hold, and conditions of poverty will change to prosperity.

Your mind is your own to educate and direct. You can do it by the aid of the Spirit, but you must be satisfied to work slowly. Be patient and persistent.

3. Old Clothes

As you go over your wardrobe in the spring or fall, do not keep any old, useless, or even questionable, garments, for "fear you might need them another year." Give them to the ragman, or send them to the county or city poor house. There is nothing that will keep you in a rut of shabbiness more than clinging to old clothes.

It is useless to say that you cannot afford new garments. It is because you have harped upon this idea that you are still in straitened circumstances. You believe neither in God or yourself. Possibly you were brought up to think yourself a mere worm of earth, born to poverty and sorrow.

If you were, it will of course require a continued effort to train your mind to the new thought, the thought of your divine inheritance of all God's vast universe of wealth. But you can do it.

Begin by giving away your old clothes. There may be people, poor relations, or some struggling mother of half-clad children, to whom your old garments will seem like new raiment, and to whom they will bring hope and happiness.

As a rule, it is not well to give people your discarded clothing. It has a tendency to lower their self-respect and to make them look to you, instead of to themselves, for support. It all depends upon whom the people are and how you do it.

If you can find employment for them, and arouse their hope and self-confidence and ambition, it is better than carloads of clothing or furniture or provisions.

But little children, suffering from cold, or hard-working, over-taxed men and women, will not be harmed, and may be temporarily cheered and encouraged by your gifts.

No matter if you still need your frayed-out garments—do not keep them.

Your thoughts of poverty and trouble have impregnated them so that you will continue to produce the same despondent mind stuff while you wear these garments. Get rid of them, and believe that you are to soon procure fresh, becoming raiment. Rouse all your energies, and go straight ahead with that purpose in mind. You will be surprised to find how soon the opportunity presents itself for you to obtain what you need.

There is new strength, repose of mind and inspiration in fresh apparel. God gives Nature new garments every season. We are a part of Nature. He gives us the qualities and the opportunities to obtain suitable covering for our changing needs, if we believe in the one, and use the other.

When I read of a wealthy man who boasts that he has worn one hat seven years, or a woman in affluent circumstances who has worn one bonnet for various seasons, I feel sorry for their ignorance and ashamed of their penuriousness.

Look at the apple tree, with its delicate spring drapery, its luxurious summer foliage, its autumn richness of coloring, its winter draperies of white! Surely the Creator did not intend the tree to have more variety than man!

The tree trusts, and grows, and takes storm and sun as divinely sent, and believes in its right to new apparel, and it comes. It will come to you if you do the same.

4. High Noon

Every woman who passes thirty ought to keep her brain, heart and mind alive and warm with human sympathy and emotion. She ought to interest herself in the lives of others, and make her friendship valuable to the young.

She should keep her body supple, and avoid losing the lines of grace: and she should select some study or work to occupy her spare hours and to lend a zest to the coming years. Every woman in the comfortable walks in life can find time for such a study. No woman of tact, charm, refinement and feeling need ever let her husband, unless she has married a clod, become indifferent or commonplace in his treatment of her. Man reflects to an astonishing degree woman's sentiments for him.

Keep sentiment alive in your own heart, madam, and in the heart of your husband. If he sees that other men admire you he will be more alert to the necessity of remaining your lover.

Take the happy, safe, medium path between a gray and a gay life by keeping it radiant and bright. Read and think and talk of cheerful, hopeful, interesting subjects. Avoid small gossip, and be careful in your criticism of neighbors. Sometimes we must criticize, but speak *to* people whose faults you feel a word of counsel may amend, not *of* them to others.

Make your life after it reaches its noon, glorious with sunlight, rich with harvests, and bright with color. Be alive in mind, heart and body. Be joyous without giddiness, loving without silliness, attractive without being flirtatious, attentive to others' needs without being officious, and instructive without too great a display of erudition. Be a noble, loving, lovable woman.

If is never too late in life to make a new start. No matter how small a beginning may be, it is so much begun for a new incarnation if it is cut off here by death.

If I were one hundred years old, and in possession of my faculties, I would not hesitate to undertake a new enterprise which offered a hope of bettering my condition.

Thought is eternal in its effects, and every hopeful thought which enters the mind sets vibrations in motion, which shall help minds millions of miles distant and lives yet unborn.

It is folly to mourn over a failure to provide opportunities and luxuries for children. We have only to look at the children of the rich, to see how little enduring happiness money gives, and how seldom great advantages result in great characters. The majority of the really great people of the world, in all lines of achievement, have sprung from poverty. I do not mean from pauper homes, but from the homes where only the mere necessities of life could be obtained, and where early in their youth the children felt it necessary to go into the world and make their own way. Self-dependence, self- reliance, energy, ambition, were all developed in this way.

How rarely do we find these qualities in the children of wealth. How rarely do great philosophers, great statesman, great thinkers and great characters develop from the wealthy classes.

Pauperism—infant labor—the wage-earning women—are all evils which ought to be abolished. But next to that evil I believe the worst thing possible for a human soul is to be born to wealth. It is an obstacle to greatness which few are strong enough to surmount, and it rarely results in happiness to the recipient.

5. Obstacles

However great the obstacles between you and your goal may be or have been, do not lay the blame of your failure upon them. Other people have succeeded in overcoming just as great obstacles. Remove such hindrances from the path for others, if you can, or tell them a way to go around. Even lead them a little distance and cheer them on.

But so far as you yourself are concerned, do not stop to excuse any delinquency or half- heartedness or defeat by the plea of circumstance or environment. The great nature makes its own environment, and dominates circumstance. It all depends upon the amount of force in your own soul.

While you apply this rule to yourself and make no scapegoat of "fate," you must have consideration for the weakness of others, and you must try and better the conditions of the world as you go along.

You are robust and possessed of all your limbs. You can mount over the great boulder which has fallen in the road to success, and go on your way to your goal all the stronger for the experience.

But behind you comes a one-legged man—a blind man—a man bowed to the earth with a heavy burden, which he cannot lay down. It will require weeks, months, years of effort on their part to climb over that rock which you surmounted in a few hours.

So it is right and just for you to call other strong ones to your aid and roll the boulder away or blast it out of the path. That is just exactly the way you should think of the present industrial conditions. In spite of them, the strong, well-poised, earnest and determined soul can reach any desired success.

But there are boulders in the road which do not belong there, boulders which cause hundreds of the pilgrims who are lame or blind or burdened, to fall by the wayside and perish. It is your duty to aid in removing these obstacles and in making the road a safe and clear thoroughfare for all who journey.

Do not sit down by the roadside and say you have been hindered by these difficulties, that is to confess yourself weak. Do not mount over them and rush to your goal and say coldly to the throngs behind you, "Oh, everybody can climb over that rock who really tries—didn't I?" That is to announce yourself selfish and unsympathetic.

No doubt the lame, the blind and the burdened *could* attain the goal despite the rocks if they were fired by a consciousness of the divine force within them; that consciousness can achieve *all things under all circumstances*. But there will always be thousands of pilgrims toiling wearily toward the goal who have not come to this realization.

If there are unjust, unfair and unkind restrictions placed about them, see to it that you do all in your power to right what is wrong. But never wait to attain your own success because of these restrictions or obstacles.

Believe absolutely in your own God-given power to overcome anything and everything. Think of yourself as performing miracles with God's aid.

Desire success so intensely that you attract it as the magnet attracts the steel.

Help to adjust things as you go along, but never for a moment believe that the lack of adjustment can cause you to fail.

6. Thought Force

Your spirit and mine are both part of the stupendous cause. We have always been, and always will be. First in one form, then in another.

Every thought, word and deed is helping decide your next place in the Creator's magnificent universe. You will be beautiful or ugly, wise or ignorant, fortunate or unfortunate, according to what use you make of yourself here and now.

Unselfish thoughts, training your mind to desire only universal good, the cultivation of the highest attributes, such as love, honesty, gratitude, faith, reverence and good will, all mean a life of usefulness and happiness in another incarnation, as well as satisfaction and self-respect in this sphere.

Even if you escape the immediate results of the opposite course of action here, you must face the law of cause and effect in the next state. It is inevitable. God, the maker of all things, does not change His laws. "As you sow you reap." "As a man thinketh so is he." There is no "revenge" in God's mind. He simply makes His laws, and we work our destinies for good or ill according to our adherence to them or violation of them.

Each one of us is a needed part of His great plan. Let each soul say: "He has need of me or I would not be. I am here to strengthen the plan." Remember that always in your most discouraged hours.

The Creator makes no mistakes. There is a divine purpose in your being on earth. Think of yourself as necessary to the great design. It is an inspiring thought. And then consider the immensity of the universe and how accurately the Maker planned it all.

Do not associate with pessimists. If you are unfortunate enough to be the son or daughter, husband or wife of one, put cotton wool (either real or spiritual) in your ears, and shut out the poison words of discouragement and despondency. No tie of blood or law should compel you to listen to what means discomfort and disaster to you. Get out and away, into the society of optimistic people.

Before you go, insist on saying cheerful, hopeful and bright things, sowing the seed, as it were, in the mental ground behind you. But do not sit down to see it grow. Never feel that it is your duty to stay closely and continuously in the atmosphere of the despondent.

You might as well think it your duty to stay in deep water with one who would not make the least effort to swim. Get on shore and throw out a life-line, but do not remain and be dragged under. If you find anyone determined to talk failure and sickness and misfortune and disaster, walk away.

You would not permit the dearest person on earth to administer slow poison to you if you knew it. Then why think it your duty to take mental potions which paralyze your courage and kill your ambition?

Despondency is one phase of immorality. It is blasphemous and an insult to the Creator.

You are justified in avoiding the people who send you from their presence with less hope and force and strength to cope with life's problems than when you met them. Do what you can to change their current of thought. But do not associate intimately with them until they have learned to keep silent—at least, if they cannot speak hopefully.

Learn how to walk, how to poise your body, how to breathe, how to hold your head, how to focus your mind on things of universal importance. Believe your tender, loving thoughts and wishes for good to all humanity have power to help the struggling souls of earth to rise to higher and better conditions. No matter how limited your sphere of action may seem to you and how small your town appears on the map, if you develop your mental and spiritual forces through *love thoughts* you can be a power to move the world along. Rise up and realize your strength. Not only will you be more useful and happy, but you will grow more beautiful and keep your youth.

7. Opulence

Do not go through the world talking poverty and asking everyone you deal with to show you special consideration because you are "poor" and "unfortunate." If you do this with an idea of saving a few dollars here and there, you will always have to do it, because you are creating poverty conditions by your constant assertions.

It is a curious fact that the people who are always demanding consideration in money matters demand the best that is going at the same time. I have known a woman to make a plea for cut prices in a boarding house because she was so poor, yet she wanted the sunniest room and the best location the house afforded.

It is the charity patients who make the most complaint of a physician's skill or a nurse's attention.

If you cannot afford to do certain things, or buy certain objects, don't. But when you decide you must, decide, too, that you will pay the price, and make no whining plea of poverty.

There are two extremes of people in the world, one as distasteful as the other. One is represented by the man who boasts of the costliness of every possession, and invites the whole world to behold his opulence and expenditure. His clothes, his house, his servants, his habits, seem no different to the observer from his neighbor's, yet, according to his story, they cost ten times the amount.

The other extreme is the man who dresses well, lives well, enjoys all the comforts and pleasures of his associates, yet talks poverty continually, and expects the entire community to show him consideration in consequence.

Another thing to avoid is the role of the chronically injured person. We all know him. He has a continual grievance. He has been cheated, abused, wronged, insulted, disappointed and deceived. We wonder how or why he has managed to exist, as we listen to the story of his troubles. No one ever treats him fairly, either in business or social life. Everybody is ungrateful, unkind, selfish, and he could not be made to believe that these experiences were of his own making.

All of us meet with occasional blows from fate, in the form of insults, or ingratitude, or trickery from an unexpected source. But if we get nothing else but those disappointing experiences from life, we may rest assured the fault lies somewhere in ourselves. We are not sending out the right kind of mental stuff, or we would get better returns.

"You never can tell what your thoughts will do
In bringing you hate or love,
For thoughts are things, and their airy wings
Are swift as a carrier dove.
They follow the law of the universe—
Each thing must create its kind,
And they speed o'er the track to bring you back
Whatever went out from your mind."

In the main, we must of necessity get from humanity what we give to it. If we question our ability to win friends or love, people will also question it.

If we doubt our own judgment and discretion in business, others will doubt it, and the shrewd and unprincipled will take the opportunity given by our doubts of ourselves, to spring upon us. If in consequence we distrust every person we meet, we create an unwholesome and unfortunate atmosphere about ourselves, which will bring to us the unworthy and deceitful.

   Stand firm in the universe. Believe in yourself. Believe in others. If you make a mistake, consider it only an incident. If someone wrongs you, cheats, misuses or insults you, let it pass as one of the lessons you had to learn, but do not imagine that you are selected by fate for only such lessons. Keep wholesome, hopeful and sympathetic with the world at large, whatever individuals may do. Expect life to use you better every year, and it will not disappoint you in the long run. For life is what we make it.

8. Eternity

   Do you know what a wonderfully complicated thing a human being is? Every feature, every portion of your body, every motion you make, reflects your mental organization.

   I know a woman past middle life who has always been on the opposite side of every question discussed in her presence. She was agnostic with the orthodox, reverential with atheists, liberal with the narrow, bigoted with the liberal. Whatever belief anyone expressed on any subject, she invariably took the other extreme. She loved to disagree with her fellow-men. It was her pastime. Now, to walk with that woman in silence is merely to carry on a wordless argument. You cannot regulate your steps so they will harmonize with hers. She will be just ahead or just behind you, and if you want to turn to the left, she pulls to the right. A promenade with her is more exhausting than a day's labor. She is not conscious of it, and would think anyone very unreasonable and unjust who told her of her peculiarities.

   I know a woman who all her life has been looking afar for happiness and peace and content, and has never found any of them, because she did not look in her own soul. She was a restless girl, and she married, believing in domestic life lay the goal of her dreams. But she was not happy there, and sighed for freedom. She wanted to move, and did move, once, twice, thrice, to different points of the United States. She was discontented with each change. She is today possessed of all comforts and luxuries which life can afford, yet she is the same restless soul. She likes to read, but it is always the book which she does not possess which she craves. If she is in the library with shelves book-filled, she goes into the garret and hunts in old boxes for a book or a paper which has been cast aside. If she is in a picture gallery, she wants to go to the window and look out on the street, but when she is on the street it bores her, and she longs to go in the house. If a member of the family is absent, she gets no enjoyment out of the society of those at home; yet when that absent one returns her mind strays elsewhere, seeking some imagined happiness not found here.

   I wonder if such souls ever find it, even in the spirit realm, or if they go on there seeking and always seeking something just beyond.

It is a great gift to learn to enjoy the present—to get all there is out of it, and to think of today as a piece of eternity. Begin now to teach yourself this great art if you have not thought of it before. To be able to enjoy heaven, one must learn first to enjoy earth.

9. Morning Influences

What do you think about the very first thing in the morning? Your thoughts during the first half-hour of the morning will greatly influence the entire day. You may not realize this, but it is nevertheless a fact.

If you set out with worry, and depression, and bitterness of soul toward fate or man, you are giving the keynote to a day of discords and misfortunes. If you think peace, hope and happiness, you are sounding a note of harmony and success.

The result may not be felt at once, but it will not fail to make itself evident eventually. Control your morning thoughts. You can do it. The first moment on waking, no matter what your mood, say to yourself: "I will get all the comfort and pleasure possible out of this day, and I will do something to add to the measure of the world's happiness or well-being. I will control myself when tempted to be irritable or unhappy, I will look for the bright side of every event."

Once you say these things over to yourself in a calm, earnest way, you will begin to feel more cheerful. The worries and troubles of the coming day will seem less colossal.

Then say: "I shall be given help to meet anything that comes today. Everything will be for the best. I shall succeed in whatever I undertake. I cannot fail."

Do not let it discourage you if the moment you leave your room you encounter a trouble or a disaster. This usually happens. When we make any boast, spiritually or physically, we are put to the test. The occult forces about us are not unlike human beings. When a, schoolboy boasts of his strength, and says he can "lick any boy in school," he generally gets a chance to prove it.

When we declare we are brave enough to overcome any fate, we find our strength put to the test at once. But that is all right. Prove your words to be true. Regard the troubles and cares you encounter as the "punching bags" of fate, given you to develop your spiritual muscle.

Go at them with courage and keep to your morning resolve. By and by the troubles will lessen, and you will find yourself master of Circumstances.

10. The Philosophy of Happiness

There are natures born to happiness just as there are born musicians, mechanics and mathematicians. They are usually children who came into life under right pre-natal conditions. That is, children conceived and born in love. The mother who thanks God for the little life she is about to bring to earth, gives her child a more blessed endowment than if it were heir to a kingdom or a fortune.

As the majority of people, however, born under "civilized" conditions, are unwelcome to their mothers, it is rarely we encounter one who has a birthright of happiness.

Youth possesses a certain buoyancy and exhilaration which passes for happiness, until the real disposition of the individual asserts itself with the passing of time. Good health and strong vitality are great aids to happiness; yet that they, wealth and honors added, do not produce that much desired state of mind we have but to look about us to observe.

One who is not born a musician needs to toil more assiduously to acquire skill in the art, however strong his desire or great his taste, than the natural genius.

So the man not endowed with joyous impulses needs to set himself the task of acquiring the habit of happiness. I believe it can be done. To the sad or restless or discontented being I would say: Begin each morning by resolving to find something in the day to enjoy. Look in each experience which comes to you for some grain of happiness. You will be surprised to find how much that has seemed hopelessly disagreeable possesses either an instructive or an amusing side.

There is a certain happiness to be found in the most disagreeable duty when you stop to realize that you are getting it out of the way. If it is one of those duties which has the uncomfortable habit of repeating itself continually, you can at least say you are learning patience and perseverance, which are two great virtues and essential to any permanent happiness in life.

Do not anticipate the happiness of tomorrow, but discover it in today. Unless you are in the profound depths of some great sorrow, you will find it if you look for it.

Think of yourself each morning as an explorer in a new realm. I know a man whose time is gold, and he carefully arranged his plans to take three hours for a certain pleasure. He lost his way and missed his pleasure, but was full of exuberant delight over his "new experience." "I saw places and met with adventures I might have missed my whole life." He was a true philosopher and optimist and such a man gets the very kernel out of the nut of life.

I know a woman who had since her birth every material blessing, health, wealth, position, travel and a luxurious home. She was forever complaining of the cares and responsibilities of the latter. Finally she prevailed upon the family to rent the home for a series of years and to live in hotels. Now she goes about posing as a martyr, "a homeless woman." It is impossible for such a selfishly perverted nature to know happiness.

A child should be taught from its earliest life to find entertainment in every kind of condition or weather. If it hears its elders cursing and bemoaning a rainy day the child's plastic mind is quick to receive the impression that a rainy day is a disaster. How much better to expatiate in its presence on the blessing of rain, end to teach it the enjoyment of all nature's varying moods, which other young animals feel.

Happiness must come from within in order to respond to that which comes from without, just as there must be a musical ear and temperament to enjoy music. Cultivate happiness as an art or science.

11. A Worn-Out Creed

I have a, letter from an "orthodox Christian," who says the only hope for humanity lies in the "old-fashioned religion." Then be proceeds to tell me how carefully he has studied human nature, "in business, in social life, and in himself," and that he finds it all vile—selfish—sinful. Of course he does, because he studies it from a false and harmful standpoint, and looks for "the worm of earth" and "the poor, miserable sinner," instead of the *divine man*.

We find what we look for in this world. I have always been looking for the noble qualities in human beings, and I have found them. There are great souls all along the highway of life, and there are great qualities even in the people who seem common and weak to us ordinarily.

One of the grandest souls I know is a man who served his term in prison for sins committed while in drink. He was not "born bad;" he simply drifted into bad company and formed bad habits. He paid the awful penalty of five years behind prison bars, but the divine man within him asserted itself, and today I have no friend I feel prouder to call that name.

Mr. John L. Tait, secretary of the Central Howard Association, of Chicago, writes me regarding his knowledge of ex-convicts: "According to my experience with a number of men of this class during the last two years, more than 90 per cent of them are worthy of the most cordial support and assistance."

If this can be said of men who have been criminals, surely humanity is not so vile as my "orthodox" correspondent would have me believe. A "Christian" of that order ought to be put under restraint, and not allowed to associate with mankind. He carries a moral malaria with him, which poisons the air. He suggests evil to minds which have not thought it. He is a dangerous hypnotist, while pretending to be a disciple of Christ.

The man who believes that all men are vicious, selfish and immoral is projecting pernicious mind stuff into space, which is as dangerous to the peace of the community as dynamite bombs. The world has been kept back too long by this false, unholy and blasphemous "religion." It is not the religion of Christ—it is the religion of ignorant translators, ignorant readers.

Thank God, its supremacy is past. A wholesome and holy religion has taken its place with the intelligent progressive minds of the day, a religion which says: "I am all goodness, love, truth, mercy, health. I am a necessary part of God's universe. I am a divine soul, and only good can come through me or to me. God made me, and He could make nothing but goodness and purity and worth. I am a reflection of all His qualities."

This is the "new" religion; yet it is older than the universe. It is God's own thought put into practical form.

12. Common Sense

If you are suffering from physical ills, ask yourself if it is not your own fault. There is scarcely one person in one hundred who does not overeat or drink. I know an entire family who complains of gastric troubles, yet who keep the coffee pot continually on the range and drink large quantities of that beverage at least twice a day. No one can be well who does that. Almost every human ailment can be traced to foolish diet.

Eat only two meals in twenty-four hours. If you are not engaged in active physical labor, make it one meal. Drink two or three or four quarts of milk at intervals during the day to supply good blood to the system. You will thrive upon it, and you will not miss the other two meals after the first week. And your ailments will gradually disappear.

Meantime, if you are self-supporting, your bank account will increase. Think of the waste of money which goes into indigestible food! It is appalling when you consider it. Heaven speed the time when men and women find out how little money it requires to sustain the body in good health and keep the brain clear and the eye bright!

The heavy drinker is today looked upon with pity and scorn. The time will come when the heavy eater will be similarly regarded.

Once find the delight of a simple diet, the benefit to body and mind and purse, and life will assume new interest, and toil will be robbed of its drudgery, for it will cease to be a mere matter of toiling for a bare existence.

Again, are you unhappy? Stop and ask yourself why. If you have a great sorrow, time will be your consoler. And there is an ennobling and enriching effect of sorrow well borne. It is the education of the soul. But if you are unhappy over petty worries and trials, you are wearing yourself to no avail; and if you are allowing small things to irritate and harass you and to spoil the beautiful days for you, take yourself in hand and change your ways.

You can do it if you choose. It is pitiful to observe what sort of troubles most unhappy people are afflicted with. I have seen a beautiful young woman grow care-lined and faded just from imagining she was being "slighted" or neglected by her acquaintances. Someone nodded coldly to her, another one spoke superciliously, a third failed to invite her, a fourth did not pay her a call, and so on—always a grievance to relate until one is prepared to look sympathetic at the sight of her.

And such petty, petty grievances for this great, good life to be marred by! And all the result of her own disposition. Had she chosen to look for appreciation and attention and good will she would have found it everywhere.

Then, about your temper? Is it flying loose over a trifle? Are you making yourself and everyone else wretched if a chair is out of place, or a meal a moment late, or some member of the family is tardy at dinner, or your shoe string is in a tangle or your collar button mislaid? Do you go to pieces nervously if you are obliged to repeat a remark to someone who did not understand you? I have known a home to be ruined by just such infinitesimal annoyances. It is a habit, like the drug or alcohol habit—this irritability.

All you need do is to stop it. Keep your voice from rising, and speak slowly and calmly when you feel yourself giving way to it. Realize how ridiculous and disagreeable you will be if you continue, what an unlovely and hideous old age you are preparing for yourself. And realize that a loose temper is a sign of vulgarity and lack of culture.

Think of the value of each day of life, how much it means and what possibilities of happiness and usefulness it contains if well spent.

But if you stuff yourself like an anaconda, dwell on the small worries and grow angry at the least trifle, you are committing as great and inexcusable a folly as if you flung your furniture and garments and food and fuel into the sea in a spirit of wanton cruelty. You are wasting life for nothing. Every sick, gloomy day you pass is a sin against life. Get health, be cheerful, keep calm.

Clear your mind of every gloomy, selfish angry or revengeful thought. Allow no resentment or grudge toward man or fate to stay in your heart overnight. Wake in the morning with a blessing for every living thing on your lips and in your soul. Say to yourself: "Health, luck, usefulness, success, are mine. I claim them." Keep thinking that thought, no matter what happens, just as you would put one foot before another if you had a mountain to climb. Keep on, keep on, and suddenly you will find you are on the heights, with luck beside you.

Whoever follows this recipe *cannot fail* of happiness, good fortune and a useful life. But saying the words over *once* and then drifting back to anger, selfishness, revenge and gloom will do no good.

The words must be said over and over, and *thought* and *lived* when not said.

13. Literature

The world is full of "New Thought" Literature. It is helpful and inspiring to read. It is worth many dollars to anyone who will *live* its philosophy.

I talked to a man who has been studying along these lines for some years. "Oh, I know all that philosophy," he said; "it is nothing new. I am perfectly familiar with it." Yet this man was continually allowing himself to grow angry over the least trifle; he was quick to see and speak of the faults in others; he was demanding more of those he associated with in the way of consideration and justice than he was willing to give, and he was untidy in his person and improvident in his use of money.

Now it is the merest waste of time for this man to read "New Thought" literature or practice "deep breathing," since he will not put into daily and hourly practice what is taught by the New Religion. He is like the orthodox Christian who mumbles through the Lord's Prayer and then goes forth to do exactly as he would not be done by in business, social and domestic life.

Man is what he thinks. Not what he says, reads or hears. By persistent thinking you can undo any condition which exists. You can free yourself from any chains, whether of poverty, sin, ill health or unhappiness. If you have been thinking these thoughts half a lifetime you must not expect to batter down the walls you have built, in a week, or a month, or a year. You must work and wait, and grow discouraged and stumble and pick yourself up and go on again.

You cannot in an hour gain control over a temper which you have let fly loose for twenty years. But you *can* control it eventually, and learn to think of a burst of anger as a vulgarity like drunkenness or profanity, something you could not descend to.

If you have allowed yourself to think despondent thoughts and believe that poverty and sickness were your portion for years, it will take time to train your mind to more cheerful and hopeful ideas; but you can do it by repeated assertions and by reading and thinking and living the beautiful New Thought Philosophy.

14. Optimism

Not long ago I read the following gloomy bit of pessimism from the pen of a man bright enough to know better than to add to the mental malaria of the world. He said:

"Life is a hopeless battle in which we are foredoomed to defeat. And the prize for which we strive 'to have and to hold' -- What is it? A thing that is neither enjoyed while had, nor missed when lost. So worthless it is, so unsatisfying, so inadequate to purpose, so false to hope and at its best so brief, that for consolation and compensation we set up fantastic faiths of an aftertime in a better world from which no confirming whisper has ever reached us out of the void. Heaven is a prophecy uttered by the lips of despair, but Hell is an inference from history."

This is morbid and unwholesome talk which can do no human being any good to utter, or listen to. But it can depress and discourage the weak and struggling souls, who are striving to make the best of circumstances, and it can nerve to suicide the hand of some half-crazed being, who needed only a word of encouragement and cheer to brace up and win the race.

This is the unpardonable sin—to talk discouragingly to human souls, hungering for hope. When the man without brains does it, he can be pardoned for knowing no better. When the man with brains does it, he should be ashamed to look his fellow mortals in the eyes. It is a sin ten times deeper dyed than giving a stone to those who ask for bread. It is giving poison to those who plead for a cup of cold water.

Fortunately the remarks above quoted contain not one atom of truth! The writer may speak for himself, but he has no right to speak for others. It is all very well for a man who is marked with smallpox to say his face has not one unscarred inch on the surface of it. But he has no premises to stand upon when he says there is not a face in the world which is free from small-pox scars.

Life is not "a hopeless battle in which we are doomed to defeat." Life is a glorious privilege, and we can make anything we choose of it, if we begin early and are in deep earnest, and realize our own divine powers. Nothing can hinder us or stay us. We can do and be whatsoever we will.

The prize of life is not "a thing which is neither enjoyed while had nor missed when lost." It is enjoyed by millions of souls today—this great prize of life. I for one declare that for every day of misery in my existence I have had a week of joy and happiness. For every hour of pain, I have had a day of pleasure. For every moment of worry, an hour of content.

I cannot be the only soul so endowed with the appreciation of life! I know scores of happy people who enjoy the many delights of earth, and there are thousands whom I do not know.

Of course "life is not missed when lost"—because it is never lost. It is indestructible. Life ever was, and ever will be. It is a continuous performance.

It is not "worthless" to the wholesome, normal mind. It is full of interest, and rich with opportunities for usefulness. When any man says his life is worthless, it is because he has eyes and sees not, and ears and hears not. It is his own fault, not the fault of God, fate or accident.

If every life seems at times "unsatisfactory" and "inadequate" it is only due to the cry of the immortal soul longing for larger opportunities and fewer limitations.

Neither is life "false to hope." He who trusts the divine Source of Life, shall find his hopes more than realized here upon earth. I but voice the knowledge of thousands of souls, when I make this assertion. I know whereof I speak.

All that our dearest hopes desire will come to us, if we believe in ourselves as rightful heirs to Divine Opulence, and work and think always on those lines.

If "no whisper has ever reached us out of the void" confirming our faith in immortality, then one-third of the seemingly intelligent and sane beings of our acquaintance must be fools or liars. For we have the assertion of fully this number that such whispers have come, besides the Biblical statistics of numerous messages from the other realm. "As it was in the beginning, is now and shall be ever more, world without end, Amen."

15. Preparation

Every day I hear middle-aged people bemoaning the fact that they were not given advantages or did not seize the opportunities for an education in early youth. They believe that their lives would be happier, better and more useful had an education been obtained. Scarcely one of these people realizes that middle life is the schooltime for old age, and that just as important an opportunity is being missed or ignored day by day for the storing up of valuable knowledge which will be of great importance in rendering old age endurable.

Youth is the season to acquire knowledge, middle life is the time to acquire wisdom. Old age is the season to enjoy both, but wisdom is far the more important of the two. By wisdom I mean the philosophy which enables us to control our tempers, curb our tendency to severe criticism, and cultivate our sympathies.

The majority of people after thirty-five consider themselves privileged to be cross, irritable, critical and severe, because they have lived longer than the young, because they have had more trials and disappointments, and because they believe they understand the world better. Those are excellent reasons why they should be patient, kind, broad and sympathetic.

The longer we live the more we should realize the folly and vulgarity of ill-temper, the cruelty of severe criticism and the necessity for a broad-minded view of life, manners, morals and customs.

Unless we adapt ourselves to the changing habits of the world, unless we adopt some of the new ideas that are constantly coming to the front, we will find ourselves carping, disagreeable and lonely old people as the years go by.

The world will not stand still for us. Society will not wear the same clothes or follow the same pleasures, or think the same thoughts when we are eighty that were prevalent when we were thirty. We must keep moving with the world or stand still and solitary. After thirty we must seize every hour and educate ourselves to grow into agreeable old age.

It requires at least twenty years to become well educated in book and college lore. If we begin to study at seven we are rarely through with all our common schools, seminaries, high schools and colleges have to offer under a score of years. The education for old age needs fully as many years. We need to begin at thirty to be tolerant, patient, serene, trustful, sympathetic and liberal. Then, at fifty, we may hope to have "graduated with honors" from life's school of wisdom, and to be prepared for another score of years of usefulness and enjoyment in the practice of these qualities.

Instead of wasting our time in bemoaning the loss of early opportunities for obtaining an education, let us devote ourselves to the cultivation of wisdom, since that is free to all who possess self-control, will power, faith and perseverance. Begin today, at home. Be more tolerant of the faults of the other members of your household. Restrain your criticisms on the conduct of your neighbors.

Try and realize the causes which led some people who have gone wrong to err. Look for the admirable qualities in everyone you meet.

Sympathize with the world. Be interested in progress, be interested in the young. Keep in touch with each new generation, and do not allow yourself to grow old in thought or feeling. Educate yourself for a charming old age.   There is no time to lose.

16. Dividends

Our thoughts are shaping unmade spheres,
And, like a blessing or a curse,
They thunder down the formless years
And ring throughout the universe.

The more we realize the tremendous responsibility of our mental emanations the better for the world and ourselves. The sooner we teach little children what a mighty truth lies in the Bible phrase "As a man thinketh, so is he," the better for future generations. If a man thinks sickness, poverty and misfortune, he will meet them and claim them all eventually as his own. But he will not acknowledge the close relationship, he will deny his own children and declare they were sent to him by an evil fate.

Walter Atkinson tells us that "he who hates is an assassin." Every kindergarten and public school teacher ought to embody this idea in the daily lessons for children. It may not be possible to teach a child to "love every neighbor as himself," for that is the most difficult of Commandments to follow to the letter; but it is possible to eliminate hatred from a nature if we awaken sympathy for the object of dislike.

That which we pity we cannot hate. The wonderful Intelligence which set this superb system of worlds in action must have been inspired by love for all it created. So much grandeur and magnificence, so much perfection of detail, could only spring from Love.

Whatever is out of harmony in our little world has been caused by man's substituting hate and fear for love and faith. Every time we allow either hate or fear to dominate our minds we disarrange the order of the universe and make trouble for humanity, and ourselves.

It may be a little late in reaching us, but it is sure to come back to the Mind which sent forth the cause.

Every time we entertain thoughts of love, sympathy, forgiveness and faith we add to the well-being of the world, and create fortunate and successful conditions for ourselves. Those, too, may be late in coming to us—*but they will come.*

Right thinking is not attained in a day or a week. We must train the mind to reject the brood of despondent, resentful, fearful and prejudiced thoughts which approach it, and to invite and entertain cheerful, broad and wholesome thoughts instead, just as we overcome false tones and cultivate musical ones in educating the voice for singing.

When we once realize that by driving away pessimistic, angry and bitter thoughts we drive away sickness and misfortune to a great extent, and that by seeking the kinder and happier frame of mind we seek at the same time success and health and good luck, we will find a new impetus in the control of our mental forces. For we all love to be paid for our worthy deeds, even while we believe in being good for good's sake only. And nothing in life is surer than this: RIGHT THINKING PAYS LARGE DIVIDENDS.

Think success, prosperity, usefulness. It is much more profitable than thinking self-destruction or the effort at self-destruction, for that is an act which aims at an impossibility. You can destroy the body, but the *you* who suffers in mind and spirit will suffer still, and live still. You will only change your location from one state to another. You did not make yourself, you cannot unmake yourself. You can merely put yourself among the spiritual tramps who hang about the earth's borders, because they have not prepared a better place for themselves.

Suicide is cheap, vulgar and cowardly. Because you have made a wreck of a portion of this life, do not make a wreck of the next. Mend up your broken life here, go along bravely and with sympathy and love in your heart, determined to help everybody you can, and to better your condition as soon as possible. Men have done this after fifty, and lived thirty good years to enjoy the results.

Do not feel hurt by the people who slight you, or who refer to your erring past. Be sorry for them. I would rather be a tender-hearted reformed sinner than a hard-hearted model of good behavior. I would rather learn sympathy through sin than never learn it at all.
There is nothing we cannot live down, and rise above, and overcome. There is nothing we cannot be in the way of nobility and worth.

17. Royalty

We get what we give. I have never known this rule to fail in the long run. If we give sympathy, appreciation, goodwill, charitable thoughts, admiration and love—we receive all these back from humanity in time. We may bestow them unworthily, as the sower of good seed may cast it on a rocky surface; but the winds of heaven will scatter it broadcast, and, while the rock remains barren, the fields shall yield a golden harvest. *The seed must be good*, however.

If I say to myself without any real regard for another in my heart, "I want that person to like me, I will do all in my power to please him," I need not be surprised if my efforts fail or prove of only temporary efficacy.

Neither need I feel surprised or pained if I find by-and-by that other people are bestowing policy friendship upon me, actions with no feeling for a foundation. No matter how kind and useful I make my conduct toward an individual, if in my secret heart I am criticizing him severely and condemning him, I must expect criticism and condemnation from others as my portion.

We reap what we sow. Some harvests are longer in growing than others, but they will all grow in time.

Servility in love, or friendship, or duty, is never commendable. I do not believe God Himself feels complimented when the beings He created as the highest type of His workmanship declare themselves worthless worms, unworthy of His regard!

We are heirs of God's kingdom, and rightful inheritors of happiness, and health, and success. What monarch would feel pleasure in having his children crawl in the dust, saying, "We are less than nothing, miserable, unworthy creatures"? Would he not prefer to hear them say, proudly: "We are of royal blood"?

We ought always to believe in our best selves, in our right to love and be loved, to give and receive happiness, and to toil and be rewarded, And then we should bestow our love, our gifts and our toil with no anxious thought about the returns. If we chance to love a loveless individual, to give to one bankrupt in gratitude, to toil for the unappreciative, it is but a temporary deprivation for us. The love, the gratitude and the recompense will all come to us in time from some source, or many sources. It cannot fail.

18. Heredity

American parents, as a rule, can be put in two extreme classes, those who render the children insufferably conceited and unbearable by overestimating their abilities and over-praising their achievements, and those who render them morbid and self-depreciating by a lack of wholesome praise. It is rare indeed, when we find parents wise and sensible enough to strengthen the best that is in their children by discreet praise, and at the same time to control the undesirable qualities by judicious and kind criticism.

I heard a grandmother not long ago telling callers in the presence of a small boy what a naughty, bad child he was, and how impossible it seemed to make him mind. Wretched seed to sow in the little mind, and the harvest is sure to be sorrow. I have heard parents and older children expatiate on the one stupid trait and the one plain feature of a bright and handsome child, intending to keep it from forming too good an opinion of itself.

To all young people I would say, cultivate a belief in yourself. Base it on self-respect and confidence in God's love for his own handiwork. Say to yourself, "I will be what I will to be." Not because the human will is all-powerful, but because the Divine will is back of you. Analyze your own abilities and find what you are best fitted to do. Then set about the task of doing your chosen work to the very best of your ability, and do not for an instant doubt your own capabilities. Perhaps they may be dwarfed and enfeebled by years of morbid thought; but if you persist in a self-respecting and self-reliant and God-trusting course of thinking your powers will increase and your capabilities strengthen.

It is no easy matter to overcome a habit of self-depreciation. It is like straightening out a limb which has been twisted by a false attitude or correcting a habit of sitting round-shouldered. It requires a steady and persistent effort. When the depressing and doubtful thoughts come, drive them away like malaria-breeding insects. Say, "This is not complimentary to my Maker. I am His work. I must be worthy of my own respect and of that of others. I must and will succeed."

19. Invincibility

If we persistently desire good things to come to us for unselfish purposes, and at the same time faithfully perform the duties which lie nearest, we will eventually find our desires being realized in the most unexpected manner. Our thought force has proved to be a wedge, opening the seemingly inaccessible Wall of Circumstance.

To read good books, to think and ponder on what you read, to cultivate every agreeable quality you observe in others, and to weed from your nature every unworthy and disagreeable trait, to study humanity with an idea of being helpful and sympathetic, all these efforts will help you to the ultimate attainment of your wishes.

It is a proven fact that if we devote a few moments each day to reaching exercises, standing with loose garments and stretching the body muscles to reach some point above us, we increase our stature. Just so if we mentally and spiritually are continually reaching to a higher plane, we are growing.

Every least thought of the brain is a chisel, chipping away at our characters, and our characters are building our destinies. The incessant and persistent demand of our hearts and minds MUST be granted.

20. That Mental Chisel

During a trolley ride through a thrifty New England locality, where church spires were almost as plentiful as trees, I studied the faces of the people who came into the car during my two hours' journey. The day was beautiful, and all along the route our numbers were recruited by bevies of women, young, middle aged and old, who were bent on shopping expeditions or setting forth to make social calls. They went and came at each village through which our coach of democracy passed, and they represented all classes.

The young girls were lovely, as young girls are the world over: their complexion possessed that soft tender luster, peculiar to seashore localities, for the salty breath of Father Neptune is the greatest of cosmetics. Many of the young faces were formed in classic mould, their features clearly cut and refined, and severe, like the thoughts and principles of their ancestors. Often I observed a mother and some female relative, presumably an aunt, in company with a young relative; and always the sharpening and withering process of the years of set and unelastic thought was discernible upon their faces, which had once been young, and classic and attractive.

In the entire two hours I saw but three lovely faces which were matured by time. I saw scores of well-dressed and evidently well-cared-for women of middle age, whose countenances were furrowed, drawn, pinched, sallow, and worn, beyond excuse; for time, sorrow, and sickness are not plausible excuses for such ravages upon a face God drew in lines of beauty.

Time should mature a woman's beauty as it does that of a tree. Sorrow should glorify it as does the frost the tree, and sickness should not be allowed to lay a lingering touch upon it, until death calls the spirit away.

Without question the great majority of the women I saw were earnest orthodox Christians. I heard snatches of conversation regarding Church and Charities and I have no doubt that each woman among them believed herself to be a disciple of Christ. Yet where was the result of the loving, tender, sweet spirit of Christ's teaching? It surely was not visible upon those pinched and worried faces, and those faces were certain and truthful chronicles of the work done by the minds within.

One face said to me in every line, "I talk about God's goodness and loving-kindness, but I worry over the dust in the spare room, I fret about our expenses, I am troubled about my lungs, and I fear my husband has an unregenerate heart. I never know an hour's peace, for even in my sleep, I worry, worry, worry, but of course I know I will be saved by the blood of Christ!"

Another said, "I am in God's fold, well and safe, but I hate and despise my nearest neighbor, for she wears clothes that I am sure she cannot pay for, and her children are always dressed better than mine. I quarrel with my domestics, and am always in trouble of some kind, just because human beings are so full of sin and no one but myself is ever right. I shall be so glad to leave this world of woe and go to heaven, but I hope I will not meet many of my present acquaintances there!"

Another said, "If I only had good health—but I was born to sickness and suffering, and it is God's will that I should suffer!" Oh the pity of it, and to imagine this is religion!

Thank God the wave of "New Thought" is sweeping over the land, and washing away those old blasphemous errors of mistaken creeds. The "New Thought" is to give us a new race of beautiful middle-aged and old people. Today in any part of the land among rich, poor, ignorant or intellectual, orthodox or materialists the beautiful mature face is rarer than a white blackbird in the woods. It is impossible to be plain, ugly, or uninteresting in late life, if the mind keeps itself occupied with right thinking.

The withered and drawn face of fifty indicates withered emotions and drawn and perverted ambitions. The dried and sallow face tells its story of dried-up sympathies and hopes. The furrowed face tells of acid cares eating into the heart. All this is irreligious! Yet all this prevails extensively in our most conservative and churchy communities.

He who in truth trusts God cannot worry. He who loves God and mankind, cannot become dried and withered at fifty, for love will re-create his blood, and renew the fires of his eye. He who understands his own divine nature will grow more beautiful with the passing of time, for the God within will become each year more visible.

The really reverent soul accepts its sorrows as blessings in disguise, and he who so accepts them is beautified and glorified by them, within and without.

Are you growing more attractive as you advance in life? Is your eye softer and deeper, is your mouth kinder, your expression more sympathetic, or are you screwing up your face in tense knots of worry? Are your eyes growing hopeless and dull, is your mouth drooping at the corners, and becoming a set thin line in the centre, and is your skin dry, and sallow, and parched?

Study yourself and answer these questions to your own soul, for in the answer depends the decision whether you really love and trust God, and believe in your own immortal spirit, or whether you are a mere impostor in the court of faith.

21. The Object of Life

What do you believe to be the object of your life? To be happy and successful, perhaps you are thinking, even if you do not answer in those words. That is the idea of the many. Meanwhile others, who have been educated in the melancholy faith of their ancestors, believe the object of this life is to be miserable, poor, and full of sorrow, that they may wear a crown of glory hereafter. But the clear thinker and careful observer must realize that there is one and only one main object in life—*the building of character*.

He who sets out in early youth with that ambition and purpose, and keeps to it, will not only attain his object, but he will, too, attain happiness and true success—for there is no such thing as failure for the man or woman of character.

We often apply the two words character and success, unworthily. We speak of a man of "much character" when he is merely self-assertive and stubborn, and we call a man successful, who has accumulated a fortune, or achieved fame and a position, by doubtful methods.

Then what is character, and what is success? Character is the result of the cultivation of the highest and noblest dualities in human nature, and putting those qualities to practical use. Success is the conquest of the lower and baser self, and the ability to be useful to one's fellow men.

There are men of brain, wealth and position who are failures, and there are men of limited abilities and in humble places who are yet successful, inasmuch as they make the utmost of themselves, and their opportunities.

It makes no difference how lowly your sphere in life may be, and no matter how limited your environment, you can build your character if you will. You need no outlay of money, no assistance from those in power, no influence.

Character Building must be done alone, and by yourself. The ground must be cleansed of debris, and the structure must be erected stone by stone. It is dull, slow, hard work, especially the preparation.

All preparation is drudgery. When this little whirling globe of ours began to cool in space think what a task lay before it! Think of the mass of chaos which had to slowly shape itself into mighty, green, glad and snowcapped mountains, fertile vales, and noble forests.

Each one of us is a little world, whirling alone on an individual orbit, but the divine power is within us, to grow into symmetry, beauty, and perfection if only we realize it. And the happiness of the work, once we begin it, is beyond the power of description. There is no other satisfaction can compare with that of looking back across the years and finding that you have grown in self-control, in charity of judgment, in a sense of justice, in generosity, and in unselfishness. If you are conscious of this growth, let no lack of material success for one moment disturb you. That will come, enough for your need, in time.

The man of symmetrically developed character is never a pauper. He is never dependent for more than a temporary period. To possess character is to be useful, and to be useful is to be independent, and to be useful and independent, is to be happy, even in the midst of sorrow; for sorrow is not necessarily unhappiness. The man who has made the development of a noble and harmonious character the business of his life, accepts his sorrows as means of greater growth, and finds in them an exaltation of spirit which is closely allied to happiness. To such a nature, absolute wretchedness would only be possible through the loss of self-respect; the lowering of an ideal or the failure of a principle.

Would you be happy and successful? Then set yourself to *build character*. Seek to be worthy of your own highest commendation.

22. Wisdom

A great many people are attracted to the New Thought of the day, by its declaration of our right to material wealth, and by its claim that the mind of man can create, command, and control conditions which produce wealth. There is no question concerning the truth of this claim. But woe unto him who cultivates his mental and spiritual powers only for this purpose. His gold shall turn to dross, his pleasure to Dead Sea fruit. He shall be as one who drags a beautiful garment through the mud of the streets, and while clothed in purple and fine linen is yet a repulsive object.

Into the Great Scheme of Existence, as first conceived by the Creator, money did not enter. He made this beautiful Universe, and all that it contains was meant for the enjoyment of His creatures. There was no millionaire and no pauper soul created by God.

Each soul contains the spark of the divine spirit, and by the realization of that spark, and all it means, whatever is desired by mortal man may come to him.

But wise is he who remembers the injunction, "Seek first the kingdom of heaven and all other things shall be added unto you." Wise is he who understands the meaning of the words, "Unto him that hath, more shall be given."

Not until you obtain the faculty of being happy through your spiritual and mental faculties, independent of material conditions, not until you learn to value wealth only as a means of helpfulness, can you safely turn your powers of concentration upon the idea of opulence.

To demand, assert, and command wealth for its mere sensual benefits, to focus your mind upon it because you desire to shine, lead, and triumph, is to play spiritual football with spiritual dynamite. You may obtain what you seek, you may accumulate riches, but at the cost of all that is worth living for.

The merely ignorant, or stupid, or wholly material man who stumbles into a fortune, through inheritance, dogged persistent industry, or chance, may enjoy it in his own fashion, and do no harm in the world. But the man who knows and who has developed his spiritual powers only for the purpose of commanding material gain, might better have a millstone tied about his neck. For he makes himself a spiritual outcast, and his money shall never bring him happiness.

Make, therefore, your assertion of opulence the last in your list, as you make Love first. Call unto yourself spiritual insight, absolute unselfishness, desire for universal good, wisdom, justice, and usefulness, and last of all opulence. Think of yourself as possessed of all these qualities before you picture financial independence. For without love for your kind, without the desire for usefulness and the spiritual insight and the wisdom to be just before being generous, your money would bring you only temporary pleasure, and would do the world no good.

Neither should you labor under the impression that God's work is lying undone because you have no fortune to command and wisely distribute where most needed. Rest assured if you do the work which lies nearest to you, relieve such distress as is possible to you, and keep your faith in the ultimate justice of God's ways, that the world will move on, and humanity will slowly attain its destined goal, even if you never become a millionaire.

23. Self-Conquest

Every New Idea, or supposed New Idea, is a light which attracts the moths. The "New Thought" is no exception. About it flutter hysterical women, unbalanced men: the erratic and the irresponsible.

The possibilities of performing miracles, of healing the sick, hypnotizing the well, transforming poverty into wealth, and changing age to youth, are the rays of light which flicker through the darkness and draw them into the circle of radiance.

The self-indulgent fat woman subscribes to New Thought literature, pays for a course of lectures, and goes forth into the ranks of the unbelievers, proclaiming her power to become a sylph, and to cause others to become sylphs.

The extravagant and inconsiderate rush forth after having heard a discourse upon the power of mind over matter, and declare that they possess the secret of accumulating a fortune by occult means. The lovers of the marvelous believe that they will become great healers in a brief space of time. Not one of these moth converts realizes that the very first step to take in the direction of "New Thought" is self-conquest.

The gourmand does not know that self-indulgence and a gross appetite are incompatible with mental or spiritual growth, and will be insurmountable obstacles in her path toward symmetry. The spendthrift does not take into consideration the fact that good sense, thrift and industry, must aid his mental assertion of wealth, and the miracle lover does not understand that something greater and more difficult is required than a mere wish to heal before healing powers can be obtained.

That the physical body and material conditions can be dominated by the divine spirit in man, is an incontrovertible fact. But first, last and always, the lesser self must be subjugated, and the weak and unworthy qualities overcome.

The woman who desires to reduce her flesh cannot do so by reading occult literature, or joining mystic circles, or attending lectures, unless she permeates herself so thoroughly with spiritual truths that she no longer craves six courses at dinner, and three meals a day, and unless she overcomes her dislike for exercise.

The man who wishes to control circumstances must love better things than money before he can succeed. He must love, and respect, and believe in his Creator, and trust the Divine Man within himself, and he must illustrate this love and trust by his daily conduct, and in his home circle, and in his business relations.

Once in a century, perhaps, is a man born with great powers already developed to heal the sick, or to do other seeming miracles. Such beings are old souls, who have obtained diplomas in former lives; but the majority of us are still in school, and we cannot become "seniors" until we pass through the lower grades. We must change ourselves before we can change material conditions: we must heal our own thoughts and make them sane and normal, before we can heal bodily disease in others.

It is not an immediate process. I have heard an old lady declare that she "got religion" in the twinkling of an eye, and she believed all people would be damned and burn in hell fire, who did not pass through this sudden illumination.

It is possible that the religion which can worship a God cruel enough to burn his children in fire, can only be obtained in the twinkling of an eye; but the reverent, wholesome, and beautiful religion of "New Thought" must be grown into little by little, through patience, faith, and practice.

All that it claims to do it can do, but not instantaneously, not rapidly. We must first make ourselves over; after absolute control of our minds has been obtained, then, and only then, may we hope to influence circumstances and health.

24. The Important Trifles

You will find, in the effort to reach a higher spirituality in your daily life, that the small things try your patience and your strength more than the greater ones. Home life, like business life, is composed of an accumulation of trifles.

There are people who bear great sorrows with resignation, and seem to gain a certain dignity and force of character through trouble, but who are utterly vanquished by trivial annoyances. The old-fashioned orthodox "Christian" was frequently of this order. Death, poverty, and misfortune he bore without complaining, and became ofttimes a more agreeable companion in times of deepest sorrow. He regarded all such experiences as the will of God, and bowed to them. Yet, if his dinner was late, his coffee below the standard, if his eye-glasses were misplaced, or his toe trodden upon, he became a raging lion, and his roar drove his affrighted household into dark corners.

There have been neighborhood Angels, who watched beside the dying sinner, sustained orphans and widows, and endured great troubles sublimely like martyrs. But if a dusty shoe trod upon a freshly washed floor, or husband or child came tardily to the breakfast-table, or lingered outside the door after regulation hour for retiring—lo, the Angel became a virago, or a droning mosquito with persistent sting.

The New Philosophy demands serenity and patience through small trials, as well as fortitude in meeting life's larger ills. It demands, too, that we seek to avoid giving others unnecessary irritation by a thoughtless disregard of the importance of trifles. A man is more likely to keep calm if he wakes in the night and discovers that the house is on fire, than he is if, on being fully prepared to retire, he finds the only mug on the third story is missing from his wash-stand, or the cake of toilet-soap he asked for the day before has been forgotten.

A mother bears the affliction of a crippled child with more equanimity than she is able to bring to bear upon the continual thoughtlessness of a strong one. To be kind, means to be thoughtful. The kindest and most loving heart will sometimes forget and be careless; but it cannot be perpetually forgetful and careless of another's wishes and needs, even in the merest trifles.

25. Concentration

The New Thought includes *concentration of thought* in its teaching; and he who learns that important art is not liable to frequently forget small or large duties. It is he who scatters, instead of concentrates his mind powers, who keeps himself and others in a state of continual irritation by forgetting, mislaying, and losing, three petty vices which do much to mar domestic or business life.

Concentration is a most difficult acquirement for the mature mind which has been allowed to grow in the habit of thought scattering. Wise is the mother, and as sure as wise, who teaches her child to finish each task begun before attempting another, for that is the first step in concentration.

Prentice Mulford, that great and good pioneer in the field of practical New Thought, tells us to apply our whole mental powers to whatever we do, even if it is merely the tying of a shoe, and to think of nothing else until that shoe is tied, then to utterly forget the shoe string, when we turn to another duty or employment. The next lesson in concentration he gives us, is to repeat the word often, to impress it upon the mind. And then to declare each day that "Concentration is mine" will aid still farther in the acquisition of this great and important quality.

Meanwhile, since we can be so fortunate as to always surround ourselves with others who have acquired it, the student of the Higher Philosophy must learn to be serene and self-poised when he encounters life's pigmy worries. He must carry his religion into his bedroom and his office, and not forget it utterly when he loses his collar-button, or misses his car, or finds his office boy has taken a parcel to the wrong address.

To build character necessitates a constant watch upon ourselves. The New Thought is not a religion of Sundays, but of every day.

26. Destiny

Never say that you wish your situation were different! Never wish you had some other person's life or troubles or worries. Accept your own as a *working basis*, the best for you. Then go ahead and *change whatever* displeases you. Remember you are the maker and molder of your own destiny. You do not recall the fact, but you brought about the present conditions of your destiny in former incarnations.

Even if you do not believe this, you must acknowledge that *you are here*, and that the situation in which you find yourself seems to be inevitable for the present. But it is not inevitable for the future, unless you lie down in the furrow and whine, and wish you were a millionaire, or a genius, and rail at the partiality of Providence.

There is no partiality in the Universe. The whole scheme is well balanced. If you were allowed to change lots with anyone on the face of the earth, you would complain and find fault in a short time.

One of our best known millionaires, born to opulence, complains that he has been robbed of the privilege of making his own fortune. He is no happier than you. His confession betrays his weakness of character just as your repining and fault-finding betrays yours. The real worthwhile character thanks God for its destiny and says, "I will show the world what I can do with my life."

Not long ago there was a great trotting-race at Brighton Beach. The blind conqueror "Rythmic" won five consecutive races. Think of it! He did not, like a mortal man, shrink back and say "I am blind—that is a terrible destiny—I am cursed of God—I will not try to win the race." He just trusted the hand of the Master at the reins, did his best and won the honors of the season.

We are all blind racers on the track of earth. The king, the millionaire, the statesman, the law-maker, the beggar, the laborer, the cripple, we are all in the dark. The only thing is to trust the hand of the Master, and *do our best*.

Believe your position is the right starting point for *you*, merely the starting point. It is the shapeless block of stone from which you are to fashion the perfect statue. Or it is the mere mud from which you are to mould the clay image, and later that is to be put into enduring marble.

What is uglier or more unattractive than mud? Yet think of the glorious conceptions which it imprisons. Take the mud of your present environment and thank God for it, and make the image of the future you desire. You can do it—you must do it—you will do it.

27. Sympathy

Are you of a sympathetic nature? If so, do not let your sympathies help to add to the world's miseries. That may seem a strange expression, but it can be explained if you will listen.

Much of the misery in the world is the result of imagination. All of it is the result of selfishness and ignorance. But hundreds and thousands of people believe themselves sick, sorrowful and poverty stricken, who would be well, glad and prosperous, if they only thought themselves so. Every time you pour out your sympathy upon these self-made sufferers, you add to their burden of wrong thought, and make it just so much more difficult for them to rise out of their troubles.

I do not believe all the misfortune in the world is caused by wrong thinking in this life, or can be done away with by right thinking. The three-year-old child who toddles in front of a trolley car and loses a leg, while the tired mother is bending over the washtub to keep the wolf of hunger at bay, cannot be blamed for wrong thinking as the cause of its trouble. Neither can the deaf mute or the child born blind or deformed. We must go farther back, to former lives, to find the first cause of such misfortunes.

No "New Thought," no amount of optimistic theology or philosophy can restore the child's leg, or ears, or eyes. It is utter nonsense to say that miracles like these can be performed. There are scores of individuals whom we meet handicapped in life's race by such dire calamities that we spontaneously pour forth our sympathy. But, even to these, it were kinder and wiser to give diverting thoughts, and a new outlook, and to open up avenues for pleasure, and entertainment, and profit, in place of tears and condolence.

Sympathy, without alleviating actions to a sufferer, is like a cloud without rain to the parched earth. But the great majority of people whom we encounter are making their own crosses, and we who offer them sympathy, and condolence, are but adding to the burden's weight.

I do not recommend coldness, indifference, or ridicule as a substitute for sympathy. But instead of leading the sick man on to tell you the details of his illness, and to describe all his symptoms, while your own body responds with sympathetic aches and pains as you listen, it is kinder to divert his attention to some cheerful and merry topic, or to refer to some case like his own which resulted in perfect restoration to health. Instead of going down into his underground cave of depression, bring him out into the wholesome sunlight of your own healthful state, even if for a moment only, and impress upon his mind that health belongs to him, and must return to him.

To the man in business trouble the same advice applies. Tell him you are sorry for him, but do not take on his despondency to prove it. Talk of the future and all the possibilities it holds for a determined man or woman. Make him laugh. Speak of trouble as the gymnasium where our moral muscles are developed. Answer him that everything he desires is his if he will be persistent and determined in demanding his own. If you put force in your words you will leave an impression.

Do not go away from the house of trouble in tears, but leave the troubled ones you called upon smiling as you depart. That is true sympathy.

28. The Breath

A man reproved me for my interest in New Thought creeds. "The old religion I learned at my mother's knee is good enough for me!" he said. "It is good enough for anybody!" Yet this man's mother had always "enjoyed poor health," as the old lady expressed it, and the man himself was forever talking of his diseases, his ill luck, his poverty, which he said he had been enabled to endure only through the sustaining power of the religion "learned at his mother's knee."

It would be difficult to convince the man that had his mother taught him the creed of the "New Religion" he could have changed all these unfortunate conditions. Life-long ill health would have been impossible for his mother, or for him. The old-fashioned religion allowed and still allows a human being to breathe like a canary bird. Little children go to Sunday-School all their young lives, and grow up to be devout church members, and never hear one word about the importance of deep breathing.

Possibly you may think breathing lessons belong to physical culture, and have no place in religious teachings. There is where you err. In order to develop your whole being, you must learn how to control body and mind through the spirit. Thousands of years ago, men who gave their entire lives to the study of these things learned the great importance of deep breathing as an aid to religious meditation. By this practice, systematically observed, the body is calmed, the mind is brought into subjection, and the spirit rises into control. And in addition, absolute health is achieved. A large portion of our physical ailments result from unused lung cells, and consequent imperfect circulation of the blood.

Fill the lungs full—every cell—with fresh air, two or three times daily, and do not overload the digestive organs, and sickness will fly away to the dark regions where it belongs. At least ten minutes morning and night should be given to the breathing exercises. Sit upright in a comfortable chair, alone, facing the east in the morning and the west at night, because great magnetic force comes from the direction of the sun. Have a window or a door opening to the outer air. Place your hands lightly on your knees, and close your eyes and mouth. Leave your spine free, not touching the chair. Wear no compressing garments or bands. Inflate the chest and abdominal regions as you inhale deep breaths through the nostrils, while counting seven slowly. Exhale while you count seven. Repeat this exercise seven times.

Think as you inhale of whatever qualities you would like to possess, and believe that you are inhaling them. Select seven qualities—Love, Health, Wisdom, Usefulness, Power to Do Good, Success, and Opulence will cover the average human desires. The very unworldly will substitute spiritual knowledge for opulence. Fill your mind with the idea that you are drawing in these qualities with your breaths, and exhaling all that is weak or unworthy. After a few moments you will be conscious of a security and peace new and uplifting. And after a few weeks of steady, persistent practice of these exercises, you will find life growing more beautiful to you, and your strength will be increased tenfold, both physically and spiritually.

29. Generosity

Have you ever observed how invariably your "last dollar" is restored to you, with additions, when you have given it for some worthy purpose? Even if the purpose did not prove to be a worthy one, yet if you thought it so, and gave your last dollar with spontaneous sympathy and good will, you were not long left penniless. Money is much like a man. If you do not hold it too jealously it returns to you the more readily.

Never hesitate to give aid where you feel there is sore and pressing need, for fear you will be left in want yourself. You will not be. This does not mean that indiscriminate charity is commendable. It does not mean that you should lend money to everyone who asks, or lift and carry the burdens of everyone who is ready to lean upon you. It is as wrong to encourage the man addicted to the vice of borrowing, as the one with the vice of alcohol or drugs. One depends upon his acquaintances to tide him over hard places, instead of upon his own strength of character, and the other depends upon stimulants for the same purpose. The too-ready lender is almost as great an evil to humanity as rum or opium, since he too helps a man to kill his own better nature and destroy his self-respect.

If you were able and willing to pay rents of all the poor people you know, and clothe their children, you would soon produce a condition of settled pauperism among them. Large and frequent favors of a financial nature are an injury to anyone, even if it is your son or brother. Let no man lean on anyone save God and his own divine self.

But little helps, when they are unexpected, arouse hope and awaken new faith and new ambition in a discouraged soul. Look about you for such souls, the worn and weary father of a brood of hungry children, the widow struggling with adverse fate in an effort to clothe and educate a child, the tired shop girl who uses all her earnings to sustain her parents, the ambitious boy or girl eager for a chance in life, and the poor cripple or invalid seeking health. You will find them all about you. Do not be afraid to use a dollar here or there to give these worthy ones a happy surprise, no matter how poor you are. It is an insult to the Opulent Creator to suppose you will suffer want and poverty if you help those who are in temporary misfortune. You will not.

Ofttimes we read and hear of the open-handed generous man who "helped everybody," and who "never refused to aid a needy brother," and who ended his life in penury because of his generosity. Never believe these tales until you investigate them. Invariably you will find not generosity but extravagance and utter lack of forethought, caused the man's financial ruin.

I recall a gifted young woman who gave freely to all who asked her assistance and who died a lingering death as a charity patient in a hospital. Yet this young woman had expended ten dollars on foolish and rapid living where she gave one in charity; it was her wasteful extravagance, not her open heart of sympathy, which made her a pauper.

It has been my observation that dollars planted in the soil of benevolence grow into harvests of prosperity. The man who is not afraid to use his small means to assist others need not fear poverty.

30. Woman's Opportunity

The greatest opportunity to better the world which can come to any woman is through the experience of maternity. The power of prenatal influence which a mother possesses is awe-inspiring to realize. It has been said upon excellent authority that Napoleon's mother read Roman history with absorbing interest during the months preceding his birth. Think of the nations and the centuries influenced by that one woman's mental concentration! The geography of the world was changed by her power of focused thought.

In all probability Napoleon's mother did not know what she was doing; she was not conscious of the destiny her mind was shaping for her unborn child, nor of the law governing such conditions. Women have been strangely ignorant of this vital truth; until recent years it has not been considered a "proper" theme for tongue or pen, and today the great majority of young women marry absolutely uninformed upon the subject of prenatal influence.

Men are equally oblivious of any knowledge regarding the matter, and consequently make no special effort to keep the expectant mother of their offspring happy, hopeful, or free of anxiety and worry during this period. Often they do not strive to aid them in their own attempts to bestow a desirable temperament upon the unborn child, but heedlessly and needlessly aggravate or grieve the mind which is stamping its impress upon an unborn soul.

It is just here that the "New Thought" can perform its greatest miracles of good. Even the woman who has not been enlightened upon the law of ante-birth-influence will, if a true disciple of the Religion of Right-living, bring healthy and helpful children into the world, because her normal state of mind will be inclusive of those three qualities; and her continued and repeated assertions of her own divine nature will shape the brain of her child in optimistic and reverential mold.

There is the old law of the continual falling of the drop of water upon the stone to be verified in the spiritual plane. Continual assertions of a mother that her child will be all that she desires it to be, will wear away the stone of inherited tendencies, and bring into physical being a malleable nature wholly amenable to the after influences and efforts she may bring to bear upon it. It is a tremendous responsibility which rests upon the woman who knows she is to be a mother of a human being.

A hundred ancestors may have contributed certain qualities to that invisible and formless atom which contains an immortal soul, yet the mother's mind has the power to remake and rebuild all those characteristics, and to place over them her own dominating impulse, whether for good or ill.

Surely, if success in the arts or the sciences is worthy of years of devoted attention and interested effort, the molding of a noble human being is worth eight or nine months of concentrated thought and unflagging zeal of purpose. Every expectant mother should set herself about the important business God has entrusted her with, unafraid, and confident of her divine mission. She should direct her mind into wholesome and optimistic channels; she should read inspiring books and think loving and large thoughts. She should pray and aspire! and always should she carry in her mind the ideal of the child she would mother, and command from the great Source of all Opulence the qualities she would desire to perpetuate. And they will be given.

31. Balance

Avoid all strained and abstruse language, when conversing with people who may not have entered this realm of thought. Do not allow anyone to think of you as a lunatic, or a crank, unnecessarily. Of course there are people in the world who consider everyone a lunatic who holds an opinion differing from their own. But it can do you, or your philosophy, no good to thrust its most difficult phases before the minds of the unawakened, by vague and high flown expressions.

I once chanced to call upon a lady who had, quite unknown to me, entered upon the study of Christian Science. She remarked to me, almost as soon as the greetings were exchanged, "I had a claim to meet for three days this week, but I have come through it and am victorious." I supposed the lady referred to some business matter, perhaps a legal affair, and waited an explanation. After considerable rambling conversation, I managed to grasp the fact that the woman had been sick in the house three days, but now was well. She considered her illness a mere "claim" her "mortal mind" had made which she had to meet and combat.

This sort of talk is very ridiculous. We need not talk about every ailment which attacks us as we move along toward the condition of perfect health which belongs to us! But if we do speak of indisposition, let us use common sense language.

What we want to realize is, that we are in the body, but that the spirit can control bodily conditions, if we give it the ascendancy, to the extent of keeping us well, moral, useful, and comfortable even in the midst of sickness, vice, indolence and poverty. We can rise above these false elements, and subjugate them.

Meanwhile we cannot live without food, clothes and money. Despise and ignore these vulgar things as we may assume to do, we yet must have them. It brings only ridicule upon ourselves and our ideas to make this pretense of despising the necessities of life. To make them secondary in our thoughts to spiritual knowledge is right and wise, but this is better illustrated by our lives and conduct than by our words.

ON THE DUTY OF CIVIL DISOBEDIENCE
Henry David Thoreau

I heartily accept the motto, -- "That government is best which governs least"; and I should like to see it acted up to more rapidly and systematically. Carried out, it finally amounts to this, which also I believe, -- "That government is best which governs not at all"; and when men are prepared for it, that will be the kind of government which they will have. Government is at best but an expedient; but most governments are usually, and all governments are sometimes, inexpedient. The objections which have been brought against a standing army, and they are many and weighty, and deserve to prevail, may also at last be brought against a standing government. The standing army is only an arm of the standing government. The government itself, which is only the mode which the people have chosen to execute their will, is equally liable to be abused and perverted before the people can act through it. Witness the present Mexican war, the work of comparatively a few individuals using the standing government as their tool; for, in the outset, the people would not have consented to this measure.

This American government -- what is it but a tradition, though a recent one, endeavoring to transmit itself unimpaired to posterity, but each instant losing some of its integrity? It has not the vitality and force of a single living man; for a single man can bend it to his will. It is a sort of wooden gun to the people themselves. But it is not the less necessary for this; for the people must have some complicated machinery or other, and hear its din, to satisfy that idea of government which they have. Governments show thus how successfully men can be imposed on, even impose on themselves, for their own advantage. It is excellent, we must all allow. Yet this government never of itself furthered any enterprise, but by the alacrity with which it got out of its way. It does not keep the country free. It does not settle the West. It does not educate. The character inherent in the American people has done all that has been accomplished; and it would have done somewhat more, if the government had not sometimes got in its way. For government is an expedient by which men would fain succeed in letting one another alone; and, as has been said, when it is most expedient, the governed are most let alone by it. Trade and commerce, if they were not made of India rubber, would never manage to bounce over the obstacles which legislators are continually putting in their way; and, if one were to judge these men wholly by the effects of their actions, and not partly by their intentions, they would deserve to be classed and punished with those mischievous persons who put obstructions on the railroads.

But, to speak practically and as a citizen, unlike those who call themselves no-government men, I ask for, not at once no government, but at once a better government. Let every man make known what kind of government would command his respect, and that will be one step toward obtaining it.

After all, the practical reason why, when the power is once in the hands of the people, a majority are permitted, and for a long period continue, to rule, is not because they are most likely to be in the right, nor because this seems fairest to the minority, but because they are physically the strongest. But a government in which the majority rule in all cases cannot be based on justice, even as far as men understand it. Can there not be a government in which majorities do not virtually decide right and wrong, but conscience? -- in which majorities decide only those questions to which the rule of expediency is applicable? Must the citizen ever for a moment, or in the least degree, resign his conscience to the legislator? Why has every man a conscience, then? I think that we should be men first, and subjects afterward. It is not desirable to cultivate a respect for the law, so much as for the right. The only obligation which I have a right to assume is to do at any time what I think right. It is truly enough said that a corporation has no conscience; but a corporation of conscientious men is a corporation with a conscience. Law never made men a whit more just; and, by means of their respect for it, even the well-disposed are daily made the agents of injustice. A common and natural result of an undue respect for law is, that you may see a file of soldiers, colonel, captain, corporal, privates, powder-monkeys, and all, marching in admirable order over hill and dale to the wars, against their wills, ay, against their common sense and consciences, which makes it very steep marching indeed, and produces a palpitation of the heart. They have no doubt that it is a damnable business in which they are concerned; they are all peaceably inclined. Now, what are they? Men at all? or small movable forts and magazines, at the service of some unscrupulous man in power? Visit the Navy Yard, and behold a marine, such a man as an American government can make, or such as it can make a man with its black arts -- a mere shadow and reminiscence of humanity, a man laid out alive and standing, and already, as one may say, buried under arms with funeral accompaniments, though it may be

> "Not a drum was heard, not a funeral note,
> As his corse to the rampart we hurried;
> Not a soldier discharged his farewell shot
> O'er the grave where our hero we buried."

The mass of men serve the state thus, not as men mainly, but as machines, with their bodies. They are the standing army, and the militia, jailers, constables, posse comitatus, etc. In most cases there is no free exercise whatever of the judgment or of the moral sense; but they put themselves on a level with wood and earth and stones; and wooden men can perhaps be manufactured that will serve the purpose as well. Such command no more respect than men of straw or a lump of dirt. They have the same sort of worth only as horses and ogs. Yet such as these even are commonly esteemed good citizens. Others, as most legislators, politicians, lawyers, ministers, and office-holders, serve the state chiefly with their heads; and, as they rarely make any moral distinctions, they are as likely to serve the devil, without intending it, as God. A very few, as heroes, patriots, martyrs, reformers in the great sense, and men, serve the state with their consciences also, and so necessarily resist it for the most part; and they are commonly treated as enemies by it. A wise man will only be useful as a man, and will not submit to be "clay," and "stop a hole to keep the wind away," but leave that office to his dust at least:--

"I am too high-born to be propertied,
To be a secondary at control,
Or useful serving-man and instrument
To any sovereign state throughout the world."

He who gives himself entirely to his fellow-men appears to them useless and selfish; but he who gives himself partially to them is pronounced a benefactor and philanthropist.

How does it become a man to behave toward this American government to-day? I answer, that he cannot without disgrace be associated with it. I cannot for an instant recognize that political organization as my government which is the slave's government also.

All men recognize the right of revolution; that is, the right to refuse allegiance to, and to resist, the government, when its tyranny or its inefficiency are great and unendurable. But almost all say that such is not the case now. But such was the case, they think, in the Revolution of '75. If one were to tell me that this was a bad government because it taxed certain foreign commodities brought to its ports, it is most probable that I should not make an ado about it, for I can do without them. All machines have their friction; and possibly this does enough good to counterbalance the evil. At any rate, it is a great evil to make a stir about it. But when the friction comes to have its machine, and oppression and robbery are organized, I say, let us not have such a machine any longer. In other words, when a sixth of the population of a nation which has undertaken to be the refuge of liberty are slaves, and a whole country is unjustly overrun and conquered by a foreign army, and subjected to military law, I think that it is not too soon for honest men to rebel and revolutionize. What makes this duty the more urgent is the fact that the country so overrun is not our own, but ours is the invading army.

Paley, a common authority with many on moral questions, in his chapter on the "Duty of Submission to Civil Government," resolves all civil obligation into expediency; and he proceeds to say that "so long as the interest of the whole society requires it, that is, so long as the established government cannot be resisted or changed without public inconveniency, it is the will of God... that the established government be obeyed, and no longer.... This principle being admitted, the justice of every particular case of resistance is reduced to a computation of the quantity of the danger and grievance on the one side, and of the probability and expense of redressing it on the other." Of this, he says, every man shall judge for himself. But Paley appears never to have contemplated those cases to which the rule of expediency does not apply, in which a people, as well as an individual, must do justice, cost what it may. If I have unjustly wrested a plank from a drowning man, I must restore it to him though I drown myself. This, according to Paley, would be inconvenient. But he that would save his life, in such a case, shall lose it. This people must cease to hold slaves, and to make war on Mexico, though it cost them their existence as a people.

In their practice, nations agree with Paley; but does any one think that Massachusetts does exactly what is right at the present crisis?

"A drab of state, a cloth-o'-silver slut,

To have her train borne up, and her soul trail in the dirt." Practically speaking, the opponents to a reform in Massachusetts are not a hundred thousand politicians at the South, but a hundred thousand merchants and farmers here, who are more interested in commerce and agriculture than they are in humanity, and are not prepared to do justice to the slave and to Mexico, cost what it may. I quarrel not with far-off foes, but with those who, near at home, co-operate with, and do the bidding of those far away, and without whom the latter would be harmless. We are accustomed to say, that the mass of men are unprepared; but improvement is slow, because the few are not materially wiser or better than the many. It is not so important that many should be as good as you, as that there be some absolute goodness somewhere; for that will leaven the whole lump. There are thousands who are in opinion opposed to slavery and to the war, who yet in effect do nothing to put an end to them; who, esteeming themselves children of Washington and Franklin, sit down with their hands in their pockets, and say that they know not what to do, and do nothing; who even postpone the question of freedom to the question of free-trade, and quietly read the prices-current along with the latest advices from Mexico, after dinner, and, it may be, fall asleep over them both. What is the price-current of an honest man and patriot to-day? They hesitate, and they regret, and sometimes they petition; but they do nothing in earnest and with effect. They will wait, well disposed, for others to remedy the evil, that they may no longer have it to regret. At most, they give only a cheap vote, and a feeble countenance and Godspeed, to the right, as it goes by them. There are nine hundred and ninety-nine patrons of virtue to one virtuous man; but it is easier to deal with the real possessor of a thing than with the temporary guardian of it.

All voting is a sort of gaming, like checkers or backgammon, with a slight moral tinge to it, a playing with right and wrong, with moral questions; and betting naturally accompanies it. The character of the voters is not staked. I cast my vote, perchance, as I think right; but I am not vitally concerned that that right should prevail. I am willing to leave it to the majority. Its obligation, therefore, never exceeds that of expediency. Even voting for the right is doing nothing for it. It is only expressing to men feebly your desire that it should prevail. A wise man will not leave the right to the mercy of chance, nor wish it to prevail through the power of the majority. There is but little virtue in the action of masses of men. When the majority shall at length vote for the abolition of slavery, it will be because they are indifferent to slavery, or because there is but little slavery left to be abolished by their vote. They will then be the only slaves. Only his vote can hasten the abolition of slavery who asserts his own freedom by his vote.

I hear of a convention to be held at Baltimore, or elsewhere, for the selection of a candidate for the Presidency, made up chiefly of editors, and men who are politicians by profession; but I think, what is it to any independent, intelligent, and respectable man what decision they may come to? Shall we not have the advantage of his wisdom and honesty, nevertheless? Can we not count upon some independent votes? Are there not many individuals in the country who do not attend conventions? But no: I find that the respectable man, so called, has immediately drifted from his position, and despairs of his country, when his country has more reason to despair of him. He forthwith adopts one of the candidates thus selected as the only available one, thus proving that he is himself available for any purposes of the demagogue. His vote is of no more worth than that of any unprincipled foreigner or hireling native, who may have been bought. Oh for a man who is a man, and, as my neighbor says, has a bone in his back which you cannot pass your hand through! Our statistics are at fault: the population has been returned too large. How many men are there to a square thousand miles in this country? Hardly one. Does not America offer any inducement for men to settle here? The American has dwindled into an Odd Fellow -- one who may be known by the development of his organ of gregariousness, and a manifest lack of intellect and cheerful self-reliance; whose first and chief concern, on coming into the world, is to see that the almshouses are in good repair; and, before yet he has lawfully donned the virile garb, to collect a fund for the support of the widows and orphans that may be; who, in short ventures to live only by the aid of the Mutual Insurance company, which has promised to bury him decently.

It is not a man's duty, as a matter of course, to devote himself to the eradication of any, even the most enormous wrong; he may still properly have other concerns to engage him; but it is his duty, at least, to wash his hands of it, and, if he gives it no thought longer, not to give it practically his support. If I devote myself to other pursuits and contemplations, I must first see, at least, that I do not pursue them sitting upon another man's shoulders. I must get off him first, that he may pursue his contemplations too. See what gross inconsistency is tolerated. I have heard some of my townsmen say, "I should like to have them order me out to help put down an insurrection of the slaves, or to march to Mexico; -- see if I would go"; and yet these very men have each, directly by their allegiance, and so indirectly, at least, by their money, furnished a substitute. The soldier is applauded who refuses to serve in an unjust war by those who do not refuse to sustain the unjust government which makes the war; is applauded by those whose own act and authority he disregards and sets at naught; as if the state were penitent to that degree that it hired one to scourge it while it sinned, but not to that degree that it left off sinning for a moment. Thus, under the name of Order and Civil Government, we are all made at last to pay homage to and support our own meanness. After the first blush of sin comes its indifference; and from immoral it becomes, as it were, unmoral, and not quite unnecessary to that life which we have made.

The broadest and most prevalent error requires the most disinterested virtue to sustain it. The slight reproach to which the virtue of patriotism is commonly liable, the noble are most likely to incur. Those who, while they disapprove of the character and measures of a government, yield to it their allegiance and support are undoubtedly its most conscientious supporters, and so frequently the most serious obstacles to reform. Some are petitioning the State to dissolve the Union, to disregard the requisitions of the President. Why do they not dissolve it themselves -- the union between themselves and the State -- and refuse to pay their quota into its treasury? Do not they stand in the same relation to the State, that the State does to the Union? And have not the same reasons prevented the State from resisting the Union, which have prevented them from resisting the State?

How can a man be satisfied to entertain an opinion merely, and enjoy it? Is there any enjoyment in it, if his opinion is that he is aggrieved? If you are cheated out of a single dollar by your neighbor, you do not rest satisfied with knowing that you are cheated, or with saying that you are cheated, or even with petitioning him to pay you your due; but you take effectual steps at once to obtain the full amount, and see that you are never cheated again. Action from principle -- the perception and the performance of right -- changes things and relations; it is essentially revolutionary, and does not consist wholly with anything which was. It not only divides states and churches, it divides families; ay, it divides the individual, separating the diabolical in him from the divine.

Unjust laws exist; shall we be content to obey them, or shall we endeavor to amend them, and obey them until we have succeeded, or shall we transgress them at once? Men generally, under such a government as this, think that they ought to wait until they have persuaded the majority to alter them. They think that, if they should resist, the remedy would be worse than the evil. But it is the fault of the government itself that the remedy is worse than the evil. It makes it worse. Why is it not more apt to anticipate and provide for reform? Why does it not cherish its wise minority? Why does it cry and resist before it is hurt? Why does it not encourage its citizens to be on the alert to point out its faults, and do better than it would have them? Why does it always crucify Christ, and excommunicate Copernicus and Luther, and pronounce Washington and Franklin rebels?

One would think, that a deliberate and practical denial of its authority was the only offence never contemplated by government; else, why has it not assigned its definite, its suitable and proportionate, penalty? If a man who has no property refuses but once to earn nine shillings for the State, he is put in prison for a period unlimited by any law that I know, and determined only by the discretion of those who placed him there; but if he should steal ninety times nine shillings from the State, he is soon permitted to go at large again.

If the injustice is part of the necessary friction of the machine of government, let it go, let it go; perchance it will wear smooth -- certainly the machine will wear out. If the injustice has a spring, or a pulley, or a rope, or a crank, exclusively for itself, then perhaps you may consider whether the remedy will not be worse than the evil; but if it is of such a nature that it requires you to be the agent of injustice to another, then, I say, break the law. Let your life be a counter friction to stop the machine. What I have to do is to see, at any rate, that I do not lend myself to the wrong which I condemn.

As for adopting the ways which the State has provided for remedying the evil, I know not of such ways. They take too much time, and a man's life will be gone. I have other affairs to attend to. I came into this world, not chiefly to make this a good place to live in, but to live in it, be it good or bad. A man has not everything to do, but something; and because he cannot do everything, it is not necessary that he should do something wrong. It is not my business to be petitioning the Governor or the Legislature any more than it is theirs to petition me; and if they should not hear my petition, what should I do then? But in this case the State has provided no way; its very Constitution is the evil. This may seem to be harsh and stubborn and unconciliatory; but it is to treat with the utmost kindness and consideration the only spirit that can appreciate or deserves it. So is an change for the better, like birth and death which convulse the body.

I do not hesitate to say, that those who call themselves Abolitionists should at once effectually withdraw their support, both in person and property, from the government of Massachusetts, and not wait till they constitute a majority of one, before they suffer the right to prevail through them. I think that it is enough if they have God on their side, without waiting for that other one. Moreover, any man more right than his neighbors constitutes a majority of one already.

I meet this American government, or its representative, the State government, directly, and face to face, once a year—no more -- in the person of its tax-gatherer; this is the only mode in which a man situated as I am necessarily meets it; and it then says distinctly, Recognize me; and the simplest, the most effectual, and, in the present posture of affairs, the indispensablest mode of treating with it on this head, of expressing your little satisfaction with and love for it, is to deny it then. My civil neighbor, the tax-gatherer, is the very man I have to deal with—for it is, after all, with men and not with parchment that I quarrel—and he has voluntarily chosen to be an agent of the government. How shall he ever know well what he is and does as an officer of the government, or as a man, until he is obliged to consider whether he shall treat me, his neighbor, for whom he has respect, as a neighbor and well-disposed man, or as a maniac and disturber of the peace, and see if he can get over this obstruction to his neighborliness without a ruder and more impetuous thought or speech corresponding with his action? I know this well, that if one thousand, if one hundred, if ten men whom I could name—if ten honest men only—ay, if one HONEST man, in this State of Massachusetts, ceasing to hold slaves, were actually to withdraw from this copartnership, and be locked up in the county jail therefor, it would be the abolition of slavery in America. For it matters not how small the beginning may seem to be: what is once well done is done forever. But we love better to talk about it: that we say is our mission. Reform keeps many scores of newspapers in its service, but not one man. If my esteemed neighbor, the State's ambassador, who will devote his days to the settlement of the question of human rights in the Council Chamber, instead of being threatened with the prisons of Carolina, were to sit down the prisoner of Massachusetts, that State which is so anxious to foist the sin of slavery upon her sister—though at present she can discover only an act of inhospitality to be the ground of a quarrel with her -- the Legislature would not wholly waive the subject the following winter.

Under a government which imprisons any unjustly, the true place for a just man is also a prison. The proper place to-day, the only place which Massachusetts has provided for her freer and less desponding spirits, is in her prisons, to be put out and locked out of the State by her own act, as they have already put themselves out by their principles. It is there that the fugitive slave, and the Mexican prisoner on parole, and the Indian come to plead the wrongs of his race, should find them; on that separate, but more free and honorable ground, where the State places those who are not with her, but against her -- the only house in a slave State in which a free man can abide with honor. If any think that their influence would be lost there, and their voices no longer afflict the ear of the State, that they would not be as an enemy within its walls, they do not know by how much truth is stronger than error, nor how much more eloquently and effectively he can combat injustice who has experienced a little in his own person. Cast your whole vote, not a strip of paper merely, but your whole influence. A minority is powerless while it conforms to the majority; it is not even a minority then; but it is irresistible when it clogs by its whole weight. If the alternative is to keep all just men in prison, or give up war and slavery, the State will not hesitate which to choose. If a thousand men were not to pay their tax-bills this year, that would not be a violent and bloody measure, as it would be to pay them, and enable the State to commit violence and shed innocent blood. This is, in fact, the definition of a peaceable revolution, if any such is possible. If the tax-gatherer, or any other public officer, asks me, as one has done, "But what shall I do?" my answer is, "If you really wish to do anything, resign your office." When the subject has refused allegiance, and the officer has resigned his office, then the revolution is accomplished. But even suppose blood should flow. Is there not a sort of blood shed when the conscience is wounded? Through this wound a man's real manhood and immortality flow out, and he bleeds to an everlasting death. I see this blood flowing now.

I have contemplated the imprisonment of the offender, rather than the seizure of his goods -- though both will serve the same purpose -- because they who assert the purest right, and consequently are most dangerous to a corrupt State, commonly have not spent much time in accumulating property. To such the State renders comparatively small service, and a slight tax is wont to appear exorbitant, particularly if they are obliged to earn it by special labor with their hands. If there were one who lived wholly without the use of money, the State itself would hesitate to demand it of him. But the rich man -- not to make any invidious comparison -- is always sold to the institution which makes him rich. Absolutely speaking, the more money, the less virtue; for money comes between a man and his objects, and obtains them for him; and it was certainly no great virtue to obtain it. It puts to rest many questions which he would otherwise be taxed to answer; while the only new question which it puts is the hard but superfluous one, how to spend it. Thus his moral ground is taken from under his feet. The opportunities of living are diminished in proportion as what are called the "means" are increased. The best thing a man can do for his culture when he is rich is to endeavor to carry out those schemes which he entertained when he was poor. Christ answered the Herodians according to their condition. "Show me the tribute-money," said he; -- and one took a penny out of his pocket; -- if you use money which has the image of Caesar on it, and which he has made current and valuable, that is, if you are men of the State, and gladly enjoy the advantages of Caesar's government, then pay him back some of his own when he demands it; "Render therefore to Caesar that which is Caesar's, and to God those things which are God's" -- leaving them no wiser than before as to which was which; for they did not wish to know.

When I converse with the freest of my neighbors, I perceive that, whatever they may say about the magnitude and seriousness of the question, and their regard for the public tranquillity, the long and the short of the matter is, that they cannot spare the protection of the existing government, and they dread the consequences to their property and families of disobedience to it. For my own part, I should not like to think that I ever rely on the protection of the State. But, if I deny the authority of the State when it presents its tax-bill, it will soon take and waste all my property, and so harass me and my children without end. This is hard. This makes it impossible for a man to live honestly, and at the same time comfortably in outward respects. It will not be worth the while to accumulate property; that would be sure to go again. You must hire or squat somewhere, and raise but a small crop, and eat that soon. You must live within yourself, and depend upon yourself always tucked up and ready for a start, and not have many affairs. A man may grow rich in Turkey even, if he will be in all respects a good subject of the Turkish government. Confucius said, "If a state is governed by the principles of reason, poverty and misery are subjects of shame; if a state is not governed by the principles of reason, riches and honors are the subjects of shame." No: until I want the protection of Massachusetts to be extended to me in some distant Southern port, where my liberty is endangered, or until I am bent solely on building up an estate at home by peaceful enterprise, I can afford to refuse allegiance to Massachusetts, and her right to my property and life. It costs me less in every sense to incur the penalty of disobedience to the State than it would to obey. I should feel as if I were worth less in that case.

Some years ago, the State met me in behalf of the Church, and commanded me to pay a certain sum toward the support of a clergyman whose preaching my father attended, but never I myself. "Pay," it said, "or be locked up in the jail." I declined to pay. But, unfortunately, another man saw fit to pay it. I did not see why the schoolmaster should be taxed to support the priest, and not the priest the schoolmaster: for I was not the State's schoolmaster, but I supported myself by voluntary subscription. I did not see why the lyceum should not present its tax-bill, and have the State to back its demand, as well as the Church. However, at the request of the selectmen, I condescended to make some such statement as this in writing:-- "Know all men by these presents, that I, Henry Thoreau, do not wish to be regarded as a member of any incorporated society which I have not joined." This I gave to the town clerk; and he has it. The State, having thus learned that I did not wish to be regarded as a member of that church, has never made a like demand on me since; though it said that it must adhere to its original presumption that time. If I had known how to name them, I should then have signed off in detail from all the societies which I never signed on to; but I did not know where to find a complete list.

I have paid no poll-tax for six years. I was put into a jail once on this account, for one night; and, as I stood considering the walls of solid stone, two or three feet thick, the door of wood and iron, a foot thick, and the iron grating which strained the light, I could not help being struck with the foolishness of that institution which treated me as if I were mere flesh and blood and bones, to be locked up. I wondered that it should have concluded at length that this was the best use it could put me to, and had never thought to avail itself of my services in some way. I saw that, if there was a wall of stone between me and my townsmen, there was a still more difficult one to climb or break through, before they could get to be as free as I was. I did not for a moment feel confined, and the walls seemed a great waste of stone and mortar. I felt as if I alone of all my townsmen had paid my tax. They plainly did not know how to treat me, but behaved like persons who are underbred. In every threat and in every compliment there was a blunder; for they thought that my chief desire was to stand the other side of that stone wall. I could not but smile to see how industriously they locked the door on my meditations, which followed them out again without let or hindrance, and they were really all that was dangerous. As they could not reach me, they had resolved to punish my body; just as boys, if they cannot come at some person against whom they have a spite, will abuse his dog. I saw that the State was half-witted, that it was timid as a lone woman with her silver spoons, and that it did not know its friends from its foes, and I lost all my remaining respect for it, and pitied it.

Thus the State never intentionally confronts a man's sense, intellectual or moral, but only his body, his senses. It is not armed with superior wit or honesty, but with superior physical strength. I was not born to be forced. I will breathe after my own fashion. Let us see who is the strongest. What force has a multitude? They only can force me who obey a higher law than I. They force me to become like themselves. I do not hear of men being forced to have this way or that by masses of men. What sort of life were that to live? When I meet a government which says to me, "Your money or your life," why should I be in haste to give it my money? It may be in a great strait, and not know what to do: I cannot help that. It must help itself; do as I do. It is not worth the while to snivel about it. I am not responsible for the successful working of the machinery of society. I am not the son of the engineer. I perceive that, when an acorn and a chestnut fall side by side, the one does not remain inert to make way for the other, but both obey their own laws, and spring and grow and flourish as best they can, till one, perchance, overshadows and destroys the other. If a plant cannot live according to its nature, it dies; and so a man.

The night in prison was novel and interesting enough. The prisoners in their shirt-sleeves were enjoying a chat and the evening air in the doorway, when I entered. But the jailer said, "Come, boys, it is time to lock up"; and so they dispersed, and I heard the sound of their steps returning into the hollow apartments. My room-mate was introduced to me by the jailer as "a first-rate fellow and a clever man." When the door was locked, he showed me where to hang my hat, and how he managed matters there. The rooms were whitewashed once a month; and this one, at least, was the whitest, most simply furnished, and probably the neatest apartment in the town. He naturally wanted to know where I came from, and what brought me there; and, when I had told him, I asked him in my turn how he came there, presuming him to be an honest man, of course; and, as the world goes, I believe he was. "Why," said he, "they accuse me of burning a barn; but I never did it." As near as I could discover, he had probably gone to bed in a barn when drunk, and smoked his pipe there; and so a barn was burnt. He had the reputation of being a clever man, had been there some three months waiting for his trial to come on, and would have to wait as much longer; but he was quite domesticated and contented, since he got his board for nothing, and thought that he was well treated.

He occupied one window, and I the other; and I saw that if one stayed there long, his principal business would be to look out the window. I had soon read all the tracts that were left there, and examined where former prisoners had broken out, and where a grate had been sawed off, and heard the history of the various occupants of that room; for I found that even here there was a history and a gossip which never circulated beyond the walls of the jail. Probably this is the only house in the town where verses are composed, which are afterward printed in a circular form, but not published. I was shown quite a long list of verses which were composed by some young men who had been detected in an attempt to escape, who avenged themselves by singing them.

I pumped my fellow-prisoner as dry as I could, for fear I should never see him again; but at length he showed me which was my bed, and left me to blow out the lamp.

It was like travelling into a far country, such as I had never expected to behold, to lie there for one night. It seemed to me that I never had heard the town-clock strike before, nor the evening sounds of the village; for we slept with the windows open, which were inside the grating. It was to see my native village in the light of the Middle Ages, and our Concord was turned into a Rhine stream, and visions of knights and castles passed before me. They were the voices of old burghers that I heard in the streets. I was an involuntary spectator and auditor of whatever was done and said in the kitchen of the adjacent village-inn -- a wholly new and rare experience to me. It was a closer view of my native town. I was fairly inside of it. I never had seen its institutions before. This is one of its peculiar institutions; for it is a shire town. I began to comprehend what its inhabitants were about.

In the morning, our breakfasts were put through the hole in the door, in small oblong-square tin pans, made to fit, and holding a pint of chocolate, with brown bread, and an iron spoon. When they called for the vessels again, I was green enough to return what bread I had left; but my comrade seized it, and said that I should lay that up for lunch or dinner. Soon after he was let out to work at haying in a neighboring field, whither he went every day, and would not be back till noon; so he bade me good-day, saying that he doubted if he should see me again.

When I came out of prison -- for some one interfered, and paid that tax -- I did not perceive that great changes had taken place on the common, such as he observed who went in a youth and emerged a tottering and gray-headed man; and yet a change had to my eyes come over the scene -- the town, and State, and country -- greater than any that mere time could effect. I saw yet more distinctly the State in which I lived. I saw to what extent the people among whom I lived could be trusted as good neighbors and friends; that their friendship was for summer weather only; that they did not greatly propose to do right; that they were a distinct race from me by their prejudices and superstitions, as the Chinamen and Malays are; that in their sacrifices to humanity, they ran no risks, not even to their property; that after all they were not so noble but they treated the thief as he had treated them, and hoped, by a certain outward observance and a few prayers, and by walking in a particular straight though useless path from time to time, to save their souls. This may be to judge my neighbors harshly; for I believe that many of them are not aware that they have such an institution as the jail in their village.

It was formerly the custom in our village, when a poor debtor came out of jail, for his acquaintances to salute him, looking through their fingers, which were crossed to represent the grating of a jail window, "How do ye do?" My neighbors did not thus salute me, but first looked at me, and then at one another, as if I had returned from a long journey. I was put into jail as I was going to the shoemaker's to get a shoe which was mended. When I was let out the next morning, I proceeded to finish my errand, and, having put on my mended shoe, joined a huckleberry party, who were impatient to put themselves under my conduct; and in half an hour -- for the horse was soon tackled -- was in the midst of a huckleberry field, on one of our highest hills, two miles off, and then the State was nowhere to be seen.

This is the whole history of "My Prisons."

I have never declined paying the highway tax, because I am as desirous of being a good neighbor as I am of being a bad subject; and as for supporting schools, I am doing my part to educate my fellow-countrymen now. It is for no particular item in the tax-bill that I refuse to pay it. I simply wish to refuse allegiance to the State, to withdraw and stand aloof from it effectually. I do not care to trace the course of my dollar, if I could, till it buys a man or a musket to shoot one with -- the dollar is innocent -- but I am concerned to trace the effects of my allegiance. In fact, I quietly declare war with the State, after my fashion, though I will still make what use and get what advantage of her I can, as is usual in such cases.

If others pay the tax which is demanded of me, from a sympathy with the State, they do but what they have already done in their own case, or rather they abet injustice to a greater extent than the State requires. If they pay the tax from a mistaken interest in the individual taxed, to save his property, or prevent his going to jail, it is because they have not considered wisely how far they let their private feelings interfere with the public good.

This, then, is my position at present. But one cannot be too much on his guard in such a case, lest his action be biased by obstinacy or an undue regard for the opinions of men. Let him see that he does only what belongs to himself and to the hour.

I think sometimes, Why, this people mean well; they are only ignorant; they would do better if they knew how: why give your neighbors this pain to treat you as they are not inclined to? But I think, again, This is no reason why I should do as they do, or permit others to suffer much greater pain of a different kind. Again, I sometimes say to myself, When many millions of men, without heat, without ill-will, without personal feeling of any kind, demand of you a few shillings only, without the possibility, such is their constitution, of retracting or altering their present demand, and without the possibility, on your side, of appeal to any other millions, why expose yourself to this overwhelming brute force? You do not resist cold and hunger, the winds and the waves, thus obstinately; you quietly submit to a thousand similar necessities. You do not put your head into the fire. But just in proportion as I regard this as not wholly a brute force, but partly a human force, and consider that I have relations to those millions as to so many millions of men, and not of mere brute or inanimate things, I see that appeal is possible, first and instantaneously, from them to the Maker of them, and, secondly, from them to themselves. But, if I put my head deliberately into the fire, there is no appeal to fire or to the Maker of fire, and I have only myself to blame. If I could convince myself that I have any right to be satisfied with men as they are, and to treat them accordingly, and not according, in some respects, to my requisitions and expectations of what they and I ought to be, then, like a good Mussulman and fatalist, I should endeavor to be satisfied with things as they are, and say it is the will of God. And, above all, there is this difference between resisting this and a purely brute or natural force, that I can resist this with some effect; but I cannot expect, like Orpheus, to change the nature of the rocks and trees and beasts.

 I do not wish to quarrel with any man or nation. I do not wish to split hairs, to make fine distinctions, or set myself up as better than my neighbors. I seek rather, I may say, even an excuse for conforming to the laws of the land. I am but too ready to conform to them. Indeed, I have reason to suspect myself on this head; and each year, as the tax-gatherer comes round, I find myself disposed to review the acts and position of the general and State governments, and the spirit of the people, to discover a pretext for conformity.

> "We must affect our country as our parents,
> And if at any time we alienate
> Our love or industry from doing it honor,
> We must respect effects and teach the soul
> Matter of conscience and religion,
> And not desire of rule or benefit."

I believe that the State will soon be able to take all my work of this sort out of my hands, and then I shall be no better a patriot than my fellow-countrymen. Seen from a lower point of view, the Constitution, with all its faults, is very good; the law and the courts are very respectable; even this State and this American government are, in many respects, very admirable and rare things, to be thankful for, such as a great many have described them; but seen from a point of view a little higher, they are what I have described them; seen from a higher still, and the highest, who shall say what they are, or that they are worth looking at or thinking of at all?

However, the government does not concern me much, and I shall bestow the fewest possible thoughts on it. It is not many moments that I live under a government, even in this world. If a man is thought-free, fancy-free, imagination-free, that which is not never for a long time appearing to be to him, unwise rulers or reformers cannot fatally interrupt him.

I know that most men think differently from myself; but those whose lives are by profession devoted to the study of these or kindred subjects, content me as little as any. Statesmen and legislators, standing so completely within the institution, never distinctly and nakedly behold it. They speak of moving society, but have no resting-place without it. They may be men of a certain experience and discrimination, and have no doubt invented ingenious and even useful systems, for which we sincerely thank them; but all their wit and usefulness lie within certain not very wide limits. They are wont to forget that the world is not governed by policy and expediency. Webster never goes behind government, and so cannot speak with authority about it. His words are wisdom to those legislators who contemplate no essential reform in the existing government; but for thinkers, and those who legislate for all time, he never once glances at the subject. I know of those whose serene and wise speculations on this theme would soon reveal the limits of his mind's range and hospitality. Yet, compared with the cheap professions of most reformers, and the still cheaper wisdom and eloquence of politicians in general, his are almost the only sensible and valuable words, and we thank Heaven for him. Comparatively, he is always strong, original, and, above all, practical. Still, his quality is not wisdom, but prudence. The lawyer's truth is not truth, but consistency or a consistent expediency. Truth is always in harmony with herself, and is not concerned chiefly to reveal the justice that may consist with wrong-doing. He well deserves to be called, as he has been called, the Defender of the Constitution. There are really no blows to be given by him but defensive ones. He is not a leader, but a follower. His leaders are the men of '87. "I have never made an effort," he says, "and never propose to make an effort; I have never countenanced an effort, and never mean to countenance an effort, to disturb the arrangement as originally made, by which the various States came into the Union." Still thinking of the sanction which the Constitution gives to slavery, he says, "Because it was a part of the original compact -- let it stand." Notwithstanding his special acuteness and ability, he is unable to take a fact out of its merely political relations, and behold it as it lies absolutely to be disposed of by the intellect -- what, for instance, it behooves a man to do here in America to-day with regard to slavery, but ventures, or is driven, to make some such desperate answer as the following, while professing to speak absolutely, and as a private man -- from which what new and singular code of social duties might be inferred? "The manner," says he, "in which the governments of those States where slavery exists are to regulate it is for their own consideration, under their responsibility to their constituents, to the general laws of propriety, humanity, and justice, and to God. Associations formed elsewhere, springing from a feeling of humanity, or any other cause, have nothing whatever to do with it. They have never received any encouragement from me, and they never will."

They who know of no purer sources of truth, who have traced up its stream no higher, stand, and wisely stand, by the Bible and the Constitution, and drink at it there with reverence and humility; but they who behold where it comes trickling into this lake or that pool, gird up their loins once more, and continue their pilgrimage toward its fountain-head.

No man with a genius for legislation has appeared in America. They are rare in the history of the world. There are orators, politicians, and eloquent men, by the thousand; but the speaker has not yet opened his mouth to speak who is capable of settling the much-vexed questions of the day. We love eloquence for its own sake, and not for any truth which it may utter, or any heroism it may inspire. Our legislators have not yet learned the comparative value of free-trade and of freedom, of union, and of rectitude, to a nation. They have no genius or talent for comparatively humble questions of taxation and finance, commerce and manufacturers and agriculture. If we were left solely to the wordy wit of legislators in Congress for our guidance, uncorrected by the seasonable experience and the effectual complaints of the people, America would not long retain her rank among the nations. For eighteen hundred years, though perchance I have no right to say it, the New Testament has been written; yet where is the legislator who has wisdom and practical talent enough to avail himself of the light which it sheds on the science of legislation?

The authority of government, even such as I am willing to submit to -- for I will cheerfully obey those who know and can do better than I, and in many things even those who neither know nor can do so well -- is still an impure one: to be strictly just, it must have the sanction and consent of the governed. It can have no pure right over my person and property but what I concede to it. The progress from an absolute to a limited monarchy, from a limited monarchy to a democracy, is a progress toward a true respect for the individual. Even the Chinese philosopher was wise enough to regard the individual as the basis of the empire. Is a democracy, such as we know it, the last improvement possible in government? Is it not possible to take a step further towards recognizing and organizing the rights of man? There will never be a really free and enlightened State until the State comes to recognize the individual as a higher and independent power, from which all its own power and authority are derived, and treats him accordingly. I please myself with imagining a State at least which can afford to be just to all men, and to treat the individual with respect as a neighbor; which even would not think it inconsistent with its own repose if a few were to live aloof from it, not meddling with it, nor embraced by it, who fulfilled all the duties of neighbors and fellow-men. A State which bore this kind of fruit, and suffered it to drop off as fast as it ripened, would prepare the way for a still more perfect and glorious State, which also I have imagined, but not yet anywhere seen.

Ode: Intimations of Immortality
from Recollections of Early Childhood

William Wordsworth

There was a time when meadow, grove, and stream,
The earth, and every common sight,
To me did seem
Apparelled in celestial light,
The glory and the freshness of a dream.
It is not now as it hath been of yore;--
Turn wheresoe'er I may,
By night or day,
The things which I have seen I now can see no more.

The Rainbow comes and goes,
And lovely is the Rose,
The Moon doth with delight
Look round her when the heavens are bare,
Waters on a starry night
Are beautiful and fair;
The sunshine is a glorious birth;
But yet I know, where'er I go,
That there hath past away a glory from the earth.

Now, while the birds thus sing a joyous song,
And while the young lambs bound
As to the tabor's sound,
To me alone there came a thought of grief:
A timely utterance gave that thought relief,
And I again am strong:
The cataracts blow their trumpets from the steep;
No more shall grief of mine the season wrong;
I hear the Echoes through the mountains throng,
The Winds come to me from the fields of sleep,
And all the earth is gay;
Land and sea
Give themselves up to jollity,
And with the heart of May
Doth every Beast keep holiday;--
Thou Child of Joy,
Shout round me, let me hear thy shouts, thou happy
Shepherd-boy!

Ye blessed Creatures, I have heard the call
Ye to each other make; I see
The heavens laugh with you in your jubilee;
My heart is at your festival,

My head hath its coronal,
The fulness of your bliss, I feel--I feel it all.
Oh evil day! if I were sullen
While Earth herself is adorning,
This sweet May-morning,
And the Children are culling
On every side,
In a thousand valleys far and wide,
Fresh flowers; while the sun shines warm,
And the Babe leaps up on his Mother's arm:--
I hear, I hear, with joy I hear!
--But there's a Tree, of many, one,
A single Field which I have looked upon,
Both of them speak of something that is gone:
The Pansy at my feet
Doth the same tale repeat:
Whither is fled the visionary gleam?
Where is it now, the glory and the dream?

Our birth is but a sleep and a forgetting:
The Soul that rises with us, our life's Star,
Hath had elsewhere its setting,
And cometh from afar:
Not in entire forgetfulness,
And not in utter nakedness,
But trailing clouds of glory do we come
From God, who is our home:
Heaven lies about us in our infancy!
Shades of the prison-house begin to close
Upon the growing Boy,
But He beholds the light, and whence it flows,
He sees it in his joy;
The Youth, who daily farther from the east
Must travel, still is Nature's Priest,
And by the vision splendid
Is on his way attended;
At length the Man perceives it die away,
And fade into the light of common day.

Earth fills her lap with pleasures of her own;
Yearnings she hath in her own natural kind,
And, even with something of a Mother's mind,
And no unworthy aim,
The homely Nurse doth all she can
To make her Foster-child, her Inmate Man,
Forget the glories he hath known,
And that imperial palace whence he came.

Behold the Child among his new-born blisses,
A six years' Darling of a pigmy size!
See, where 'mid work of his own hand he lies,
Fretted by sallies of his mother's kisses,
With light upon him from his father's eyes!
See, at his feet, some little plan or chart,
Some fragment from his dream of human life,
Shaped by himself with newly-learned art;
A wedding or a festival,
A mourning or a funeral;
And this hath now his heart,
And unto this he frames his song:
Then will he fit his tongue
To dialogues of business, love, or strife;
But it will not be long
Ere this be thrown aside,
And with new joy and pride
The little Actor cons another part;
Filling from time to time his "humorous stage"
With all the Persons, down to palsied Age,
That Life brings with her in her equipage;
As if his whole vocation
Were endless imitation.

Thou, whose exterior semblance doth belie
Thy Soul's immensity;
Thou best Philosopher, who yet dost keep
Thy heritage, thou Eye among the blind,
That, deaf and silent, read'st the eternal deep,
Haunted for ever by the eternal mind,--
Mighty Prophet! Seer blest!
On whom those truths do rest,
Which we are toiling all our lives to find,
In darkness lost, the darkness of the grave;
Thou, over whom thy Immortality
Broods like the Day, a Master o'er a Slave,
A Presence which is not to be put by;
Thou little Child, yet glorious in the might
Of heaven-born freedom on thy being's height,
Why with such earnest pains dost thou provoke
The years to bring the inevitable yoke,
Thus blindly with thy blessedness at strife?
Full soon thy Soul shall have her earthly freight,
And custom lie upon thee with a weight
Heavy as frost, and deep almost as life!

O joy! that in our embers
Is something that doth live,

That nature yet remembers
What was so fugitive!
The thought of our past years in me doth breed
Perpetual benediction: not indeed
For that which is most worthy to be blest--
Delight and liberty, the simple creed
Of Childhood, whether busy or at rest,
With new-fledged hope still fluttering in his breast:--
Not for these I raise
The song of thanks and praise;
But for those obstinate questionings
Of sense and outward things,
Fallings from us, vanishings;
Blank misgivings of a Creature
Moving about in worlds not realised,
High instincts before which our mortal Nature
Did tremble like a guilty Thing surprised:
But for those first affections,
Those shadowy recollections,
Which, be they what they may,
Are yet the fountain light of all our day,
Are yet a master light of all our seeing;
Uphold us, cherish, and have power to make
Our noisy years seem moments in the being
Of the eternal Silence: truths that wake,
To perish never;
Which neither listlessness, nor mad endeavour,
Nor Man nor Boy,
Nor all that is at enmity with joy,
Can utterly abolish or destroy!
Hence in a season of calm weather
Though inland far we be,
Our Souls have sight of that immortal sea
Which brought us hither,
Can in a moment travel thither,
And see the Children sport upon the shore,
And hear the mighty waters rolling evermore.

Then sing, ye Birds, sing, sing a joyous song!
And let the young Lambs bound
As to the tabor's sound!
We in thought will join your throng,
Ye that pipe and ye that play,
Ye that through your hearts to-day
Feel the gladness of the May!
What though the radiance which was once so bright
Be now for ever taken from my sight,
Though nothing can bring back the hour

Of splendour in the grass, of glory in the flower;
We will grieve not, rather find
Strength in what remains behind;
In the primal sympathy
Which having been must ever be;
In the soothing thoughts that spring
Out of human suffering;
In the faith that looks through death,
In years that bring the philosophic mind.

And O, ye Fountains, Meadows, Hills, and Groves,
Forebode not any severing of our loves!
Yet in my heart of hearts I feel your might;
I only have relinquished one delight
To live beneath your more habitual sway.
I love the Brooks which down their channels fret,
Even more than when I tripped lightly as they;
The innocent brightness of a new-born Day
Is lovely yet;
The Clouds that gather round the setting sun
Do take a sober colouring from an eye
That hath kept watch o'er man's mortality;
Another race hath been, and other palms are won.
Thanks to the human heart by which we live,
Thanks to its tenderness, its joys, and fears,
To me the meanest flower that blows can give
Thoughts that do often lie too deep for tears.

As a Man Thinketh

James Allen

*Mind is the Master power that moulds and makes,
And Man is Mind, and evermore he takes
The tool of Thought, and, shaping what he wills,
Brings forth a thousand joys, a thousand ills:--
He thinks in secret, and it comes to pass:
Environment is but his looking-glass.*

CONTENTS

Thought and Character

Effect of Thought on Circumstances

Effect of Thought on Health and Body

Thought and Purpose

The Thought-Factor in Achievement

Visions and Ideals

Serenity

FOREWORD

THIS little volume (the result of meditation and experience) is not intended as an exhaustive treatise on the much-written-upon subject of the power of thought. It is suggestive rather than explanatory, its object being to stimulate men and women to the discovery and perception of the truth that--

"They themselves are makers of themselves."

by virtue of the thoughts, which they choose and encourage; that mind is the master-weaver, both of the inner garment of character and the outer garment of circumstance, and that, as they may have hitherto woven in ignorance and pain they may now weave in enlightenment and happiness.

James Allen
Broad Park Avenue
Ilfracombe
England

Thought and Character

THE aphorism, "As a man thinketh in his heart so is he," not only embraces the whole of a man's being, but is so comprehensive as to reach out to every condition and circumstance of his life. A man is literally *what he thinks*, his character being the complete sum of all his thoughts.

As the plant springs from, and could not be without, the seed, so every act of a man springs from the hidden seeds of thought, and could not have appeared without them. This applies equally to those acts called "spontaneous" and "unpremeditated" as to those, which are deliberately executed.

Act is the blossom of thought, and joy and suffering are its fruits; thus does a man garner in the sweet and bitter fruitage of his own husbandry.

"Thought in the mind hath made us, What we are by thought was wrought and built. If a man's mind Hath evil thoughts, pain comes on him as comes The wheel the ox behind. . . . If one endure In purity of thought, joy follows him As his own shadow—sure."

Man is a growth by law, and not a creation by artifice, and cause and effect is as absolute and undeviating in the hidden realm of thought as in the world of visible and material things. A noble and Godlike character is not a thing of favour or chance, but is the natural result of continued effort in right thinking, the effect of long-cherished association with Godlike thoughts. An ignoble and bestial character, by the same process, is the result of the continued harbouring of groveling thoughts.

Man is made or unmade by himself; in the armoury of thought he forges the weapons by which he destroys himself; he also fashions the tools with which he builds for himself heavenly mansions of joy and strength and peace. By the right choice and true application of thought, man ascends to the Divine Perfection; by the abuse and wrong application of thought, he descends below the level of the beast. Between these two extremes are all the grades of character, and man is their maker and master.

Of all the beautiful truths pertaining to the soul which have been restored and brought to light in this age, none is more gladdening or fruitful of divine promise and confidence than this—that man is the master of thought, the moulder of character, and the maker and shaper of condition, environment, and destiny.

As a being of Power, Intelligence, and Love, and the lord of his own thoughts, man holds the key to every situation, and contains within himself that transforming and regenerative agency by which he may make himself what he wills.

Man is always the master, even in his weaker and most abandoned state; but in his weakness and degradation he is the foolish master who misgoverns his "household." When he begins to reflect upon his condition, and to search diligently for the Law upon which his being is established, he then becomes the wise master, directing his energies with intelligence, and fashioning his thoughts to fruitful issues. Such is the *conscious* master, and man can only thus become by discovering *within himself* the laws of thought; which discovery is totally a matter of application, self analysis, and experience.

Only by much searching and mining, are gold and diamonds obtained, and man can find every truth connected with his being, if he will dig deep into the mine of his soul; and that he is the maker of his character, the moulder of his life, and the builder of his destiny, he may unerringly prove, if he will watch, control, and alter his thoughts, tracing their effects upon himself, upon others, and upon his life and circumstances, linking cause and effect by patient practice and investigation, and utilizing his every experience, even to the most trivial, everyday occurrence, as a means of obtaining that knowledge of himself which is Understanding, Wisdom, Power. In this direction, as in no other, is the law absolute that "He that seeketh findeth; and to him that knocketh it shall be opened;" for only by patience, practice, and ceaseless importunity can a man enter the Door of the Temple of Knowledge.

Effect of Thought on Circumstances

MAN'S mind may be likened to a garden, which may be intelligently cultivated or allowed to run wild; but whether cultivated or neglected, it must, and will, *bring forth*. If no useful seeds are *put* into it, then an abundance of useless weed-seeds will *fall* therein, and will continue to produce their kind.

Just as a gardener cultivates his plot, keeping it free from weeds, and growing the flowers and fruits which he requires, so may a man tend the garden of his mind, weeding out all the wrong, useless, and impure thoughts, and cultivating toward perfection the flowers and fruits of right, useful, and pure thoughts. By pursuing this process, a man sooner or later discovers that he is the master-gardener of his soul, the director of his life. He also reveals, within himself, the laws of thought, and understands, with ever-increasing accuracy, how the thought-forces and mind elements operate in the shaping of his character, circumstances, and destiny.

Thought and character are one, and as character can only manifest and discover itself through environment and circumstance, the outer conditions of a person's life will always be found to be harmoniously related to his inner state. This does not mean that a man's circumstances at any given time are an indication of his *entire* character, but that those circumstances are so intimately connected with some vital thought-element within himself that, for the time being, they are indispensable to his development.

Every man is where he is by the law of his being; the thoughts which he has built into his character have brought him there, and in the arrangement of his life there is no element of chance, but all is the result of a law which cannot err. This is just as true of those who feel "out of harmony" with their surroundings as of those who are contented with them.

As a progressive and evolving being, man is where he is that he may learn that he may grow; and as he learns the spiritual lesson which any circumstance contains for him, it passes away and gives place to other circumstances.

Man is buffeted by circumstances so long as he believes himself to be the creature of outside conditions, but when he realizes that he is a creative power, and that he may command the hidden soil and seeds of his being out of which circumstances grow, he then becomes the rightful master of himself.

That circumstances grow out of thought every man knows who has for any length of time practised self-control and self-purification, for he will have noticed that the alteration in his circumstances has been in exact ratio with his altered mental condition. So true is this that when a man earnestly applies himself to remedy the defects in his character, and makes swift and marked progress, he passes rapidly through a succession of vicissitudes.

The soul attracts that which it secretly harbours; that which it loves, and also that which it fears; it reaches the height of its cherished aspirations; it falls to the level of its unchastened desires,--and circumstances are the means by which the soul receives its own.

Every thought-seed sown or allowed to fall into the mind, and to take root there, produces its own, blossoming sooner or later into act, and bearing its own fruitage of opportunity and circumstance. Good thoughts bear good fruit, bad thoughts bad fruit.

The outer world of circumstance shapes itself to the inner world of thought, and both pleasant and unpleasant external conditions are factors, which make for the ultimate good of the individual. As the reaper of his own harvest, man learns both by suffering and bliss.

Following the inmost desires, aspirations, thoughts, by which he allows himself to be dominated, (pursuing the will-o'-the-wisps of impure imaginings or steadfastly walking the highway of strong and high endeavour), a man at last arrives at their fruition and fulfilment in the outer conditions of his life. The laws of growth and adjustment everywhere obtains.

A man does not come to the almshouse or the jail by the tyranny of fate or circumstance, but by the pathway of groveling thoughts and base desires. Nor does a pure-minded man fall suddenly into crime by stress of any mere external force; the criminal thought had long been secretly fostered in the heart, and the hour of opportunity revealed its gathered power. Circumstance does not make the man; it reveals him to himself No such conditions can exist as descending into vice and its attendant sufferings apart from vicious inclinations, or ascending into virtue and its pure happiness without the continued cultivation of virtuous aspirations; and man, therefore, as the lord and master of thought, is the maker of himself the shaper and author of environment. Even at birth the soul comes to its own and through every step of its earthly pilgrimage it attracts those combinations of conditions which reveal itself, which are the reflections of its own purity and, impurity, its strength and weakness.

Men do not attract that which they *want*, but that which they *are*. Their whims, fancies, and ambitions are thwarted at every step, but their inmost thoughts and desires are fed with their own food, be it foul or clean. The "divinity that shapes our ends" is in ourselves; it is our very self. Only himself manacles man: thought and action are the gaolers of Fate--they imprison, being base; they are also the angels of Freedom--they liberate, being noble. Not what he wishes and prays for does a man get, but what he justly earns. His wishes and prayers are only gratified and answered when they harmonize with his thoughts and actions.

In the light of this truth, what, then, Is the meaning of "fighting against circumstances?" It means that a man is continually revolting against an *effect* without, while all the time he is nourishing and preserving its *cause* in his heart. That cause may take the form of a conscious vice or an unconscious weakness; but whatever it is, it stubbornly retards the efforts of its possessor, and thus calls aloud for remedy.

Men are anxious to improve their circumstances, but are unwilling to improve themselves; they therefore remain bound. The man who does not shrink from self-crucifixion can never fail to accomplish the object upon which his heart is set. This is as true of earthly as of heavenly things. Even the man whose sole object is to acquire wealth must be prepared to make great personal sacrifices before he can accomplish his object; and how much more so he who would realize a strong and well-poised life?

Here is a man who is wretchedly poor. He is extremely anxious that his surroundings and home comforts should be improved, yet all the time he shirks his work, and considers he is justified in trying to deceive his employer on the ground of the insufficiency of his wages. Such a man does not understand the simplest rudiments of those principles which are the basis of true prosperity, and is not only totally unfitted to rise out of his wretchedness, but is actually attracting to himself a still deeper wretchedness by dwelling in, and acting out, indolent, deceptive, and unmanly thoughts.

Here is a rich man who is the victim of a painful and persistent disease as the result of gluttony. He is willing to give large sums of money to get rid of it, but he will not sacrifice his gluttonous desires. He wants to gratify his taste for rich and unnatural viands and have his health as well. Such a man is totally unfit to have health, because he has not yet learned the first principles of a healthy life.

Here is an employer of labour who adopts crooked measures to avoid paying the regulation wage, and, in the hope of making larger profits, reduces the wages of his workpeople. Such a man is altogether unfitted for prosperity, and when he finds himself bankrupt, both as regards reputation and riches, he blames circumstances, not knowing that he is the sole author of his condition.

I have introduced these three cases merely as illustrative of the truth that man is the causer (though nearly always is unconsciously) of his circumstances, and that, whilst aiming at a good end, he is continually frustrating its accomplishment by encouraging thoughts and desires which cannot possibly harmonize with that end. Such cases could be multiplied and varied almost indefinitely, but this is not necessary, as the reader can, if he so resolves, trace the action of the laws of thought in his own mind and life, and until this is done, mere external facts cannot serve as a ground of reasoning.

Circumstances, however, are so complicated, thought is so deeply rooted, and the conditions of happiness vary so, vastly with individuals, that a man's entire soul-condition (although it may be known to himself) cannot be judged by another from the external aspect of his life alone. A man may be honest in certain directions, yet suffer privations; a man may be dishonest in certain directions, yet acquire wealth; but the conclusion usually formed that the one man fails *because of his particular honesty*, and that the other *prospers because of his particular dishonesty*, is the result of a superficial judgment, which assumes that the dishonest man is almost totally corrupt, and the honest man almost entirely virtuous. In the light of a deeper knowledge and wider experience such judgment is found to be erroneous. The dishonest man may have some admirable virtues, which the other does, not possess; and the honest man obnoxious vices which are absent in the other. The honest man reaps the good results of his honest thoughts and acts; he also brings upon himself the sufferings, which his vices produce. The dishonest man likewise garners his own suffering and happiness.

It is pleasing to human vanity to believe that one suffers because of one's virtue; but not until a man has extirpated every sickly, bitter, and impure thought from his mind, and washed every sinful stain from his soul, can he be in a position to know and declare that his sufferings are the result of his good, and not of his bad qualities; and on the way to, yet long before he has reached, that supreme perfection, he will have found, working in his mind and life, the Great Law which is absolutely just, and which cannot, therefore, give good for evil, evil for good. Possessed of such knowledge, he will then know, looking back upon his past ignorance and blindness, that his life is, and always was, justly ordered, and that all his past experiences, good and bad, were the equitable outworking of his evolving, yet unevolved self.

Good thoughts and actions can never produce bad results; bad thoughts and actions can never produce good results. This is but saying that nothing can come from corn but corn, nothing from nettles but nettles. Men understand this law in the natural world, and work with it; but few understand it in the mental and moral world (though its operation there is just as simple and undeviating), and they, therefore, do not co-operate with it.

Suffering is *always* the effect of wrong thought in some direction. It is an indication that the individual is out of harmony with himself, with the Law of his being. The sole and supreme use of suffering is to purify, to burn out all that is useless and impure. Suffering ceases for him who is pure. There could be no object in burning gold after the dross had been removed, and a perfectly pure and enlightened being could not suffer.

The circumstances, which a man encounters with suffering, are the result of his own mental in harmony. The circumstances, which a man encounters with blessedness, are the result of his own mental harmony. Blessedness, not material possessions, is the measure of right thought; wretchedness, not lack of material possessions, is the measure of wrong thought. A man may be cursed and rich; he may be blessed and poor. Blessedness and riches are only joined together when the riches are rightly and wisely used; and the poor man only descends into wretchedness when he regards his lot as a burden unjustly imposed.

Indigence and indulgence are the two extremes of wretchedness. They are both equally unnatural and the result of mental disorder. A man is not rightly conditioned until he is a happy, healthy, and prosperous being; and happiness, health, and prosperity are the result of a harmonious adjustment of the inner with the outer, of the man with his surroundings.

A man only begins to be a man when he ceases to whine and revile, and commences to search for the hidden justice which regulates his life. And as he adapts his mind to that regulating factor, he ceases to accuse others as the cause of his condition, and builds himself up in strong and noble thoughts; ceases to kick against circumstances, but begins to *use* them as aids to his more rapid progress, and as a means of discovering the hidden powers and possibilities within himself.

Law, not confusion, is the dominating principle in the universe; justice, not injustice, is the soul and substance of life; and righteousness, not corruption, is the moulding and moving force in the spiritual government of the world. This being so, man has but to right himself to find that the universe is right; and during the process of putting himself right he will find that as he alters his thoughts towards things and other people, things and other people will alter towards him.

The proof of this truth is in every person, and it therefore admits of easy investigation by systematic introspection and self-analysis. Let a man radically alter his thoughts, and he will be astonished at the rapid transformation it will effect in the material conditions of his life. Men imagine that thought can be kept secret, but it cannot; it rapidly crystallizes into habit, and habit solidifies into circumstance. Bestial thoughts crystallize into habits of drunkenness and sensuality, which solidify into circumstances of destitution and disease: impure thoughts of every kind crystallize into enervating and confusing habits, which solidify into distracting and adverse circumstances: thoughts of fear, doubt, and indecision crystallize into weak, unmanly, and irresolute habits, which solidify into circumstances of failure, indigence, and slavish dependence: lazy thoughts crystallize into habits of uncleanliness and dishonesty, which solidify into circumstances of foulness and beggary: hateful and condemnatory thoughts crystallize into habits of accusation and violence, which solidify into circumstances of injury and persecution: selfish thoughts of all kinds crystallize into habits of self-seeking, which solidify into circumstances more or less distressing. On the other hand, beautiful thoughts of all kinds crystallize into habits of grace and kindliness, which solidify into genial and sunny circumstances: pure thoughts crystallize into habits of temperance and self-control, which solidify into circumstances of repose and peace: thoughts of courage, self-reliance, and decision crystallize into manly habits, which solidify into circumstances of success, plenty, and freedom: energetic thoughts crystallize into habits of cleanliness and industry, which solidify into circumstances of pleasantness: gentle and forgiving thoughts crystallize into habits of gentleness, which solidify into protective and preservative circumstances: loving and unselfish thoughts crystallize into habits of self-forgetfulness for others, which solidify into circumstances of sure and abiding prosperity and true riches.

A particular train of thought persisted in, be it good or bad, cannot fail to produce its results on the character and circumstances. A man cannot *directly* choose his circumstances, but he can choose his thoughts, and so indirectly, yet surely, shape his circumstances.

Nature helps every man to the gratification of the thoughts, which he most encourages, and opportunities are presented which will most speedily bring to the surface both the good and evil thoughts.

Let a man cease from his sinful thoughts, and all the world will soften towards him, and be ready to help him; let him put away his weakly and sickly thoughts, and lo, opportunities will spring up on every hand to aid his strong resolves; let him encourage good thoughts, and no hard fate shall bind him down to wretchedness and shame. The world is your kaleidoscope, and the varying combinations of colours, which at every succeeding moment it presents to you are the exquisitely adjusted pictures of your ever-moving thoughts.

"So You will be what you will to be;
Let failure find its false content
In that poor word, 'environment,'
But spirit scorns it, and is free.

"It masters time, it conquers space;
It cowes that boastful trickster, Chance,
And bids the tyrant Circumstance
Uncrown, and fill a servant's place.

"The human Will, that force unseen,
The offspring of a deathless Soul,
Can hew a way to any goal,
Though walls of granite intervene.

"Be not impatient in delays
But wait as one who understands;
When spirit rises and commands
The gods are ready to obey."

Effect of Thought on Health and the Body

THE body is the servant of the mind. It obeys the operations of the mind, whether they be deliberately chosen or automatically expressed. At the bidding of unlawful thoughts the body sinks rapidly into disease and decay; at the command of glad and beautiful thoughts it becomes clothed with youthfulness and beauty.
 Disease and health, like circumstances, are rooted in thought. Sickly thoughts will express themselves through a sickly body. Thoughts of fear have been known to kill a man as speedily as a bullet, and they are continually killing thousands of people just as surely though less rapidly. The people who live in fear of disease are the people who get it. Anxiety quickly demoralizes the whole body, and lays it open to the, entrance of disease; while impure thoughts, even if not physically indulged, will soon shatter the nervous system.
 Strong, pure, and happy thoughts build up the body in vigour and grace. The body is a delicate and plastic instrument, which responds readily to the thoughts by which it is impressed, and habits of thought will produce their own effects, good or bad, upon it.
 Men will continue to have impure and poisoned blood, so long as they propagate unclean thoughts. Out of a clean heart comes a clean life and a clean body. Out of a defiled mind proceeds a defiled life and a corrupt body. Thought is the fount of action, life, and manifestation; make the fountain pure, and all will be pure.
 Change of diet will not help a man who will not change his thoughts. When a man makes his thoughts pure, he no longer desires impure food.
 Clean thoughts make clean habits. The so-called saint who does not wash his body is not a saint. He who has strengthened and purified his thoughts does not need to consider the malevolent microbe.

If you would protect your body, guard your mind. If you would renew your body, beautify your mind. Thoughts of malice, envy, disappointment, despondency, rob the body of its health and grace. A sour face does not come by chance; it is made by sour thoughts. Wrinkles that mar are drawn by folly, passion, and pride.

I know a woman of ninety-six who has the bright, innocent face of a girl. I know a man well under middle age whose face is drawn into inharmonious contours. The one is the result of a sweet and sunny disposition; the other is the outcome of passion and discontent.

As you cannot have a sweet and wholesome abode unless you admit the air and sunshine freely into your rooms, so a strong body and a bright, happy, or serene countenance can only result from the free admittance into the mind of thoughts of joy and goodwill and serenity.

On the faces of the aged there are wrinkles made by sympathy, others by strong and pure thought, and others are carved by passion: who cannot distinguish them? With those who have lived righteously, age is calm, peaceful, and softly mellowed, like the setting sun. I have recently seen a philosopher on his deathbed. He was not old except in years. He died as sweetly and peacefully as he had lived.

There is no physician like cheerful thought for dissipating the ills of the body; there is no comforter to compare with goodwill for dispersing the shadows of grief and sorrow. To live continually in thoughts of ill will, cynicism, suspicion, and envy, is to be confined in a self made prison-hole. But to think well of all, to be cheerful with all, to patiently learn to find the good in all—such unselfish thoughts are the very portals of heaven; and to dwell day by day in thoughts of peace toward every creature will bring abounding peace to their possessor.

Thought and Purpose

UNTIL thought is linked with purpose there is no intelligent accomplishment. With the majority the bark of thought is allowed to "drift" upon the ocean of life. Aimlessness is a vice, and such drifting must not continue for him who would steer clear of catastrophe and destruction.

They who have no central purpose in their life fall an easy prey to petty worries, fears, troubles, and self-pityings, all of which are indications of weakness, which lead, just as surely as deliberately planned sins (though by a different route), to failure, unhappiness, and loss, for weakness cannot persist in a power evolving universe.

A man should conceive of a legitimate purpose in his heart, and set out to accomplish it. He should make this purpose the centralizing point of his thoughts. It may take the form of a spiritual ideal, or it may be a worldly object, according to his nature at the time being; but whichever it is, he should steadily focus his thought-forces upon the object, which he has set before him. He should make this purpose his supreme duty, and should devote himself to its attainment, not allowing his thoughts to wander away into ephemeral fancies, longings, and imaginings. This is the royal road to self-control and true concentration of thought. Even if he fails again and again to accomplish his purpose (as he necessarily must until weakness is overcome), the *strength of character gained* will be the measure of *his true* success, and this will form a new starting-point for future power and triumph.

Those who are not prepared for the apprehension of a *great* purpose should fix the thoughts upon the faultless performance of their duty, no matter how insignificant their task may appear. Only in this way can the thoughts be gathered and focused, and resolution and energy be developed, which being done, there is nothing which may not be accomplished.

The weakest soul, knowing its own weakness, and believing this truth *that strength can only be developed by effort and practice*, will, thus believing, at once begin to exert itself, and, adding effort to effort, patience to patience, and strength to strength, will never cease to develop, and will at last grow divinely strong.

As the physically weak man can make himself strong by careful and patient training, so the man of weak thoughts can make them strong by exercising himself in right thinking.

To put away aimlessness and weakness, and to begin to think with purpose, is to enter the ranks of those strong ones who only recognize failure as one of the pathways to attainment; who make all conditions serve them, and who think strongly, attempt fearlessly, and accomplish masterfully.

Having conceived of his purpose, a man should mentally mark out a *straight* pathway to its achievement, looking neither to the right nor the left. Doubts and fears should be rigorously excluded; they are disintegrating elements, which break up the straight line of effort, rendering it crooked, ineffectual, useless. Thoughts of doubt and fear never accomplished anything, and never can. They always lead to failure. Purpose, energy, power to do, and all strong thoughts cease when doubt and fear creep in.

The will to do springs from the knowledge that we *can* do. Doubt and fear are the great enemies of knowledge, and he who encourages them, who does not slay them, thwarts himself at every step.

He who has conquered doubt and fear has conquered failure. His every, thought is allied with power, and all difficulties are bravely met and wisely overcome. His purposes are seasonably planted, and they bloom and bring forth fruit, which does not fall prematurely to the ground.

Thought allied fearlessly to purpose becomes creative force: he who *knows* this is ready to become something higher and stronger than a mere bundle of wavering thoughts and fluctuating sensations; he who *does* this has become the conscious and intelligent wielder of his mental powers.

The Thought-Factor in Achievement

ALL that a man achieves and all that he fails to achieve is the direct result of his own thoughts. In a justly ordered universe, where loss of equipoise would mean total destruction, individual responsibility must be absolute. A man's weakness and strength, purity and impurity, are his own, and not another man's; they are brought about by himself, and not by another; and they can only be altered by himself, never by another. His condition is also his own, and not another man's. His suffering and his happiness are evolved from within. As he thinks, so he is; as he continues to think, so he remains.

A strong man cannot help a weaker unless that weaker is *willing* to be helped, and even then the weak man must become strong of himself; he must, by his own efforts, develop the strength which he admires in another. None but himself can alter his condition.

It has been usual for men to think and to say, "Many men are slaves because one is an oppressor; let us hate the oppressor." Now, however, there is amongst an increasing few a tendency to reverse this judgment, and to say, "One man is an oppressor because many are slaves; let us despise the slaves."

The truth is that oppressor and slave are co-operators in ignorance, and, while seeming to afflict each other, are in reality afflicting themselves. A perfect Knowledge perceives the action of law in the weakness of the oppressed and the misapplied power of the oppressor; a perfect Love, seeing the suffering, which both states entail, condemns neither; a perfect Compassion embraces both oppressor and oppressed.

He who has conquered weakness, and has put away all selfish thoughts, belongs neither to oppressor nor oppressed. He is free.

A man can only rise, conquer, and achieve by lifting up his thoughts. He can only remain weak, and abject, and miserable by refusing to lift up his thoughts.

Before a man can achieve anything, even in worldly things, he must lift his thoughts above slavish animal indulgence. He may not, in order to succeed, give up all animality and selfishness, by any means; but a portion of it must, at least, be sacrificed. A man whose first thought is bestial indulgence could neither think clearly nor plan methodically; he could not find and develop his latent resources, and would fail in any undertaking. Not having commenced to manfully control his thoughts, he is not in a position to control affairs and to adopt serious responsibilities. He is not fit to act independently and stand alone. But he is limited only by the thoughts, which he chooses.

There can be no progress, no achievement without sacrifice, and a man's worldly success will be in the measure that he sacrifices his confused animal thoughts, and fixes his mind on the development of his plans, and the strengthening of his resolution and self-reliance.

And the higher he lifts his thoughts, the more manly, upright, and righteous he becomes, the greater will be his success, the more blessed and enduring will be his achievements.

The universe does not favour the greedy, the dishonest, the vicious, although on the mere surface it may sometimes appear to do so; it helps the honest, the magnanimous, the virtuous. All the great Teachers of the ages have declared this in varying forms, and to prove and know it a man has but to persist in making himself more and more virtuous by lifting up his thoughts.

Intellectual achievements are the result of thought consecrated to the search for knowledge, or for the beautiful and true in life and nature. Such achievements may be sometimes connected with vanity and ambition, but they are not the outcome of those characteristics; they are the natural outgrowth of long and arduous effort, and of pure and unselfish thoughts.

Spiritual achievements are the consummation of holy aspirations. He who lives constantly in the conception of noble and lofty thoughts, who dwells upon all that is pure and unselfish, will, as surely as the sun reaches its zenith and the moon its full, become wise and noble in character, and rise into a position of influence and blessedness.

Achievement, of whatever kind, is the crown of effort, the diadem of thought. By the aid of self-control, resolution, purity, righteousness, and well-directed thought a man ascends; by the aid of animality, indolence, impurity, corruption, and confusion of thought a man descends.

A man may rise to high success in the world, and even to lofty altitudes in the spiritual realm, and again descend into weakness and wretchedness by allowing arrogant, selfish, and corrupt thoughts to take possession of him.

Victories attained by right thought can only be maintained by watchfulness. Many give way when success is assured, and rapidly fall back into failure.

All achievements, whether in the business, intellectual, or spiritual world, are the result of definitely directed thought, are governed by the same law and are of the same method; the only difference lies in *the object of attainment*.

He who would accomplish little must sacrifice little; he who would achieve much must sacrifice much; he who would attain highly must sacrifice greatly.

Visions and Ideals

THE dreamers are the saviours of the world. As the visible world is sustained by the invisible, so men, through all their trials and sins and sordid vocations, are nourished by the beautiful visions of their solitary dreamers. Humanity cannot forget its dreamers; it cannot let their ideals fade and die; it lives in them; it knows them as their *realities* which it shall one day see and know.

Composer, sculptor, painter, poet, prophet, sage, these are the makers of the after-world, the architects of heaven. The world is beautiful because they have lived; without them, labouring humanity would perish.

He who cherishes a beautiful vision, a lofty ideal in his heart, will one day realize it. Columbus cherished a vision of another world, and he discovered it; Copernicus fostered the vision of a multiplicity of worlds and a wider universe, and he revealed it; Buddha beheld the vision of a spiritual world of stainless beauty and perfect peace, and he entered into it.

Cherish your visions; cherish your ideals; cherish the music that stirs in your heart, the beauty that forms in your mind, the loveliness that drapes your purest thoughts, for out of them will grow all delightful conditions, all, heavenly environment; of these, if you but remain true to them, your world will at last be built.

To desire is to obtain; to aspire is to, achieve. Shall man's basest desires receive the fullest measure of gratification, and his purest aspirations starve for lack of sustenance? Such is not the Law: such a condition of things can never obtain: "ask and receive."

Dream lofty dreams, and as you dream, so shall you become. Your Vision is the promise of what you shall one day be; your Ideal is the prophecy of what you shall at last unveil.

The greatest achievement was at first and for a time a dream. The oak sleeps in the acorn; the bird waits in the egg; and in the highest vision of the soul a waking angel stirs. Dreams are the seedlings of realities.

Your circumstances may be uncongenial, but they shall not long remain so if you but perceive an Ideal and strive to reach it. You cannot travel *within* and stand still *without*. Here is a youth hard pressed by poverty and labour; confined long hours in an unhealthy workshop; unschooled, and lacking all the arts of refinement. But he dreams of better things; he thinks of intelligence, of refinement, of grace and beauty. He conceives of,
mentally builds up, an ideal condition of life; the vision of a wider liberty and a larger scope takes possession of him; unrest urges him to action, and he utilizes all his spare time and means, small though they are, to the development of his latent powers and resources. Very soon so altered has his mind become that the workshop can no longer hold him. It has become so out of harmony with his mentality that it falls out of his life as a garment is cast aside, and, with the growth of opportunities, which fit the scope of his expanding powers, he passes out of it forever. Years later we see this youth as a full-grown man. We find him a master of certain forces of the mind, which he wields with worldwide influence and almost unequalled power. In his hands he holds the cords of gigantic responsibilities; he speaks, and lo, lives are changed; men and women hang upon his words and remould their

characters, and, sunlike, he becomes the fixed and luminous centre round which innumerable destinies revolve. He has realized the Vision of his youth. He has become one with his Ideal.

And you, too, youthful reader, will realize the Vision (not the idle wish) of your heart, be it base or beautiful, or a mixture of both, for you will always gravitate toward that which you, secretly, most love. Into your hands will be placed the exact results of your own thoughts; you will receive that which you earn; no more, no less. Whatever your present environment may be, you will fall, remain, or rise with your thoughts, your Vision, your Ideal. You will become as small as your controlling desire; as great as your dominant aspiration: in the beautiful words of Stanton Kirkham Davis, "You may be keeping accounts, and presently you shall walk out of the door that for so long has seemed to you the barrier of your ideals, and shall find yourself before an audience—the pen still behind your ear, the ink stains on your fingers and then and there shall pour out the torrent of your inspiration. You may be driving sheep, and you shall wander to the city-bucolic and open-mouthed; shall wander under the intrepid quidance of the spirit into the studio of the master, and after a time he shall say, 'I have nothing more to teach you.' And now you have become the master, who did so recently dream of great things while driving sheep. You shall lay down the saw and the plane to take upon yourself the regeneration of the world."

The thoughtless, the ignorant, and the indolent, seeing only the apparent effects of things and not the things themselves, talk of luck, of fortune, and chance. Seeing a man grow rich, they say, "How lucky he is!" Observing another become intellectual, they exclaim, "How highly favoured he is!" And noting the saintly character and wide influence of another, they remark, "How chance aids him at every turn!" They do not see the trials and failures and struggles which these men have voluntarily encountered in order to gain their experience; have no knowledge of the sacrifices they have made, of the undaunted efforts they have put forth, of the faith they have exercised, that they might overcome the apparently insurmountable, and realize the Vision of their heart. They do not know the darkness and the heartaches; they only see the light and joy, and call it "luck". They do not see the long and arduous journey, but only behold the pleasant goal, and call it "good fortune," do not understand the process, but only perceive the result, and call it chance.

In all human affairs there are *efforts*, and there are *results*, and the strength of the effort is the measure of the result. Chance is not. Gifts, powers, material, intellectual, and spiritual possessions are the fruits of effort; they are thoughts completed, objects accomplished, visions realized.

The Vision that you glorify in your mind, the Ideal that you enthrone in your heart—this you will build your life by, this you will become.

Serenity

CALMNESS of mind is one of the beautiful jewels of wisdom. It is the result of long and patient effort in self-control. Its presence is an indication of ripened experience, and of a more than ordinary knowledge of the laws and operations of thought.

A man becomes calm in the measure that he understands himself as a thought evolved being, for such knowledge necessitates the understanding of others as the result of thought, and as he develops a right understanding, and sees more and more clearly the internal relations of things by the action of cause and effect he ceases to fuss and fume and worry and grieve, and remains poised, steadfast, serene.

The calm man, having learned how to govern himself, knows how to adapt himself to others; and they, in turn, reverence his spiritual strength, and feel that they can learn of him and rely upon him. The more tranquil a man becomes, the greater is his success, his influence, his power for good. Even the ordinary trader will find his business prosperity increase as he develops a greater self-control and equanimity, for people will always prefer to deal with a man whose demeanour is strongly equable.

The strong, calm man is always loved and revered. He is like a shade-giving tree in a thirsty land, or a sheltering rock in a storm. "Who does not love a tranquil heart, a sweet-tempered, balanced life? It does not matter whether it rains or shines, or what changes come to those possessing these blessings, for they are always sweet, serene, and calm. That exquisite poise of character, which we call serenity is the last lesson of culture, the fruitage of the soul. It is precious as wisdom, more to be desired than gold—yea, than even fine gold. How insignificant mere money seeking looks in comparison with a serene life—a life that dwells in the ocean of Truth, beneath the waves, beyond the reach of tempests, in the Eternal Calm!"

How many people we know who sour their lives, who ruin all that is sweet and beautiful by explosive tempers, who destroy their poise of character, and make bad blood! It is a question whether the great majority of people do not ruin their lives and mar their happiness by lack of self-control. How few people we meet in life who are well balanced, who have that exquisite poise which is characteristic of the finished character!

Yes, humanity surges with uncontrolled passion, is tumultuous with ungoverned grief, is blown about by anxiety and doubt only the wise man, only he whose thoughts are controlled and purified, makes the winds and the storms of the soul obey him.

Tempest-tossed souls, wherever ye may be, under whatsoever conditions ye may live, know this in the ocean of life the isles of Blessedness are smiling, and the sunny shore of your ideal awaits your coming. Keep your hand firmly upon the helm of thought. In the bark of your soul reclines the commanding Master; He does but sleep: wake

Him. Self-control is strength; Right Thought is mastery; Calmness is power. Say unto your heart, "Peace, be still!"

Out in the Fields with God
Elizabeth Barrett Browning

The little cares that fretted me
I lost them yesterday
Among the fields, above the sea,
Among the winds at play,
Among the lowing of the herds,
The rustling of the trees,
Among the singing of the birds,
The humming of the bees.

The foolish fears of what might happen,
I cast them all away,
Among the clover-scented grass,
Among the new-mown hay,
Among the husking of the corn,
Where drowsy poppies nod,
Where ill thoughts die and good are born--
Out in the fields with God.

If I Can Stop One Heart from Breaking
Emily Dickinson

If I can stop one heart from breaking,
I shall not live in vain;
If I can ease one life the aching,
Or cool one pain,
Or help one fainting robin
Unto his nest again,
I shall not live in vain.

Character: The Grandest Thing in the World

Orison Swett Marden

I. A GRAND CHARACTER

If Henry Drummond was wise in calling an abstract quality, Love, the Greatest Thing in the World – then Love in the concrete, embodied in Character, is the Grandest Thing in the World. Drummond himself, in his life-story, is far grander than anything he ever wrote, for his was "the life of a radiant personality."

"You met him," says Dr. George Adam Smith, his biographer, "a graceful, well-dressed gentleman, tall and lithe, with a swing in his walk and a brightness in his face, who seemed to carry no cares, and to know neither presumption nor timidity. You spoke, and found him keen for any of a hundred interests. He fished, he shot, he skated, as few can; he played cricket; he would go any distance to see a fire or a football match. He had a new story or a new puzzle or a new joke every time he met you. Was it on the street? He drew you to watch two messenger-boys meet, grin, knock each other's hat off, lay down their baskets, and enjoy a friendly chaffer at marbles. Was it on the train? He read you a fresh tale of his favorite—Bret Harte. Was it a rainy afternoon in a country house? He described a new game, and in five minutes everybody was in the thick of it. If it was a children's party, they clamored for his sleight-of-hand." Drummond as a boy was manly, and as a man he carried a boy's heart in his breast.

"The Prince," he was called by the young men who knew him. "He had a genius for friendship," says Professor Grose. He so won the affection of workingmen that one said, after Drummond died, that he almost felt as if he must pray to him—to invoke his influence for good, from out the heavenly realms.

"His influence," says Ian Maclaren, who first knew Drummond as a boy on the cricket field, "more than that of any other man I met, was mesmeric—which means that, while other men affect their fellows by speech and example, he seized one directly by his living personality. Quite sensible and unromantic people grew uneasy in his presence, and roused themselves to resistance,--as one might do who recognized a magician, and feared his spell. Men were at once arrested, interested, fascinated by the very sight of the man, and could not take their eyes off him. It was as if the prince of one's imagination had dropped in among common folk."

He was the youth who sprang to the aid of Moody and Sankey in the Scottish stronghold, who caught hold of young men and persuaded them in untechnical phrase to do what their praying mothers on earth and God Most High would have them do; the quiet, restrained evangelist, not twenty-three, about whom all men gathered as their leader when the American evangelists left Scotland. A stalwart theologian, too, was he, who detected the natural laws that were at work in the spiritual world—a thinker simple, clear, presenting truth in the concrete. He, too, was the explorer plunging into the wilds of Africa, without giving a thought to a bookmaker's fame; and while a quarter of a million people were reading his books, he was crowding along the work of the hour at the world's end in America or Australia.

How eagerly men sought him, clung to him, and followed him as he followed the Master!

Do we ask – What is Character? Is it not that sum of qualities which distinguishes one person from another? Do we say that Drummond's versatility was his distinguishing characteristic? It was, rather, his unique combination of high qualities; and no man can acquire a far-reaching influence without a fair mental balance, with great strength upon many sides.

If it is no part of my intent, in this booklet, to catalogue those mental and moral traits of most value to mankind, yet it is my intent to name certain deep-rooted dispositions, which are essential in the mental make-up of those who set before themselves a high ideal in seeking for the Grandest Thing in the World.

II. THE LIGHT BEARERS

True worth is in being, not seeming,--
In doing, each day that goes by,
Some little good, not in the dreaming
Of great things to do by and by.
For whatever men say in their blindness,
And spite of the fancies of youth,
There's nothing so kingly as kindness,
And nothing so royal as truth.
Alice Cary

    A gentleman's first characteristic is that fineness of structure in the body which renders it capable of the most delicate sensation, and of structure in the mind which renders it capable of the most delicate sympathies; one may say, simply, "fineness of nature." -Ruskin

    There is no duty we so much underrate as the duty of being happy. . . By being happy we sow anonymous benefits upon the world, which remain unknown even to ourselves. –Stevenson

    On the steps of a public building in Florence an old, disabled soldier sat playing a violin. By his side stood a faithful dog holding in his mouth a veteran's hat, into which, now and then, a passer-by would drop a coin. A gentleman, in passing, paused, and asked for the violin; first tuning it, he then began to play.
    The sight of a well-dressed man, playing a violin in such a place, with such associations, attracted the passers-by, and they stopped. The music was so charming that they stood enchanted. The number of contributions largely increased. The hat became so heavy that the dog began to growl. It was emptied, and soon filled again. The company grew until a great congregation was gathered. The performer played one of the national airs, handed the violin back to its owner, and quickly retired.
    One of the company present said: "This is Amard Bucher, the world-renowned violinist. He did this for charity; let us follow his example." And immediately the hat was passed for a collection for the old man. Mr. Bucher did not give a penny, but he flooded the old man's day with sunshine.
    So, too, it was related that when Michael Angelo was at the height of his fame, when monarchs and popes were paying fabulous prices for his works, a little boy met him on the street, with an old pencil and a piece of dirty brown paper, and asked him for a picture. The great artist sat on the curbstone and drew a picture for his little admirer.
    A like charming story is told of Jenny Lind, the great Swedish singer, which shows her noble nature. Once when walking with a friend she saw an old woman tottering into the door of an almshouse. Her pity was at once excited, and she entered the door, ostensibly to

rest for a moment, but really to give something to the poor woman. To her surprise, the old woman began at once to talk of Jenny Lind, saying,--

"I have lived a long time in the world, and desire nothing before I die but to hear Jenny Lind."

"Would it make you happy?" inquired Jenny.

"Ay, that it would; but such folks as I can't go to the playhouse, and so I shall never hear her."

"Don't be so sure of that," said Jenny. "Sit down, my friend, and listen."

She then sang, with genuine glee, one of her best songs. The old woman was wild with delight and wonder, when she added,--

"Now you have heard Jenny Lind."

Sweeter than the perfume of roses is a reputation for a kind, charitable, unselfish nature; a ready disposition to do to others any good turn in your power. "The mind's sweetness," says Herbert, "has its operation on the body, clothes, and habitation." So Cervantes spoke of one whose face was like a benediction. "Good looking," as Horace Smith remarks, "is looking good." "Be good," says our Amesbury poet, "be womanly, be gentle, generous in your sympathies, heedful of the good breeding of all around you,--and you will not lack kind words of admiration."

Was there ever an unselfish person, of charitable and generous impulses, sociable, loving, kind, of tender spirit, thoughtful for others, who was not universally beloved? He, indeed, is the light-bearer.

Some people are born happy. No matter what their circumstances are, they are joyous, content, and satisfied with everything. They carry a perpetual holiday in their eyes, and see joy and beauty everywhere. When we meet them they impress us as having just met with some good luck, or as having some good news to tell. Like the bees that extract honey from every flower, they have a happy alchemy which transmutes even gloom into sunshine. In the sick-room they are better than the physician and more potent than drugs. All doors open to these people. They are welcome everywhere.

The most fascinating person is always the one of the most winning manners; not the one of greatest physical beauty.

We do not need an introduction to feel his greatness, if you meet a cheerful man on the street on a cold day you seem to feel the mercury rise several degrees.

The two main characteristics of a lady or of a gentleman are, according to Earl Beaconsfield, propriety and consideration for others. "Will you fall into any extreme?" asks De Sales. "Let it be on the side of gentleness." How appropriate are such sentiments for household mottoes! "Let each one strive to yield oftenest to the wishes of the other, in absolute unselfishness." "Never part without loving words."

The following was found in an old manor-house in Gloucestershire, England, written and framed, and hung over the mantel-piece of a sitting room: "The true gentleman is God's servant, the world's master, and his own man. Virtue is his business; study, his recreation; contentment, his rest; and happiness, his reward. God is his father; Jesus Christ, his Savior; the saints, his brethren; and all that need him his friends. Devotion is his chaplain; chastity, his chamberlain; sobriety, his butler; temperance, his cook; hospitality, his housekeeper; Providence, his steward; charity, his treasurer; piety, his mistress of the house; and discretion, his porter, to let in or out, as most fit. Thus is his whole family made up of virtue, and he is master of the house. He is necessitated to take the world on his way to heaven, and he walks through it as fast as he can, and all his business by the way is to make himself and others happy. Take him in two words—a man and a Christian."

III. THE GREAT-HEARTED

One act of charity will teach us more of the love of God
than a thousand sermons. –Robertson

It was a cold, dark evening, and the city lights only intensified by their sharp contrast the gloom of the storm. It was the time when wealthy shoppers were eating their hot dinners, when the stores were closing, and when the shop-girls were plodding home, many too poor to ride, tired with the long day's standing and work.

A shop-girl was hurrying home through the slush after a hard day's work. She was a delicate girl, poorly dressed, and wholly unable to keep out the winter's cold with a thin fall cloak. She was evidently very timid and self-absorbed.

A blind man was sitting in an alley by the pavement, silently offering pencils for sale to the heedless crowd. The wind and sleet beat upon him. He had no overcoat. His thin hands clasped with purple fingers the wet, sleet-covered pencils. He looked as if the cold had congealed him.

The girl passed the man, as did the rest of the hurrying crowd. When she had walked half a block away she fumbled in her pocket, and turned and walked back.

For a moment she looked intently at the vender of pencils, and when she saw that he gave no sign, she quietly dropped a ten-cent piece into his fingers, and walked on.

But she was evidently troubled, for her steps grew slower.

Then she stopped, turned, and walked rapidly back to the dark alley, and the man half hiding in it. Bending over him, she said softly, "Are you really blind?"

The man lifted his head and showed her his sightless eyes. Then with an indescribable gesture he pointed to his breast. There hung the dull badge of the Grand Army of the Republic.

"I beg your pardon, sir," she said humbly. "Please give me back my ten cents."

"Yes, ma'am," he answered, and held out the coin.

She took out her purse. It was a very thin one. It contained but two silver dollars, one-third of her week's hard earnings, all she had. She put one dollar of it into his hands with the words—"Take this instead, for the dear Lord's sake, and go home now; you ought not to sit here in this bitter wind and sleet." Then she turned her steps homeward, pitying the wretched man, and thinking that no one had seen her.

"The high desire that others may be blest savors of heaven."

A poor woman, knowing that Dr. Oliver Goldsmith had studied physic, and hearing of his great humanity, solicited him in a letter to send her something for her husband, who had lost his appetite and was reduced to a most melancholy state. The good-natured poet waited on her instantly, and after some discourse with his patient found him sinking in sickness and poverty. The doctor told him they should hear from him in an hour, when he would send them some pills which he believed would prove efficacious. He immediately went home and put ten guineas into a chip box, with the following label: "These must be used as necessities require. Be patient, and of a good heart."

At the battle of Fredericksurg, hundreds of Union soldiers lay wounded on the field a whole day and a night; the agonizing cries for water among the wounded were only answered by the roar of the guns. At last a Southern soldier who could not endure these piteous cries any longer begged his general to let him carry water to the suffering. The general told him it would be instant death to appear on the field, but the cries of the unfortunates drowned the roar of the guns to him at least, and he rushed out among the wounded and dying with a supply of water on his errand of mercy. Wondering eyes from both armies watched the brave fellow as, heedless of guns, he passed from soldier to soldier, gently raising his head and placing the cooling cup to his parched lips. The Union soldiers were so struck by the action of this boy in gray, risking his life for his enemies' sake, that they ceased firing from admiration for an hour and a half, as did the Confederates. During this whole time the boy in gray went over the entire battlefield, giving drink to the thirsty, straightening cramped and mangled limbs, putting knapsacks under the heads of sufferers, spreading coats and blankets as if they had been his own comrades.

General Gordon is said to have had a great number of medals for which he cared nothing. There was a gold one, however, given to him by the Empress of China, with a special inscription engraved upon it, for which he had a great liking. But it suddenly disappeared; no one knew where or how. Years afterwards it was found out, by a curious accident, that Gordon had erased the inscription, sold the medal for ten pounds, and sent the sum anonymously for the relief of the sufferers from the cotton famine at Manchester.

There is one anecdote—matchless if not incredible. It reads like a fable out of the Orient. It relates to a Spanish Moor, whose walk in his garden was interrupted by the inrush of a Spanish cavalier who flung himself at his feet and implored protection, saying that the pursuers were seeking his life for having slain a Moor. Refuge was promised in the garden summer-house till midnight. Unlocking the door at the appointed hour, the Moor said: "You have killed my only son. But I pledged my word not to betray you." And he placed the murderer upon a mule, saying, "Flee while darkness conceals you. God is just; my faith is unspotted, and I have resigned judgment to him."

Yet, unless it is true that a pledge is sacred, the pillars of heaven may fall. Unless generosity of spirit prevails among men there can never be upon earth an ideal life.

"The last, best fruit," says Richter, "which comes to late perfection even in the kindliest soul, is tenderness toward the hard, forbearance toward the unforbearing, warmth of heart toward the cold, philanthropy toward the misanthropic."

As we stand upon the seashore while the tide is coming in, one wave reaches up the beach far higher than any previous one, then recedes, and for some time none that follows comes up to its mark, but after a while the whole sea is there and beyond it; so now and then there comes a man head and shoulders above his fellow-men, showing that Nature has not lost her ideal of great-heartedness, and after a while even the average man will overtop the highest wave of noble manhood yet given to the world.

IV. A NORTH-STAR COURSE

Character is moral order, seen through the medium of an individual nature. –Emerson

No man has come to true greatness who has not felt in some degree that his life belongs to his race, and that what God gives him, He gives him for mankind. –Phillips Brooks

The blossom cannot tell what becomes of its odor; and no man can tell what becomes of his influence and example that roll away from him and go beyond his ken. –Beecher

Life's more than breath and the quick round of blood;
'Tis a great spirit and a busy heart.
We live in deeds, not years; in thoughts, not breaths;
In feelings, not in figures on a dial.
We should count time by heart-throbs. He most lives
Who thinks most, feels the noblest, acts the best.
-Bailey

    In a large, open square in New Orleans stands a beautiful marble statue erected by the city, and on the statue are these words: "The Statue of Margaret, of New Orleans."
    She was left an orphan by the ravages of yellow fever. She married in early womanhood, but her husband soon died, also her only child. She was poor and uneducated, and could scarcely write her name. She went to work in the Orphan Asylum for Girls. She toiled early and late, solicited groceries from merchants, and, indeed, put her whole life into the work for these orphans. When a new and beautiful asylum was built Margaret and one of the Sisters of Mercy freed it from debt. Margaret opened a dairy and bakery in the city, of her own. Everybody knew her, and patronized her milk-wagon and bakery. She worked very hard and saved every cent, to help the orphans whom in effect she had adopted as her own children. She never owned a silk dress or wore a kid glove, and she was very plain; but the city erected this beautiful monument to the orphan's friend, as a thank-offering for a beautiful, helpful, unselfish life.
    An absolute surrender, consecration and devotion of self to all that is better and purer and truer, is the secret of character-building. By a consuming zeal for all that is noble and excellent our love of self becomes softened and clarified. By constant contemplation of excellence we clear our selfhood of all dress and impurities. We let go all things which we cannot carry into the eternal life.

It is this sublime living that stamps the features. What is more beautiful than the face of Mrs. Oliphant, of Mr. Gladstone, and of a vast number of figures that are not printed for fashion plates?

"Let any one," says Charles Kingsley, "set his heart to do what is right and nothing else, and it will not be long ere his brow is stamped with all that goes to make up the heroic expression, with a noble indignation, noble self-restraint, great hope, great sorrows, perhaps even with the print of the martyr's crown of thorns."

Where certain lines in the face of Gladstone came from we learn by such incidents as that related by Sir Francis Crossley, to whom it was told by the vicar of St. Martin's-in-the-Fields. The vicar had recently been to see a crossing-sweeper in his parish, who was ill.

"Has anyone been to see you?"

"Yes, Mr. Gladstone."

"But how came he to visit you?" inquired the vicar, who could not understand why the Chancellor of the Ex-chequer, although then living in the parish, should call upon a sick crossing-tender.

"Well," answered the crossing-sweeper, "he always had a nice word for me when he passed my crossing, and when I was not there he missed me. He asked my mate, who has taken my place, where I was, and when he heard that I was ill he asked for my address, and put it down on paper. So he called to see me."

"And what did he do?" asked the vicar.

"Why, he read to me from the Bible and prayed," was the reply.

To be loyal to the highest interests of every man, how characteristic was this of the magnanimous Gladstone! Indeed, how Christ-like was such service!

So, too, there is an anecdote of Charles N. Crittendon. When his own daughter entered into Our Father's House he gave his entire time to carrying the divine message of peace and good-will to those who rarely heard it. And he established homes of refuge for those homeless women who sought to walk in new paths of life.

I never read the life-stories of Mrs. Judson, Mrs. Snow, Miss Brittain, Miss West, without feeling that the heroic age of our race has just begun.

And let me ask what member of a Christian church was ever more self-devoted than John, the felon? He was a man of coarse features, close-cropped hair, and of a shuffling gait. He asked for a position as a nurse in a yellow-fever epidemic at Memphis. The doctor refused him.

"I wish to nurse," persisted the stranger. "Try me for a week. If you don't like me, then dismiss me; if you do, pay me my wages."

"Very well," said the doctor, "I'll take you; although, to be candid, I hesitate to do so." Then he added mentally, "I'll keep my eye on him."

But the man soon proved that he needed nobody's eye upon him. In a few weeks he had become one of the most valuable nurses on that heroic force. He was tireless and self-denying. Wherever the pestilence raged most fiercely he worked hardest. The suffering and the sinking adored him. To the neglected and the forgotten his rough face was the face of an angel.

He acted so strangely on pay-days, however, that he was followed through back streets to an obscure place, where he was seen to put his whole week's earnings into a relief-box for the benefit of the yellow-fever sufferers. Not long afterwards he sickened and died of the plague; and when his body was prepared for its unnamed grave, for he never told who he was, a livid mark was found which showed that John, the nurse, had been branded as a convicted felon. How fitting his epitaph! "I was sick, and ye visited me."

"There is but one pursuit in life," says Colton, "which it is in the power of all to follow and all to attain: this is the pursuit of virtue." "It is this commanding worth, this personal power," says Emerson, "which is crowned in all companies." Nor was there ever a more signal instance of it, dear to the heart of our English-speaking people, than occurred at Lord Stratford's Crimean war dinner party, when the old officers were invited to write secretly upon a slip of paper the name connected with that war most likely to descend to posterity with renown; every paper bore the name, "Florence Nightingale." "The lady with the light"—she it was who won the highest fame in that war of the Orient.

"Within a few hours only of the arrival of herself and her little band of nurses," says the record, "many hundred wounded men were brought in from the fight at Balaklava, and a little later thousands more from the field of Inkerman. Nothing was ready, everything was to be done, and it was her task to bring order out of a chaos of misery. She sometimes stood, during her first week in charge, twenty consecutive hours issuing directions; and she made it a point, when matters were running in routine order, to give her personal attention to the worst and most appalling cases."

"Her nerve," said a surgeon who worked with her, "was wonderful. I have been with her at very severe operations; she was more than equal to the trial. The more awful to every sense any particular case, especially if it was that of a dying man, the more surely would her slight form be seen bending over him, administering to his ease in every way in her power, and seldom quitting his side till death released him."

"She would speak to one and to another, and nod and smile to as many more," said a soldier, "but she couldn't do it to all, you know,-- we lay there by hundreds; but we could kiss her shadow as it fell, and lay our heads on the pillow again content."

Another said, "Before she come, there was such cussin' and swearin'; and after that it was as holy as a church!"

How closely are these anecdotes related to the divine life in man, and how greatly they enhance the sacredness of his personality! It is this which sets one apart, and we instinctively maintain a reserve toward those whose princely lives are so honored by unique acts of fidelity to God and to man.

It is this rigid and unquestioning adherence to duty which Mrs. Anna Jameson calls "the cement which binds the whole moral edifice together: without which all power, goodness, intellect, truth, happiness, and love itself, can have no permanence."

If a man's religion is of the right sort, will it not sharpen his faculties, quicken his energies, heighten his self-respect, give solidity to his character, and enhance both his usefulness and his prospect of success? In the sublimest flights of the soul, rectitude is never surmounted, love is never outgrown.

And by it are we not akin to the highest beings in the universe, and even to the Most High? It was during our Civil war that a soldier lay long upon his dying cot, counting the days, then the hours, of his discharge; and under his pillow was found this dedication of himself which indicated his faith in the highest kinship of the soul: "I give to a patient God my patient heart."

V. INTREPIDITY OF SPIRIT

He's true to God who's true to man:
   Wherever wrong is done
To the humblest and the weakest
   "Neath the all-beholding sun,
That wrong is also done to us,
   And they are slaves most base
Whose love of right is for themselves,
   And not for all their race.
                    Lowell

Oh, may I join the choir invisible
Of those immortal dead who live again
In minds made better by their presence; live
In pulses stirred to generosity,
In deeds of daring rectitude, in scorn
For miserable aims that end with self,
In thoughts sublime that pierce the night like stars,
And with their mild persistence urge man's search
To vaster issues!
           George Eliot

In arming the Christian soldier Paul puts sincerity before everything. Not, How much do you believe? but, How much do you believe it? He is less concerned with the article than with the ardor of my faith: he is content it should be half formed, if it be whole hearted. —Mattheson

La Tour d"Auvergne, alone in the besieged castle, multiplied himself, in effect, by shooting first from one window, then from another. When the terms of surrender were arranged the "garrison" was allowed to march out with the honors of war. To the astonishment of all, one man, the "First Grenadier of France," came forth, and stacked arms. "But the garrison must abandon the castle!" expostulated the Austrian chief. "Where is the garrison?" "I am the garrison," replied La Tour proudly.

    Garibaldi's power over his men amounted to fascination. In Rome he called for forty volunteers to go where half of them would be killed and the others wounded. The whole battalion rushed forward; and they had to draw lots, so eager were all to obey.

    What is every man but a magnet, to attract, or to be attracted? Every man ultimately falls into the company with which he affiliates. And he is the strongest who draws men to himself, who creates the company; and this is through having a positive quality—moral courage and physical prowess.

There was "Gentleman George," a young officer, of whom one of our war writers has told us. He spent all his spare hours in study, and daily he read his Bible. Camp life is never private, but George took the jeers of his comrades good-naturedly. He made an exact map of the country about the camp, much to his credit with the colonel of the regiment. When an insane soldier sprang into quarters George seized him. In the day of battle George ran in between the firing-lines and brought off a wounded lieutenant. And after such exhibitions of the stuff he was made of no one joked further whenever Gentleman George sat down to read his Bible.

"The greatest man," says a recent writer, "is he who chooses right with the most invincible resolution; who resists the sorest temptations from within and without; who bears the heaviest burdens cheerfully' who is calmest in storms and most fearless under menaces and frowns; whose reliance on truth, and virtue, and on God is most unfaltering."

Such a man was Aristide the Just. When Themistocles sought to transfer the government of Greece from the hands of the Lacedaemonians into those of the Athenians, he intimated one day in the popular assembly that he had a very important design to propose; but he could not communicate it to the public at large, because the greatest secrecy was necessary to its success, and he therefore desired that they would appoint a person to whom he might explain himself on the subject. Aristides was unanimously selected by the assembly, which deferred entirely to his opinion. Themistocles, taking him aside, told him that the design he had conceived was to burn the fleet belonging to the rest of the Grecian States, which then lay in a neighboring port, when Athens would assuredly become mistress of all Greece. Aristides returned to the assembly, and declared to them that nothing could be more advantageous to the Commonwealth than the project of Themistocles, but that, at the same time, nothing in the world could be more unfair. The assembly unanimously declared that, since such was the case, Themistocles should wholly abandon his project.

Is not moral courage always quick to rebuke a wrong? When Bishop Coleridge Patterson was a boy at Eton he was captain of the eleven; and he had the courage to declare that he would resign his captaincy, and take no part in the rowing, if coarse songs were sung at the annual supper. An objectionable song was sung, and he, with others, at once rose and left the room. It was not until an apology was offered that he resumed his post. So, too, Gladstone, as a boy at Eton, turned down his glass when an improper toast was proposed. As a schoolboy, the Bishop of Salisbury was kept by Gladstone from evil ways. And the student generations drank less in the years following Gladstone's abstemious courage.

"A heart unspotted is not easily daunted."

This is true always and everywhere. In Harvard University the idea of what was the manly thing was definitely changed when Arthur Cumnock threw his athletic influence in favor of temperance in all things, fair play, courtesy, and modesty. Moral courage always tells.

Is not intrepidity of spirit as requisite in the tent as on the battlefield? "I was sitting with General Grant one day," said Clinton B. Fisk, "when a major-general in full uniform appeared, saying: 'Boys, I have a good story to tell. There are no ladies present.' 'No, but there are gentlemen present,' replied the commander-in-chief."

When God calls a man to be upright and pure and generous, he also calls him to be intelligent and skillful, and strong and brave.

"I will call this Luther a true great man," says Carlyle, "great in intellect, in courage, affection, and integrity, one of our most lovable and precious men,--great, not as a hewn obelisk, but as an Alpine mountain, so simple, spontaneous, honest, not setting up to be great at all; there for quite another purpose than being great. Ah, yes, unsubduable granite, piercing far and wide into the heavens; yet in the clefts of it fountains, green, beautiful valleys with flowers!"

VI. "A FRAGMENT OF THE ROCK OF AGES"

"One ruddy drop of manly blood the surging sea outweighs."

   Last summer two young Creek braves, Watka and Deer, met at a dance; they were suitors for the same maiden, who was present. Trouble arose; there was a short fight, resulting in the death of Deer. For this homicide Watka was tried under the laws of his tribe, was found guilty of murder, and sentenced to be shot at a date early in August. Immediately on conviction the condemned man was released on parole, as others in the same circumstances had been,--it not being an infrequent tribal custom. No bond, no surety of any kind, nothing but his pledge to report for execution was required.
   Watka could kill his rival in love in the heat of passion; but he would not violate his promise, to save his life. He married the girl on whose account he had fought and killed Deer, and when the day of execution approached, he made preparations to die, making every possible provision for his widow.
   But he was not to die at the first time appointed. He was a member of a famous Indian baseball team, and a number of games in which he was needed had been scheduled. For this reason, and this alone, he was reprieved until the last day of October, in order that he might fulfill is baseball engagements. The games ended: and on a Sunday Watka reported to the Creek authorities (in our Indian territory) to pay his debt. A press dispatch describes what followed:
   "Watka set out alone to the public execution grounds. In due time he arrived. The crowd was waiting. The prisoner assumed his position on bended knees, with arms tied behind, and a bandage over his eyes. The rifle was in the hands of a good marksman; there was a sharp crack, and the white spot marked for the heart was instantly discolored with blood."
   A story not unlike this is related of a Bay State Tory, Dick Johnson, in our Revolutionary war. After his arrest, upon his personal word to the sheriff, he went about his usual work, in and out; and when it was time for him to be tried for high treason he set off alone and walked through the forests to Springfield to be tried for his life. But a member of the Massachusetts council, knowing his character, rescued him from the rope.
   Then, too, we have that old story of the Punic captive, released that he might advise Rome to make peace. He advised Rome not to make peace. "But Regulus, what will become of you?" "I gave my word to return, and I will keep it; but do you refuse to make peace."
   Who would not go far to see such men as Damon and Pythias, the one ready to die as a substitute for his friend, and the other voluntarily ready in his lace at the death block when the hour struck?

When the sacredness of one's word is matched in the attributes of his character throughout, all that constitutes a man, then we find that there is something in a man's life greater than his occupation or his achievements; grander than acquisition or wealth; higher than genius; more enduring than fame. "The truest test of civilization," says Emerson, "is not the census, nor the size of cities, nor the crops; no, but the kind of men the country turns out." Montaigne kept his castle gates unbarred during the wars of the Fronde, because his reputation for integrity was better defence than a regiment of horses.

"Your lordships," said Wellington in Parliament, "must all feel the high and honorable character of the late Sir Robert Peel. I was long connected with him in public life. I never knew a man in whose truth and justice I had greater confidence." Are not the characters of great men the dowry of a nation? Chateaubriand said he saw Washington but once, yet it inspired his whole life. To Washington, Jefferson once wrote—"The confidence of the whole nation centers in you." Of Abraham Lincoln, his greatest antagonist, Stephen A. Douglas said that there was safety in the very atmosphere of the man.

Manhood is above all riches and overtops all titles; character is greater than any career. "Character must stand behind, and back up everything,--the sermon, the poem, the picture, the play. None of them is worth a straw without it." "I have read," Emerson says, "that they who listened to Lord Chatham felt that there was something finer in the man than anything which he said."

It was remarked by Disraeli that "we put too much faith in systems, and look too little to men." This was the ground of that wise remark of Samuel Johnson to travelers, in which he belittled the palaces and cities, and even the picture galleries and fine scenery; yet the seeing of eminent men he thought to be of the first importance. "Go," said Lord Essex to the young Earl of Rutland, "a hundred miles to speak with one wise man, rather than five miles to see a fair town."

"The prosperity of a country," says Luther, "depends not on the abundance of its revenues, nor on the strength of its fortifications, nor on the beauty of its public buildings; but it consists in the number of its cultivated citizens, in its men of education, enlightenment, and character."

The value of personal integrity to the state, at a great crisis, was singularly illustrated by George Peabody. In 1837, after he moved from America to London, there came a commercial crisis in the United States. Many banks suspended specie payments. Many mercantile houses went to the wall, and thousands more were in great distress. Edward Everett said, "The great sympathetic nerve of the commercial world, credit, as far as the United States were concerned, was for the time paralyzed." Probably not half a dozen men in Europe would have been listened to for a moment in the Bank of England upon the subject of American securities, but George Peabody was one of them. His name was already a tower of strength in the commercial world. In those dark days his integrity stood four-square in every business panic.

Peabody retrieved the credit of the State of Maryland, and, it might almost be said, of the United States. His character was the magic wand which in many a case changed almost worthless paper into gold. Merchants on both sides of the Atlantic procured large advances from him, even before the goods consigned to him had been sold.

Another illustration is given us in Cockburn's "Memorials of Francis Horner":

"The valuable and peculiar light in which Horner's history is calculated to inspire every right-minded youth is this: at the age of thirty-eight he was possessed of greater influence than any other private man, admired, beloved, and trusted; and at this early age he died, deplored by all except the heartless and the base.

"Probably no greater homage was ever paid in Parliament to any deceased member. How was this attained? By rank? He was the son of an Edinburgh merchant. By wealth? Neither he nor any of his relatives ever had a superfluous sixpence. By office? He held but one, and that for only a few years, of no influence, and with very little pay. By talents? His were not splendid, and he had no genius. Cautious and slow, his only ambition was to be right. By eloquence? He spoke in calm, good taste, without any of the oratory that either terrifies or seduces. By any fascination of manner? His was only correct and agreeable. By what was it, then? Merely by sense, industry, good principles, and a good heart, qualities which no well-constituted mind need ever despair of attaining. It was the force of his character that raised him; and this character was not impressed upon him by nature, but formed, out of no peculiarly fine elements, by himself. There were many in the House of Commons of far greater ability and eloquence. But no one surpassed him in the combination of an adequate portion of these with moral worth. Horner was born to show what moderate powers, unaided by anything whatever except culture and goodness, may achieve, even when these powers are displayed amidst the competition and jealousies of public life."

It was Horner whom Sydney Smith described as having the ten commandments stamped on his forehead.

"Nature," says Thackeray, "has written a letter of credit upon some men's faces, which is honored wherever presented. You cannot help trusting such men; their very presence gives confidence. There is a 'promise to pay' in their very faces which gives confidence, and you prefer it to another man's endorsement."

This quality, which we sometimes speak of as characterizing "a man we can tie to," is always at a premium in a democracy. If it was said of the personal character of the first Alexander of Russia that it was equivalent to a constitution, much more, in a free land, the stability of our institutions depends upon moral excellence embodied in the citizens. "One good, strong, sound man," said Old John Brown, of Ossawatomie, "is worth a thousand men without character in a building up a state."

"Give us a man, young or old, high or low," says Dean Stanley, "on whom we know we can thoroughly depend, who will stand firm when others fail; the friend faithful and true, the adviser honest and fearless, the adversary just and chivalrous,--in such a one there is a fragment of the Rock of Ages."

VII. THE WEALTH OF THE COMMONWEALTH

The purest treasure mortal times afford
Is—spotless Reputation: that away,
Men are but gilded loam, or painted clay.
                                                            -Shakespeare

Heart-life, soul-life, hope, joy, and love, are true riches. —Beecher

When wealth is lost, nothing is lost;
When health is lost, something is lost;
When character is lost, all is lost.
             -Motto over the walls of a school in Germany

We were always without a sou, but we never spoke of money, for money counted for nothing in our ambition. —Rousseau

"Meal, please your Majesty, is a halfpenny a peck at Athens, and water I get for nothing!" This was the answer made by Socrates to King Archelaus, who had pressed him to give up preaching in the dirty streets of Athens, and come live with him in his splendid courts.

"I don't want such things," said Epictetus to the rich Roman orator who was making light of his contempt for money-wealth; "and besides you are poorer than I am. You have silver vessels, but earthenware reasons, principles, appetites. My mind furnishes me with abundant occupation in lieu of your restless idleness. All your possessions seem small to you; mine seem great to me. Your desire is insatiate, mine is satisfied."

"I have a rich neighbor," said Izaak Walton, "who is always so busy that he has no leisure to laugh; the whole business of his life is to get money, and more money; he is still drudging on, and says that 'The diligent hand maketh rich;' and it is true indeed; but he considers not that it is not in the power of riches to make a man happy; or, as was wisely said by a man of great observation, 'that there may be as many miseries beyond riches as on this side of them.' The keys that keep those riches hang often heavily at the rich man's girdle. Let us be thankful for health and a competence, and for a quiet conscience."

"Money is not needful," said Professor Blackie to the young men of Edinburgh University; "power is not needful; liberty is not needful; even health is not the one thing needful; but character alone is that which can truly save us."

"The real benefactors of mankind," says Emerson, "are the men and women who can raise their fellow-beings out of the world of corn and money; who make them forget their bank account by interesting them in their higher selves; who can raise mere money-getters into the intellectual realm, where they will cease to measure greatness and happiness by dollars and cents; who can make men forget their stomachs and feast on being's banquet."

He is the richest man who enriches his country most; in whom the people feel richest and proudest; who gives himself with his money; who opens the doors of opportunity widest to those about him; who is ears to the deaf, eyes to the blind, and feet to the lame. Such a man makes every acre of land in his community worth more, and makes richer every man who lives near him. On the other hand, many a millionaire has impoverished the town in which he lived, and lessened the value of every foot of land.

What is character but the poor man's capital? Is not character an available piece of property? Is it not estimated as moral security, the noblest of possessions? "It is an estate in the general good will and respect of men; and they who invest in it will find their reward in esteem and reputation fairly and honorably won."

"Thee shall do as well by me as I do by thee," said a Quaker tanner, when he took an apprentice. The boy won his employer's confidence by his honesty, good nature, and industry. "Henry," said the Friend, "I think of making thee a fine present when thy time is out. I cannot tell thee what it is to be; but it shall be worth more to thee than a hundred pounds." When the apprenticeship expired, the Quaker said, "I will give thy present to thy father," adding, as he addressed the latter, "Thy son is the best boy I ever had. This is the present—a good name." Henry's golden visions vanished; but his father said, "I would rather hear you say that of my son than to see you give him all the money you are worth, for 'a good name is rather to be chosen than great riches.'" It was the outcome of the lad's own exertion, the reward of his own good principles and conduct. A good name: "Without it, gold has no value; birth, no distinction; station, no dignity; beauty, no charm; age, no reverence."

"Character is like stock in trade," said Dr. Hawes, of Hartford; "the more of it a man possesses the greater his facilities for making additions to it. Character is power—is influence; it makes friends, creates funds, draws patronage and support, and opens a sure and easy way to wealth, honor, and happiness."

How were a multitude of business men who lost every dollar they had in the Chicago fire enabled to resume business at once, some in a wholesale business, without money? Their record was their bank account. The commercial agencies said they were square men; that they had always paid one hundred cents on a dollar; that they had paid promptly, and that they were industrious, and dealt honorably with all men. Their record was as good as a bank account. They drew on their character. Character was the coin which enabled penniless men to buy thousands of dollars' worth of goods. Their integrity did not burn up with their stores. The best part of them was beyond reach of fire, and could not be burned.

A good character is a precious thing, above rubies, gold, crowns, or kingdoms, and the work of making it is the noblest labor on earth.

Money-getting has well been called unhealthy when it impoverishes the mind, or dries up the sources of the spiritual life; when it extinguishes the sense of beauty, and makes one indifferent to the wonders of nature and art; when it blunts the moral sense, and confuses the distinction between right and wrong, virtue and vice; when it stifles religious impulse, and blots all thoughts of God from the soul.

It is just as important to set apart time for the development of our aesthetic faculties as for cultivating the money-getting instinct. A man cannot live by bread alone. His higher life demands an impalpable food. It takes a large bill of fare to feed an immortal being. The mind and soul in a well-developed man are ever more imperious in their demand for the true and the beautiful than is the body for material food.

Character is perpetual wealth, and by the side of him who possesses it the millionaire who has it not seems a pauper. Compared with it, what are houses and lands, stocks and bonds? "It is better that great souls should live in small habitations than that abject slaves should burrow in great houses." Plain living, rich thought, and grand effort are real riches.

Neither a man's means, nor his worth, are measurable by his money. If he has a fat purse and a lean heart, a broad estate and a narrow understanding, what will his "means" do for him—what will his "worth" gain him? What sadder sight is there than an old man who has spent his whole life getting instead of growing? If he has piled up books, statuary, and paintings, with his wealth, he may be a stranger amongst them. How poor he is if his soul has shriveled to that of a miser, and if all his nobler instincts are dead!

Do you call him successful who wears a bulldog expression that but too plainly tells the story of how he gained his fortune, taking but never giving? Can you not read in that browbeating face the sad experience of widows and orphans? Do you call him a self-made man who has unmade others to make himself—who tears others down to build himself up? Can a man be really rich who makes others poorer? Can he be happy in whose every lineament chronic avarice is seen as plainly as hunger in the countenance of a wolf? How seldom are sweet, serene, beautiful faces seen on men who have been very successful as the world rates success! Nature expresses in the face and manner the sentiment which rules the heart.

"When I say, in conducting your understanding, love knowledge with a great love," says Sydney Smith, "with a vehement love, with a love coeval with life,--what do I say but love innocence, love virtue, love purity of conduct, love that which, if you are rich and great, will vindicate the blind fortune which has made you so, and make men call it justice; love that which if you are poor will render your poverty respectable, and make the proudest feel that it is unjust to laugh at the meanness of your fortunes; love that which will comfort you, adorn you, and never quit you,--which will open to you the kingdom of thought, and all the boundless regions of conception as an asylum against the cruelty, the injustice, and the pain that may be your lot in the world,--that which will make your motives habitually great and honorable, and light up in an instant a thousand noble disdains at the very thought of meanness and of fraud?"

"Character before wealth," was the motto of our Boston merchant Amos Lawrence, who inscribed on his pocketbook, "What shall it profit a man if he shall gain the whole world and lose his own soul?"

"Do you know, sir," asked a devotee of Mammon, in speaking to John Bright, "that I am worth a million sterling?" "Yes," said the irritated but calm-spirited respondent, "I do; and I know that it is all you are worth."

"Life is constantly weighing us in very sensitive scales," says Lowell, "and telling every one of us to precisely what his real weight is, to the last grain of dust."

"I ought not to allow any man, because he has broad lands, to feel that he is rich in my presence," says Emerson. "I ought to make him feel that I can do without his riches, that I cannot be bought,--neither by comfort, neither by pride,--and although I be utterly penniless, and receiving bread from him, that he is the poor man beside me."

"What do we mean," asked Henry Ward Beecher, "when we say that a man 'is made'? Is it that he has got the control of his lower instincts, so that they are only fuel to his higher feelings, giving force to his nature? That his affections are like vines, sending out on all sides blossoms and clustering fruits? That his tastes are so cultivated that all beautiful things speak to him, and bring him their delights? That his understanding is opened, so that he walks through every hall of knowledge, and gathers its treasures? That his moral feelings are so developed and quickened that he holds sweet commerce with Heaven? Oh, no—none of these things. He is cold and dead in heart, and mind, and soul. Only his passions are alive; but—he is worth five hundred thousand dollars!

"And we say a man is 'ruined.' Are his wife and children dead? Oh, no. Have they had a quarrel, and are they separated from him? Oh, no. Has he lost his reputation through crime? No. Is his reason gone? Oh, no; it is as sound as ever. Is he struck through with disease? No. He has lost his property, and he is ruined. The man ruined! When shall we learn that 'a man's life consisteth not in the abundance of things which he possesseth'?"

A bankrupt merchant, returning home one night, said to his noble wife, "My dear, I am ruined; everything we have is in the hands of the sheriff." After a few moments of silence the wife looked into his face and asked, "Will the sheriff sell you?" "Oh, no." "Will the sheriff sell me?" "Oh, no." "Will he sell the children?" "Oh, no." "Then do not say that we have lost everything. All that is the most valuable remains to us,--manhood, womanhood, childhood. We have lost but the results of our skill and industry. We can make another fortune if our hearts and hands are left us."

What power can poverty have over a home where loving hearts are beating with a consciousness of untold riches of head and heart?

A rich mind and noble spirit will cast over the humblest home a radiance of beauty which the upholsterer and decorator can never approach. Who would not prefer to be a millionaire of character, of contentment, rather than possess nothing but the vulgar coins of a Croesus? Whoever uplifts civilization is rich though he die penniless; and future generations will erect his monument.

Some men are rich in health, in constant cheerfulness, in a mercurial temperament which floats them over troubles and trials enough to sink a shipload of ordinary men. Others are rich in disposition, family, and friends. There are some men so amiable that they carry an atmosphere of jollity about them. Some are rich in integrity and character.

What are the toil-sweated productions of wealth piled up in vast profusion around a Girard, or a Rothschild, when weighed against the stores of wisdom, the treasures of knowledge, and the strength, beauty, and glory with which victorious virtue has enriched and adorned a great multitude of minds during the march of a hundred generations?

Phillips Brooks, Whittier, Thoreau, Audubon, Emerson, Beecher, Agassiz, were rich without money. They saw the splendor in the flower, the glory in the grass, books in the running brooks, sermons in stones, and good in everything. They knew that the man who owns the landscape is seldom the one who pays the taxes on it. They sucked in power and wealth at first hand from the meadows and fields, birds, brooks, mountains, and forests, as the bee sucks honey from the flowers. Every natural object seemed to bring them a special message from the great Author of the beautiful. To such rare souls every natural object is touched with power and beauty; and their thirsty souls drink it in as a traveler on a desert drinks in the God-sent water of the oasis. To extract power and spiritual wealth from the world around them seems to be their mission, and to pour it out again in refreshing showers upon a thirsting humanity.

"What is the measure of a nation's true success?" asked Lowell. "It is the amount of energy it has contributed to the thought, the moral energy, the intellectual happiness, the spiritual hope and consolation of mankind."

Thrift.

All this has been said as to the nature of true wealth, after first of all assuming that every human being has been trained in early life (when irrevocable habits are formed) in the fundamental laws of thrift; daily labor; earning a fair means of living; saving enough for pecuniary independence in days of sickness and old age; avoidance of debt; readiness to help others; and all those wholesome divine rules of frugal self-preservation that are to be as rigidly learned and obeyed as the ten commandments—six days for labor and a life without theft or a lie or covetousness.

Assuming all this, one of the first great lessons in life is to learn the true estimate of values. As the youth starts out in his career all sorts of wares will be imposed upon him, and all kinds of temptations will be used to induce him to buy. His success will depend very largely upon his ability to estimate properly, not the apparent but the real value of everything presented to him. Vulgar wealth will flaunt her banner before his eyes, and claim supremacy over everything else. A thousand schemes will thrust their claims into his face. Every occupation and vocation will present its charms. The youth who would succeed must not allow himself to be deceived, but place emphasis of life where it belongs.

Is it any wonder that our children start out with wrong ideals of life, with wrong ideas of what constitutes success? The child is "urged to get on," to "rise in the world," to "make money." success? The child is "urged to get on," to "rise in the world," to "make money." Yet one of the great lessons to teach in this century of sharp competition and the survival of the fittest is how to be rich without money, and to learn how to do without what is popularly and falsely called success.

"I believe," says Julia Ward Howe, "that many of our youth are learning that a worthy life is the best success; whether it is attended by wealth or poverty, or by that most preferable condition of all, a modest competency. Pure, upright living and steady devotion to principle are the surest foundations of any success worth having."

"No success in life," says Frances E. Willard, "is anything but and absolute failure, unless its purpose is to increase the sum of human good and happiness."

All honor to the comparative few in every walk of life who, amid the strong materialistic tendencies of our age, still speak and act earnestly, inspired by the hope of rewards other than gold or popular favor! These are our truly great men and women. They labor in their ordinary vocations with no less zeal because they give time and thought to higher things.

"A man may as soon fill a chest with grace, or a vessel with virtue," says Phillips Brooks, "as a heart with wealth."

"If you would know the power of character," says Emerson, "see how much you would impoverish the world if you could take clean out of history the lives of Milton, Shakespeare, and Plato,--these three,-- and cause them not to be."

Are we tender, loving, self-denying, and honest, trying to fashion our frail lives after that of the model man of Nazareth? Then, though our pockets are often empty, we have an inheritance which is as overwhelmingly precious as it is eternally incorruptible.

> "What constitutes a state?
> Not high-raised battlement or labored mound,
> Thick wall or moated gate;
> Not cities proud, with spires and turrets crowned;
> Not bays, and broad-armed ports,
> Where, laughing at the storm, rich navies ride;
> Not starred and spangled courts,
> Where low-browed baseness wafts perfume to pride.
> No: men, high-minded men.

VIII. THE APOLLO BELVIDERE AND VENUS DI MILO

These statues stand for symmetry—for an ideal. Is not every character to be formed upon a unique personal ideal? And is not every man a law unto himself, in making for himself a well-proportioned character?

> "I wonder if ever a song was sung
> But the singer's heart sang sweeter!
> I wonder if ever a hymn was rung,
> But the thought surpassed the meter!
> I wonder if ever a sculptor wrought,
> Till the cold stone echoed his ardent thought!
> Or if ever a painter, with light and shade,
> The dream of his inmost heart portrayed!"

"Yet the aim of every man," said Humboldt, "should be to secure the highest and most harmonious development of his powers to a complete and consistent whole."

In every painting of the masters there is one idea or figure which stands out boldly; everything else is subordinate, and finds its real significance not in itself, but in pointing to the central idea. So, in the universe of God, every object of creation is but a guideboard with an index finger pointing to the central figure—Man. Man is the only great thing in the universe; all the ages have been trying to produce a perfect model. Only one complete human life, one ideal life, has yet evolved. Is not life itself a fine art, and more difficult than sculpture, painting, music, architecture, or the creations of poetry? Do we not need to learn how to live?

Apelles hunted over Greece for many years, studying the fairest points of beautiful women, getting here an eye, there a forehead, there a nose, here a grace, and there a turn of beauty, for his famous portrait of a perfect woman which enchanted the world. So the coming man will be composite—many in one. He will absorb into himself not the weakness, not the follies, but the strength and the virtues of other types of men. He will be a man raised to the highest power. He will be self-centered, equipoised, and ever master of himself. His sensibility will not be blunted by violation of nature's laws. His whole character will be impressible, and will respond to the most delicate touches of nature.

"Did you ever watch a sculptor slowly fashioning a human countenance?" asks a modern teacher. "It is not molded at once. It is not struck out at a single blow. It is painfully and laboriously wrought. It is a work of time; but at last the full likeness comes out and stands fixed and unchanging in the solid marble. So does a man carve out his own moral likeness. Every day he adds something to the work."

"I cannot see that you have made any progress since my last visit," said a critic to Michael Angelo. "But," said the sculptor, "I have retouched this part, polished that, softened this feature, brought out that muscle, given some expression to this lip, more energy to that limb." "But these are trifles!" "It may be so, but trifles make perfection, and perfection is no trifle."

"That infinite patience which made Michael Angelo spend a week in bringing out a muscle in a statue with more fidelity to truth, or Gerhard Douw a day in giving the right effect to a dewdrop on a cabbage leaf," makes all the difference between success and failure.

A man took a large, beautiful onyx to a noted artist to see what he could do to cover up a tinge of iron rust, which seemed to make the stone almost worthless. The artist engraved out of the blemish the figure of a lovely goddess. So the successful man turns the commonest events, the homeliest of things, into that which is beautiful in his life. And if he does it by a law of symmetrical development, then love, charity, contentment, benignity, and cheerfulness will look out from the marble he works upon. Let youth be taught to look for beauty in all they see, and to embody beauty in all they do, and the imagination will be active and healthy. If one loves beauty and looks for it, he will see it everywhere. If there is music in his soul, he will hear it everywhere; every object in nature will sing to him. Life will be neither a drudgery nor a dream, but will become full of God's life and love.

If you infuse into the purpose with which you follow the various employments and professions of life, no matter how humble they may be, the sense of beauty, pleasure, and harmony, you are transformed at once from an artisan to an artist. Any discontent you feel with the work you are compelled to do comes from your doing it in the spirit of a drudge. Do it in the spirit of a master, with a perception of the beauty which inheres in all honest work, and the drudgery will disappear in delight. "It is the spirit in which we work, not the work itself, which lends dignity to labor; and many a field has been ploughed, many a house built, in a grander spirit than has sometimes attended the government of empires or the creation of epics." How few, even in this magnificent life-gallery, where nature holds perpetual carnival of harmony and beauty, see anything of value except dollars and merchandise! As Emerson says, the farmer sees his bushel and his cart, and nothing beyond, and sinks into the farmer, instead of the *man* on the farm.

Life is not mean, it is grand; if it is mean to any, he makes it so. God made it glorious. It is paved with diamonds; its banks He fringed with flowers. He overarched it with stars. Around it He spread the glory of the physical universe—suns, moons, worlds, constellations, systems—all that is magnificent is in motion, sublime in magnitude, and grand in order and obedience. God would not have attended life with this broad march of grandeur if it did not mean something.

Ruskin tells us that the earth we tread beneath our feet is composed of clay and sand and soot and water; and he tells us that, if Nature has her perfect work (in these things), the clay will become porcelain, and may be painted upon and placed in the king's palace; then, again, it may become clear and hard and white, and have the power of drawing to itself the blue and the red, the green and the purple rays of the sunlight, and become an opal. The sand will become very hard and white, and have the power of drawing to itself the blue rays of the sunlight, and become a sapphire. The soot will become the hardest and whitest substance known, and be changed into a diamond. The water in the summer is a dewdrop, and in the winter crystallizes into a star. Even so the homeliest lives, by drawing to themselves the coloring of truth, sincerity, charity, and faith, may become crystals and gems "of purest ray serene."

Every thought which enters the mind, every word we utter, every deed we perform, makes its impression upon the inmost fiber of our being, and the resultant of these impressions is our character. The study of books, of music, or of the fine arts is not essential to a lofty character. It rests with the workman whether a rude piece of marble shall be squared into a horse-block or carved into an Apollo, a Psyche, or a Venus di Milo. It is yours, if you choose, to develop a spiritual form more beautiful than any of these, instinct with immortal life, refulgent with all the glory of character. "The power of great thoughts and grand sentiments to refine the face and manner, to lift man above his surroundings, is marvelous. We see this illustrated in the faces of great scientists, great reformers, and great statesmen." The body is but a servant of the mind. A well-balanced, cultured, and well-disciplined intellect reacts very powerfully upon the physique, and tends to bring it into harmony with itself. On the other hand, a weak, vacillating, one-sided, unsteady, and ignorant mind will ultimately bring the body into sympathy with it. Every pure and uplifting thought, every noble aspiration for the good and the true, every longing of the heart for a higher and better life, every lofty purpose and unselfish endeavor, reacts upon the body, makes it stronger, more harmonious, and more beautiful.

The influence of artistic work depicting character, in sculpture or painting, comes down to us from remote ages. We never weary of the antique forms of perfected beauty. Is Michael Angelo dead? Ask the hundreds of thousands who have gazed with rapt souls upon his immortal works at Rome. In how many thousands of lives has he lived and reigned!

"There is," says Dr. J.R. Miller, "always something pouring out from our lives, like heat from a flame of perfume from a flower. Many a life has been started on a career of beauty and blessing by the influence of a noble act. Every true soul is impressed continually by the glimpses it has of loveliness, of holiness, or of nobleness in others."

There are men and women in every country who conquer before they speak, and who exert an influence out of all proportion to their ability; and people wonder what is the secret of their power over men. It is natural for all classes to believe in and to follow character, for character is power.

"When Raphael was a boy of seventeen he went to study with the artist, Perugino. It was discovered, some time afterwards, that soon after the apprenticeship of Raphael began, the style of Perugino changed. His work was chastened by an unexpected tenderness of feeling and the candor of expression; his color acquired a brightness and sweetness of modulation unknown to him before, and this because a boy had come to be taught by him, and had thrown the influence of his life about his master's heart."

Every one, however humble, is daily and hourly altering and molding the character of all with whom he mingles, and exerting a power that will reproduce itself through countless generations.

Our manners, our bearing, our presence, tell the story of our lives, though we do not speak; and the influence of every act is felt in the utmost part of the globe. Has not every man that ever lived contributed something toward making me what I am? Has not the chisel of every member of society contributed a blow to the marble of my life, and influenced its destiny?

"If we work upon marble, it will perish," said Webster; "if upon brass, time will efface it; if we rear temples, they will crumble into dust; but if we work upon immortal minds—if we imbue them with principles, with the just fear of God and love of our fellowmen—we engrave on those tablets something which will brighten through all eternity."

IX. CULTIVATING THE GROWTH OF MAN-TIMBER

God give us men. A time like this demands
Strong minds, great hearts, true faith, and ready hands:
Men whom the lust of office does not kill;
Men whom the spoils of office cannot buy;
Men who possess opinions and a will;
Men who have honor—men who will not lie;
Men who can stand before a demagogue
And scorn his treacherous flatteries without winking;
Tall men, sun-crowned, who live above the fog
I public duty, and in private thinking.

   All the world cries, "Where is the man who will save us? We want a man!" Don't look so far for this man. You have him at hand. This man—it is you, it is I; it is each one of us! . . . How to constitute one's self a man? Nothing harder, if one knows not how to will it; nothing easier, if one wills it. –Alexander Dumas

   As there is nothing in the world great but man, there is nothing truly great in man but character. –W.M. Evarts

      Life is a leaf of paper white,
      Whereon each one of us may write
      His word or two, and then comes night.
      Greatly begin! Though thou have time
      But for a line, be that sublime,--
      Not failure, but low aim, is crime. –Lowell

And I smiled to think God's greatness
Flowed around my incompleteness;
Round my restlessness, his rest. –Mrs. Browning

   "Character is everything," said Charles Sumner, when upon his dying bed.
   "First of all," said President Garfield, when a boy, "I must make myself a man; if I do not succeed in that I can succeed in nothing."
   "According to the order of nature, men being equal, their common vocation is the profession of humanity," says Rousseau, in his celebrated essay on Education. "And whoever is well educated to discharge the duty of a man cannot be badly prepared to fill any of those offices that have a relation to him. It matters little to me

whether my pupil be designed for the army, the pulpit, or the bar. Nature has destined us to the offices of human life, antecedent to our destination concerning society. To live is the profession I would teach him. When I have done with him, it is true he will be neither a soldier, a lawyer, nor a divine. LET HIM FIRST BE A MAN. Fortune may remove him from one rank to another as she pleases; he will be always found in his place."

We are, therefore, to remember, as Dr. Moxon has told us, that the main business of life is not to do, but to become; and that action itself has its finest and most enduring fruit in character.

John Stuart Mill has put this matter clearly: "The character itself should be to the individual a paramount end, simply because the existence of this ideal nobleness of character, or of a near approach to it, in any abundance, would go further than all things else toward making human life happy, both in the comparatively humble sense of pleasure and freedom from pain, and in the higher meaning of rendering life not what it now is, almost universally puerile and insignificant, but such as every human being with highly developed faculties would desire to have."

And this, says Mill, every man is to work at: "Though our character is formed by circumstances, our own desires can do much to shape those circumstances; and what is really inspiring and ennobling in the doctrine of free will is the conviction that we have real power over the formation of our own character; our will, by influencing some of our circumstances, being able to modify our future habits or capacities of willing."

How is character made up, except by our choices and our refusals? We select from life what we choose. We resemble insects which assume the color of the leaves and plants they feed upon, for sooner or later we become like the food of our minds, like the creatures that live in our hearts. Every act of our lives, every word, every association, is written with an iron pen upon the very texture of our being.

"There is dew in one flower and not in another," said Beecher, "because one opens its cup and takes it in, while the other closes itself and the drop runs off."

What will our future be but what we make it? Our purpose will give it character. One's resolution is one's prophecy. There is no bright hope, no great outlook, for the man who is not inspired by a stalwart purpose, which alone is the true interpreter of his manhood.

"There is not in the lowest depths of our hearts," said Robertson of Brighton, "a mere desire for happiness, but a craving, as natural to us as the desire for food—the craving for nobler, higher life." To satisfy this craving is good business to be in.

If a youth were to start out in the world with the fixed determination that he will make no statement but the exact truth; that every promise shall be redeemed to the letter; that every appointment shall be kept with the strictest faithfulness, and with sacred regard for other men's time; if he should hold his reputation as a priceless treasure, and feel that the eyes of the world are upon him, that he must not deviate a hair's breadth from the truth and right—if he should take such a stand at the outset—he would come to have the almost unlimited confidence of mankind.

What we are to be really, we are now potentially. As the future oak lies folded in the acorn, so in the present lies our future. Our success will be, can be, but a natural tree, developed from the seed of our own sowing; the fragrance of its blossoms and the richness of its fruitage will depend upon nourishment absorbed from our past and present.

The first requisite of all education and discipline should be MAN-TIMBER. Tough timber must come from well-grown, sturdy trees. Such wood can be turned into a mast, can be fashioned into a piano, or an exquisite carving. But it must become timber first. Time and patience develop the sapling into the tree. So, through discipline, education, experience, the sapling child is developed into hardy mental, moral, physical timber. The only real success worthy of the name is that which comes from a consciousness of growing wider, deeper, higher, in mental and moral power, as the years go on. To feel the faculties expanding and unfolding—this is the only life worth living.

And is not all this inspiration in response to a Divine touch and a Divine life? When Mendelssohn once went to see the great Freiburg organ, the custodian, not knowing who he was, would not let him touch it. After much persuasion he allowed the persistent youth to touch a few notes. The old man stood entranced; he had never heard such melody before. At length he asked the great player his name; and, when he had been told, he stood humiliated and self-condemned. A greater musician than Mendelssohn, unknown to us, perhaps, has stood by the human organ which very possibly has given our only "wolf-notes" before to the world, pleading with us to let Him touch the strings and bring out the music divine.

And what a grace it is to come into touch with God! I have read of a girl whose wonderful grace and purity of character charmed everyone who knew her. One day a friend touched the spring of a little gold locket which she always wore on her neck, but which she had let no one see, and in it were these words: "Whom, not having seen, I love."

Mrs. Livermore has said that Miss Willard was ever conscious of being encompassed round by unseen presences and helpers. She lived in perfect spiritual reciprocity with the unseen world.

How beautiful it all is, after the blunders and the high aspirations of youth, and the struggles of manhood, if life's discipline has brought us nearer and nearer to God and the ideal life! "What are our yearnings," asks Beecher, "but homesickness for heaven? Our sighings are sighings for God, just as children cry themselves asleep away from home, and sob in their slumber, not knowing that they sob for their parents. The soul's inarticulate moanings are the affections yearning for the Infinite, and having no one to tell them what it is that ails them."

Do you not remember the legend, how the inhabitants of an ancient hamlet proposed to welcome their king, when it was announced that he would honor them with his presence? Early and late they toiled to beautify their village, to make their homes pleasing in his sight. At length, their utmost done, they rested on the eve of their sovereign's coming. But lo, in the night, while they slept, the angels came down and transformed all their work. The morning sunlight unfolded a scene of radiant splendor. On the sites of lowly cottages stately mansions rose. Snow-white marble gleamed where simply wood had been. Golden pinnacles shone aloft in the bright sunlight. Fountains sent forth their wealth of spray. Palm trees, in graceful loveliness, stood around their village green. Though but a fable, this story is substantially true; since it is thus that God, with the smile of approval, enriches, ennobles, and beautifies the labors of those who love Him, and out of love serve Him.

When, at the evening of our little day, He comes to us, or sends His messenger to bid us come home, not the great things we have done, but faithfulness in doing the little duties that He has placed upon our hands, will win His approval.

"Follow the Star! It may not lead thy feet
  Through pleasant vales where bloom and fragrance wait;
Nor may it lead thee to those mountain heights
  Where worldly fame and honor hold their state;
Yet follow thou! Forget not 't is the Star!
  And it shall lead to no one less than God,
And it shall lead to God, though God be far."

Thanks for your company! We hope that you enjoyed the book, and we wish you all the best, all through your life!

livinglifefully.com

www.ingramcontent.com/pod-product-compliance
Lightning Source LLC
Chambersburg PA
CBHW051755040426
42446CB00007B/374